# Embracing Stability and Satisfaction in Remarriage

Ms. Alice,

May you get some
insights to help you
and your loved ones
from this Book.
A lot to learn from
the participants.

Peace & God's Blessings

Fr. Joseph

# Embracing Stability and Satisfaction in Remarriage

by

**Rev. Joseph Kabali, Ph.D., LMFT, STL.**

Nihil Obstat: Rev. John G. Hillier, Ph.D

Imprimatur: + Most Rev. James F. Checchio, JCD, MBA
Bishop of the Diocese of Metuchen, NJ
October 19, 2018

The Nihil Obstat and Imprimatur are official declarations that a book or pamphlet is free of doctrinal or moral error. No implication is contained therein that those who have granted the Nihil Obstat and Imprimatur agree with the contents, opinions, or statements expressed.

Publisher: Rev. Joseph Kabali
P.o. Box 241
Parlin, NJ 08859
www.josephkabalibooks.com

Printed in the United States of America
ISBN 978-1-948828-21-5 (sc)
ISBN 978-1-948828-22-2 (e)

Self-help

2 / 25 / 2019

# EMBRACING STABILITY AND SATISFACTION IN REMARRIAGE

A Research-Based Workbook for Custodial Parents Contemplating Remarriage, Remarried Parents, Significant People in Their Lives and Professionals (Community Healers)

Includes annulment process guidelines and  healing spirituality for divorced and remarrying Catholics

# Book Reviews

This book is so comprehensive. It helps remarried people, those contemplating remarriage and their significant others to attain a deeper understanding concerning the unique and complex realities within each remarriage. The "how" to establish and maintain stability and satisfaction in remarriage is excellently discussed as well as custodial situations in remarriage. In addition to being a research-based book, it is rich with personal stories and experiences that make the text lively and interesting for the reader.

> Sueli S. Petry, Ph.D, Psychologist, Marriage and Family Therapist Highland Park, NJ. Author of publications on immigrant families and spirituality through the lifecycle, and coauthor of *Genograms: Assessment and Intervention*, 3rd edition.

As a licensed canonist who has been involved in the ministry of Tribunal for over the last thirty years, I find the chapter on the annulment process to be very informative and in agreement with the current Canon Law of the Roman Catholic Church. Additionally, the same chapter reflects the current updates on the annulment process within the Catholic Church. The chapter is particularly useful to Catholics who have undergone the pain of divorce and are seeking to be reconciled to the Church through the annulment process. The Tribunal is one avenue of help and healing for the divorced person. The Tribunal is a Church court under the direction of the Bishop and supervised by his delegate, the Judicial Vicar. Together with a specially trained staff of priests, religious and laity, we offer assistance to persons who request that the Church investigate a marriage to determine if there are possible grounds for an ecclesiastical annulment. May all who read this book find hope and healing as they continue their life journeys.

> Msgr. Richard J. Lyons JCL
> Judicial Vicar, Marriage Tribunal, Diocese of Metuchen, NJ

I am a Roman Catholic man in a second marriage for 18 years with a previous first marriage of 20 years that was never annulled. While reading the final manuscript of this book, I took particular interest in Part III, Role 2 (Annulment process in the Catholic Church). In it, the author has a way of bringing a clarity and simplicity to an area that is looked at by many divorced Catholics as one of the great mysteries of the Church. The chapter helped me to overcome the common misunderstandings about annulment and made it clear as to where the untruths lie. For the first time in nearly 50 years I understand clearly why The Catholic Church requires annulments. As a result of this clarity I have decided to apply for the annulment of my first marriage that ended in divorce. If granted annulment by the Tribunal, I will remarry my second wife in the Catholic Church in front of God, relatives and close friends. I encourage those contemplating remarriage to read this book before rushing into it.

Ronald Bibbo
Sergeantsville, NJ

As a Presbyterian and British citizen living in London, divorced and remarried as a custodial parent, I have realized that this research-based book may be useful to many people outside the United States where the research was conducted. Based on personal experiences, I find so many similarities with the participants who were interviewed by the author. Additionally, this book has helped me to reaffirm my experience that marriage is a wonderful experience and very precious. I wish all of us would only be married once. However, other factors do sometimes change that situation and we find ourselves marrying for the second time and hoping that this time we will be more successful. This book helps in "how" to make the second marriage more stable and satisfactory. I also highlight that one of the most important things to remember is that if children are involved, they cannot have lots of people telling them what to do because they will resent it. In our particular case, we discussed everything very carefully and decided that I would be the one to discipline and punish my children from the previous marriage, and my husband would talk to his children for the same reasons. Our situation was a little more complicated as my children were much younger and they lived with us.

Lesley Watchorn
London, England

This book reflects most of the realities my second husband and I have experienced and helped us over 14 years of remarriage. What sticks out for me is the comment I have read expressing that no one anticipated the problems that remarriage brings. That is so true. Therefore, preparing for remarriage is vital with the help of professionals as suggested in this book. Otherwise, find some kind of counseling before making the plunge. Finances, dealing with one's exspouse or current partner, disciplining of children and fear of another divorce are examples of unanticipated challenges. However, this book offers better approaches that reinforce stability and satisfaction in remarriage by highlighting key factors that have helped us to stay happily remarried. There are many moments when we both wanted to give up. But we stuck it out by implementing most of the factors identified in this book. For instance: committed love, maturity, spirituality, conflict resolution skills, communication, sexuality, and ongoing mutual forgiveness. I hope it will become a guide for many.

Barbara Geraghty
Ringoes, NJ

# Dedication

This book is dedicated to my mother Maria Harriett Nakamatte, a humble and loving woman for all she has taught me; and in loving memory to my father, Stephen Kalibbala, whose culturally accepted polygamous marital life exposed me to multiple stepmothers, half-siblings and extended stepfamily members.

Additionally, I dedicate this book to Dr. Sharon Davis Massey, who has persistently encouraged me to change my dissertation into a book; and to Mrs. Antonia Ndaba, a South African woman from whom I first learned in 1996 the value of being an attentive listener to people contemplating remarriage.

# Contents

Secondary Factors of Stability and Satisfaction
in Remarriage: Study Sessions 10-17

## Part III
### Roles for Divorced Persons Contemplating Remarriage

## Part IV:
### Categories of Significant People for Custodial Parents

**Part V:**
**Looking Forward**

# Preface

This workbook is based on a research study that I conducted for my dissertation in a doctoral program in family psychology. Some parts of the dissertation have been omitted or modified and others added. To make this book more accessible to people of various backgrounds, few technical words have been used and a glossary is provided at the end of the book for some of the terms.

Above all, I emphasize that for reasons of confidentiality, the names and any identifying data of the participants in the research study have been changed in this book. Any resemblance of name and/or other demographic data about anybody is a mere coincidence. However, with their authorization, some of their original words, phrases and narratives have been directly cited to highlight their retrospective experiences and suggestions to custodial parents in remarriage situations. The same citations may also be beneficial to the significant people in their lives to stimulate their thinking and take actions that may help in reinforcing the stability and satisfaction in remarriage of custodial parents.

Additionally, the gender and sexual orientation of every custodial parent who participated in the study were highly taken into consideration. All the participants identified themselves as heterosexual. The research study was focused exclusively on heterosexual custodial parents who remarried after a first divorce. Therefore, its findings may not reflect the key areas that are specific to committed partners of other sexual orientations. Consequently, they are advised to consult other resources.

The study was also designed for participants whose first and second marriages were between a man and a woman. Therefore, this book is focused on custodial parents contemplating heterosexual remarriage and/or currently living in a heterosexual remarriage. Based on the scope and findings of the research study on which this book is based, this book does not directly address the specific needs of other individuals (e.g., those who remarry after the death of a spouse, noncustodial parents, and partners who do not have any children from the previous marriage).

The study involved a small sample of 16 participants. All the participants were selected in the State of New Jersey. Therefore, their input and the resultant theory may or may not reflect a broader reality as lived by remarried parents in other States and/or other parts of the world.

Participants in the study included 8 adult men and 8 adult women aged 45 to 70 years. Each participant was remarried in a civil court and/or religious denomination after a first divorce. All the participants had spent at least 8 years in their second marriage, and were living, or had lived, with at least one biological child from the first marriage. They were recruited from New Jersey's inner cities, urban areas and suburbs. They were of different cultural backgrounds and various religious denominations, including two who were nondenominational.

A grounded theory research methodology design (Strauss & Corbin, 1998) was used. Participants were asked for their current and retrospective views of their first marriages, divorces, and remarriages. Data was collected from individuals, not couples. The grounded theoretical model that was developed from this study indicated committed love as the central theme that permeated through eight primary factors and eight secondary ones.

The primary factors (mentioned by more than 8 participants) were: integral maturity, knowledge of the complexity of remarriage, finances, collaborative parenting, sexuality, communication, spirituality, and professional help. The secondary factors (shared by fewer than 8 participants) were: marital history, motivations for remarriage, dating, house rules and roles, conflict resolution, clear boundaries, cohabitation, and permanent sites for professional remarriage services.

Each of these factors is discussed in this book and some sessions are followed by questions for personal reflection.

This book is also designed for the people who are profoundly impacted (in positive and/or negative ways) by the integral life of each custodial parent in divorce and/or remarriage situations. Examples of these significant people include but not limited to the custodian parent's ex-spouse, children, parents, other relatives, close friends, enemies, ex-in-laws, remarriage partner or spouse, stepchildren and/or their other parent, current in-laws, coworkers and employers. More often than not, custodial parents tend to seek support from one or more of these significant people in their lives before seeking professional help.

Selected categories of professionals are included as they form part of such significant others to people in divorce and remarriage situations. Examples of such professionals include: religious ministers, lawmakers, lawyers, judges, and mental health professionals, especially psychologists, marriage and family therapists, psychiatrists and social workers.

In order to help custodial parents and the significant people in their lives to understand in greater depth the complexities in remarriage situations, various authors and researchers are cited in this book to reinforce and shed more light on the ideas presented.

Why a book with questions? The questions before or after each session are intended to stimulate the reader's creative thinking and problem-solving skills and to make in-depth responses. The questions are also geared to serving as step-by-step exercises to help the reader master the main ideas within each session. If necessary, one should reread the session for greater comprehension in order to search for ways of applying it to daily living. Various spaces for writing are provided at the end of each session. The organization of the book materials also provides the reader with an opportunity for introspective and insightful self-study.

Clarification: This book has been reprinted by the author with a few modifications and a slight change in the title. His goal is to emphasize *to explore how to embrace stability and satisfaction* in remarriage not to promote remarriage over first marriage. Therefore, the new title is designed to clarify any unintended misinterpretation from first printing (still in publication) entitled: Embracing Remarriage Stability and Satisfaction.

Finally, whenever the word "Author" or "Researcher" is used throughout the book, it refers to the Author and Publisher of this book.

# Acknowledgments

Sincere thanks to my dissertation committee: The late Dr. Robert Massey (my mentor); you taught me by your support, dedication, patience, and availability. Rest in peace. Dr. Sharon Massey, you helped me to focus on remarriage stability and to understand the risks of serial monogamy. Dr. Ben Beitin, your mastery of the grounded theory, and dedication empowered me for research and clinical competence. Dr. Adriana Dunn, you taught me the importance of spirituality, marital satisfaction and committed love. Dr. Jeanne Czajka, thanks for your intuitions, focus on the storyline, dedication and support.

Relatives, whose love, sacrifices, support, words of wisdom and prayers helped me to stay focused on studies; Professors, whose wisdom has influenced my integral life; Academic companions at Seton Hall University, whose lives significantly impacted mine; Church ministers, whose support and understanding of the signs of the times in the church have empowered me; Friends and benefactors, who have supported and encouraged me in one way or another.

I am very grateful to these Consolata missionary priests (now deceased) for paving the way for me in 1998 to attend graduate studies at Seton Hall University: Fr. Alexius Lipingu, Fr. Anthony Bellagamba, Ph.D., Fr. John Berte and Fr. Maina Julius. Furthermore, I acknowledge the late Marylyn Ann Locandro. She read the very first draft of this book and encouraged me to continue writing by using the hidden wisdom within "stories" for guiding couples and as a good process of therapy. Elaborating on the value of telling stories, she highlighted in her handwritten feedback: "Isn't it the tried and true method used by Jesus? ... The parables here always carried the message."

Special thanks to all the participants in the research study: Without you, I would not have been able to write this book. Thank you for sharing your life stories and the suggestions you made to help other people embrace stable and satisfactory remarriages. I was so encouraged when almost giving up when one of the participants told me during a post-interview conversation: "Keep courage and persevere to the end. Your study is a goldmine. It is my hope that many people will benefit from your study once it is finished and written into a book." Last but not least, thanks to all the people who have helped me in different ways. Your names are written within my heart.

# Part I

## Looking Back

# Introduction

*Background Regarding Stability and Satisfaction in Remarriage*
*Knowledge Gap between Stability and Satisfaction in Remarriage after Divorce*
*Clarification of Some Phrases Used in this Book*

## *Background Regarding Stability and Satisfaction in Remarriage*

One of the reasons that motivated me to conduct research about stability and satisfaction in remarriage was witnessing within a period of twenty years the first marriage, divorce, remarriage, second divorce, second remarriage, then a third divorce and a fourth marriage of a very close friend. Above all, I recall a series of transitions in his life from being a single young adult to being a married man, then being divorced and remarried three more times. These transitions involved many challenges for him and those who cared about him. Personally, his life started to impact me with sadness, compassion, helplessness, blame, pain, anger, guilt, frustration and wishful thinking.

Because of the lack of stability in his marriages, my friend turned to me for help, but I felt unable and incompetent to assist him. As a result, I started to read a lot about marriage, divorce, single-parenthood, remarriage and stepfamilies with the hope of being able to help him to stay married. At the same time, after reading about the invitation that Pope Paul VI had made to religious ministers and people of good will to be attentive to the signs of the times (Paul VI, 1969), I realized that divorce and remarriage were increasing both in various religious denominations, and countries, especially in the United States. It seemed like divorce does not take a break!

Likewise, I became aware that some people were going through a second, third or fourth divorce experience.

Literature and research reviews also showed that during the later 1900's there was an increasing number of divorces, remarriages of divorced parents, and children living in stepfamilies as a result of divorce (cf., Carter & McGoldrick, 1998; Lofas & Sova, 1995). It was eye-opening to know the divorce rate is higher in remarriages than in first marriages (Nichols, 1996). It is no wonder, then, that Rutter (1998, p.185) called the last three decades a transition period into "the divorce revolution."

The incompetence I experienced for not being able to offer help to my friend with his marriage instabilities and the growing awareness of high divorce rates, remarriages and a series of divorces influenced me to attend a graduate program in marriage and family therapy. During the program, I shared with Dr. Adriana Dunn (one of my professors at Seton Hall University) about the need to conduct a research study focused on exploring the factors that influence remarriage stability. She listened attentively and afterward said: "Joséph, stability in remarriage is important but it is not enough. Satisfaction in remarriage is also necessary. You may have to explore the influencing factors for both stability and satisfaction in remarriage."

I took her suggestion to heart and I am so glad she gave me that great insight! Exploring those factors became the focus of the research and the results will be presented later.

During the initial stages in designing the research, I recalled that my friend had children from his first marriage and had shared custody with his former spouse after the divorce and during his first remarriage. Thinking over the dynamics and details related to his being a custodial parent after divorce, and during remarriage, what happened to his children during his third marriage helped me to start imagining the complexity of each remarriage. Eventually, I spoke with my mentor about the possibility of including custodianship in the research and limiting the study to interviewing participants in remarriage after their first divorce and the mentor agreed.

Additionally, I realized the need to conduct a study which would develop a theory that was grounded in research. Taking into account the literature I had previously read, there was an obviously significant gap between the very low numbers of competent family therapists, psychologists and other professionals in relation to the increasing numbers of custodial parents contemplating remarriage. All in all, the study was finally designed to focus on exploring the factors that influence stability and satisfaction in remarriage for custodial parents who remarry after a first divorce. Implications for theory and therapeutic practice are also results of the research.

## Knowledge Gap between Stability and Satisfaction in Remarriage after Divorce

In the previous pages, I have shared with the reader the "who," "why" and "what" that motivated me and "how" I started to explore the factors that influence stability and satisfaction in remarriage. Now I will focus on how other authors and other research studies have contributed in one way or another to the exploration of those factors. It is important to be aware of those factors and to address them before entering remarriage. Otherwise, the risk of another divorce after remarriage and/or the risk of staying in an unsatisfying remarriage are highly intensified.

During my review of the existing literature, research studies and remarriage preparation programs, I realized that they are very limited in identifying the correlation of stability and satisfaction in remarriage. They are focused mainly on the discussion of stepfamilies, remarriage after divorce or widowhood, remarriage happiness, conflicts with the ex-spouse, and the challenges between stepparents and stepchildren (Kupisch, 1987; LeBey, 2004).

McGoldrick and Carter (1998) observed that remarriage has a significant impact on the children of divorced parents. These authors underscored that there is an increasing number of stepfamilies as a result of remarriage, a situation that can be complex for the partners involved and the significant people in the lives of custodial parents or community healers (CH).

Sager (1985) clarified that second marriages are usually more complex than first marriages because an individual's lifecycle is being lived out in two or more marriage and family lifecycles. Consequently, the two marital and familial lifecycles overlap and often produce serious conflicts for the individual and his or her spouses (past and present) and for the children who live out their lives in two simultaneous familial lifecycles.

However, 64 percent of the remarriages are likely to end in divorce, and about 50 percent of remarriages terminate in less than 5 years, especially if they involve stepchildren (Kelley & Burg, 2000; McGoldrick & Carter, 1998). Nichols (1996) indicated that some of the remarried spouses divorce and remarry a second, a third, or a fourth time. Therefore, for some spouses, the cycle of divorce and remarriage has become a habitual or behavioral pattern referred to as "serial monogamy" (Brehm, 1992, p. 403).

All in all, the majority of divorced parents find it difficult to stay single for the rest of their lives. Sooner or later, a significant number of them opt for remarriage. Half of all marriages in the United States that occur each year are remarriages (Nichols, 1996; Rutter, 1998).

Consequently, in a search for how to prevent and respond to the increasing percentages of divorce after second marriages and the challenges of serial monogamy (Gottman, 1993), custodial parents preparing for remarriage need to take time for reflection. The following observation by Carter and McGoldrick (1998) is a great place to begin:

> "Courtship is probably the least likely time of all phases of the lifecycle to seek therapy. This is not because coupling is easy, but because of the tendency to idealize each other and avoid looking at the enormous longrange difficulties of establishing

an intimate relationship. While the first years of marriage are the time of the greatest overall marital satisfaction for many, they are also a time of likely divorce. The degree of mutual disappointment will usually match the degree of idealization of the relationship during courtship…" (p. 238).

Therefore, custodial parents contemplating remarriage should be encouraged to seek professional help before and during courtship. Kelley and Burg (2000, p. 139) recommended, "Settle as many issues as you can before you get married. It is easier to separate an egg before you scramble it."

Additionally, I found in the literature that a lot of emphasis was given to exploring the contributing factors that reinforce both remarriage stability and remarriage satisfaction. The rationale for this exploration was based on the clinical findings indicating that some spouses stay together as husband and wife for years, but they lack marital satisfaction (Gottman, 1993, 1994b; Johnson & Greenberg, 1994; Larson & Holman, 1994).

On the other hand, some spouses experience temporary marital satisfaction with their spouses and then decide to separate (Russell-Chapin, Chapin & Sattler, 2001). Such marital stabilities without satisfaction or marital instabilities with temporary satisfaction affect the spouses themselves. This in turn impacts all the significant people in their lives, especially the children. Children are profoundly affected by the levels of their custodial parents' marital stability and satisfaction (LeBey, 2004; Walsh, 1992).

## Clarification of Some Phrases Used in this Book

Remarriage stability: This phrase refers to the custodial parent's responsibility to develop and maintain a permanent marital commitment with his or her spouse until biological death separates them (Berger, 1998; Champlin, 1997).

Remarriage satisfaction: This phrase refers to the custodial parent's responsibilities to establish a second marriage, in which the custodial parent perceives the relationship as generating happiness and meaning through his or her interactions with his or her spouse, learning to persevere by doing his or her best to make marriage a success, and providing a mutually life-giving structure with his or her spouse and children (Gottman, 1994b; Jacobson & Greenburg, 1994).

Remarriage triad: This phrase refers to the interconnections among divorce, recoupling and stepfamily realities (Figure 1).

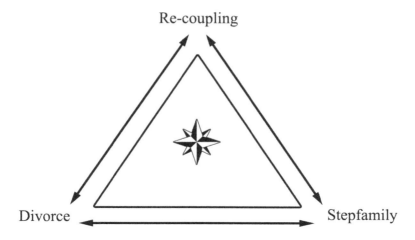

Figure 1. Remarriage triad: Interconnections among divorce, recoupling and stepfamily realities.

All in all, given the complexity of remarriage (Carter & McGoldrick, 1998; Ganong & Coleman, 1989; Gottman, 1994b; Kelley & Burg, 2000), this research-based workbook may help readers to become more aware of the major issues, concerns, and challenges affecting people involved in a remarriage triad. The results of the study helped me to acquire an insightful understanding of the complexity of the remarriage triad and consequently empowered me to write this book to reinforce stability and satisfaction in remarriage.

We prepare ourselves for many things and get training in different fields. We tend to forget to prepare ourselves for the greatest vocations and roles in society: marriage, becoming a husband or a wife, a father or a mother. Practicing on stage can be dangerous. Prepare!

# Methodology

*Narrative Style, Reflection Questions and "Keys"*

Before elaborating on the ways this workbook is designed, I would like to highlight how impactful my grandmother's stories were on my development from the time I was 7 to 19. As I reflect on them now, I realize a story is an excellent toolbox for teaching and learning. Every toolbox has different tools inside. Each tool has a different size and purpose, and may be used in many different settings. Grandma narrated various stories: short, long, full of humor, full of sadness, adventures involving one or more characters, fiction, nonfiction, emotional or loaded with complex ideas.

One thing stands out: I am able to apply most of her stories to different situations in my life. Her narrative style helped me to remember the key ideas and words of wisdom in every story and its multiple details. To this day, it is more difficult for me to recall many important ideas and details when presented in isolated statements than the way I am able to master and apply them based on a story. Therefore, based in the lessons I learned from Grandma's stories and the advanced studies in narrative therapy (White & Epson, 1990; Freedman & Combs, 1996), I have decided to include stories in this book. I have also realized that stories resonate with people and connect people at many levels, for instance: emotional, spiritual, existential, philosophical or moral.

Additionally, I remember that Grandma would sometimes narrate the story and then give her opinion. Sometimes, she would ask me to tell it back to her using my own words. Occasionally, she would ask me questions to further my thought process, gain affirmation, challenge my perceptions and motivations, question my convictions, actions, attitudes or beliefs. Whenever necessary, she would help me see the need for radical changes in my life in order to achieve better results.

Similarly, in this book, I share with the reader in a story or narrative format about a qualitative research study that I conducted. I will include some questions that you may use to further your thought process, develop your own opinions and find ways of applying them to concrete life situations.

Therefore, inspired by Grandma's style of narrating stories and profound life lessons within the stories or questions, every session or identified factor of stability and satisfaction in remarriage has been presented and discussed by using a story or narrative style.

The responses of the participants to the researcher's questions are also presented in a narrative style. The narrative presentation of each session is preceded or followed by a set of questions entitled "my experience." These questions are intended to help the reader reflect on his or her experience in regard to the factor or topic under consideration.

Finally, I have realized that whenever I misplace my keys or use the wrong keys to open a lock, I become impatient, lose my peace of mind and feel stuck. Therefore, I have also included a section entitled "keys to …" in order to facilitate the understanding and implementation of every identified factor of stability and satisfaction in remarriage.

De Shazer (1985, pp. xv-xvi) elaborates further on the metaphor of the keys: "solutions are arrived at through keys rather than locks … An intervention only needs to fit in such a way that the solution evolves. It does not need to match the complexity of the lock. Just because the complaint is complicated does not mean that the solution has to be as complicated." In other words, the section on "keys" is designed to help the reader as a toolbox for reviewing and mastering the main ideas related to the discussed topic within the session. It will also help to acquire more knowledge and needed skills to solve some of the problems one may encounter in remarriage and life.

It is important to note that the mentioned "keys" in this book are samples and not a definitive list for every identified factor of stability and satisfaction in remarriage. The reader is therefore encouraged to continue making use of the keys that work for him or her, perhaps even put them in writing. The ultimate goal is to implement some of the keys presented in this book and/or to seek help from a professional.

Supplementary information that the reader may find useful is included in the latter part of the book.

# Meet the Participants

*Grouping of the Participants and Their Demographic Data*
*Description of the Participants*
*Orientation Questions*
*Description of the Female Participants*
*Description of the Male Participants*

This section covers the factors that influence stability and satisfaction in remarriage that emerged from the collected data of the sixteen participants. Whenever possible, tables and figures have been included in this book for purposes of clarification. However, before elaborating on the results of this study, I want to emphasize once again that for reasons of confidentiality, the names of the 16 participants and their significant others have been replaced by pseudonyms. Fifteen participants out of 16 described their second marriages as stable and satisfactory. The 16th participant (Fred) said that he was unsure of the future of his remarriage. This was because 3 months before the interview, he had started to experience problems with his second wife.

Nevertheless, Fred volunteered to be interviewed, and his contributions seemed very insightful and related to the purpose of this study. The other fifteen participants also revealed that, even if at the time of the interview they had become more secure about the future of their second marriages, they had also previously experienced some moments of tension and unhappiness, especially during the first 5 years of their remarriages. Over time those tensions became less threatening and resolving them empowered the partners.

I classified the results from the collected data into primary and secondary factors that influence both stability and satisfaction. This distinction is based on the number of participants who reported on a selected factor or theme. Primary factors refer to any selected theme reported by more than 8 participants out of the total of sixteen. Any theme that was reported by less than 9 participants has been categorized as a secondary factor.

However, it is important to clarify that even if a factor has been classified as secondary, that does not mean that it is less important than any of those classified as primary ones. The distinction between primary and secondary factors is primarily the difference in frequency in which they occurred. In this study. Every reported participant's experience is valuable in its uniqueness, as well as its relationship to that of other participants. Therefore, I made every effort possible to code each participant's experiences without reducing them to numerical figures. In addition, no single participant's experiences are considered normative. Every participant had a personal story to tell and I did my best to listen attentively to each story.

The participants' specific demographics that have not been disguised are gender, age, and cultural background. However, as mentioned before, for the sake of confidentiality, other demographics have been modified or omitted. The disguise protects the participant's confidentiality but does not affect the interpretation of the results. The participants' chronological age range was from 45 to 70 years. Therefore, all the participants had lived for over one generation (40 years). It is not surprising then that the responses to my questions and volunteered suggestions seemed to me to be contributions made from long-term experiences. The responses reflected a broad knowledge base. The responses were based primarily on each participant's life experiences and wisdom that they said they had received as they aged.

All the participants in this study were parents who entered second marriages with children from a first marriage that had ended in divorce. Therefore, if some of the participants' contributions to this study resemble or contradict the factors that influence or hinder marital stability and satisfaction in first, third, fourth or any other number of marriages, that is not the intent of this study. It is beyond the scope of this study to make explicit comparisons and contrasts between second marriages and first marriages or any other rank of marriage (e.g., third, fourth, or fifth). Nevertheless, I think that certain factors (e.g., mutual love and compatibility) are likely to influence the stability and satisfaction of all marriages.

All the participants' contributions were based on their retrospective accounts of their experiences and current points of view about stability and satisfaction in remarriage. Therefore, I coded the participants' data by focusing on what each participant thought and felt comfortable to say at the time of the interviews and in follow-up sessions. Some of the participants' responses are simply reflections of what they learned during their remarriage experiences. For instance, during the interview, Bernardo emphasized strongly that remarrying partners must avoid the risk of moving into the house or apartment that belongs to one of them. This is something he learned from what he called "one of my past mistakes." Bernardo clarified:

> It was not a wise decision for me to ask my second wife to
> move into my house where I was staying as a single parent with

two children [Alice and Tom]. In a special way, my daughter [Alice] highly resented my second wife [Jessica] partly because she perceived my wife as a stranger in the house who had come to bring chaos into the home that my daughter considered her own.

## Grouping of the Participants and Their Demographic Data

The participants were divided into two groups based on their gender as shown in Figures 2 and 3 below. For each gender group, the participants are listed in the order that they were interviewed. Once I was not getting any more new information, but repetitions of the same ideas using different or similar words, the interviews ended.

## Description of the Participants

The following descriptions are primarily intended for the reader to learn more about every person as a unique individual and to honor each one's experiences. Additionally, to provide the reader with an opportunity for knowledge expansion and a positive change, one is cautioned to avoid the risk becoming judgmental or opinionated.

The reader may discover experiences from each of the participants that are familiar, eye-opening and/or expressions of profound resilience. As you read, think about what you learn from every participant and how it helps you to expand your knowledge about stability and satisfaction in remarriage. All descriptions of the participants are written in the present tense to reflect the significant variables at the time the interviews were conducted.

## Orientation Questions

The following questions are designed to orientate the reader to ponder some of the most important ideas in this book. After reading Part I and Part II of this book, the reader should be in a position to respond for himself/herself to the questions below. A profound comprehension of the significant and unique details about each participant's experiences, suggestions and results of the research study may maximize the reader's ability to write or reflect on one's personal story.

| Code | 0001F | 0002F | 0003F | 0004F | 0005F | 0006F | 0007F | 0008F | Saturation |
|---|---|---|---|---|---|---|---|---|---|
| Alphabetical pseudonyms in order of conducted interviews to saturation point | Alicia | Beatrice | Catherine | Dora | Elizabeth | Felicia | Grace | Hilda | xxxx |
| Age | 58 | 64 | 53 | 52 | 60 | 53 | 65 | 58 | |
| Cultural-ethnic background | Italian | Puerto Rican (Hispanic) | Italian & Polish | Peruvian (Hispanic) | English, German & Italian American | Puerto Rican (Hispanic) raised in U.S. | African American | German & Welsh | |
| Highest level of formal education | Some college classes | Third year of college | College Graduate | Complete college to be a nurse | One year and 6 months of college | Second year of college | Half (1/2) year of college | Post-masters (licensed terapist) | |
| Religion | Pentecostal | Roman Catholic | Roman Catholic | Roman Catholic | Roman Catholic | Roman Catholic | Baptist convert to Roman Catholic | Quaker | |
| Age at firts marriage; and duration of first marriage | 21,17 | 20,10 | 22,8 | 20,5 | 18,5 | 18, less than 1 year | 20,25 | 19,12 | |
| Children from firts marriage and from second marriage | 1,0 | 5,0 | 2,0 | 2,0 | 1,1 | 1,1 | 5,0 | 1,2 | |
| Time in years between 1st. and 2nd. marriages; and time in remarriage to present | 1,8 | 8,27 | 4,20 | 9,18 | 2,31 | 1,33 | 2,16 | 3,25 | |
| Number of step-children | 1 | 0 | 0 | 0 | 0 | 0 | 0 | 0 | |
| Current residential neighborhood | Suburban | Urban | Urban | Urban | Urban | Inner city | Inner city | Suburban | |
| Annual family income in remarriage (U.S. dollars in thousands) | Over 130 | 45-55 | 75-90 | 75-90 | 35-45 | 90-130 | 75-90 | 45-55 | |

Figure 2. Demographic summary of the female participants.

| Code | 0001M | 0002M | 0003M | 0004M | 0005M | 0006M | 0007M | 0008M | Saturation |
|---|---|---|---|---|---|---|---|---|---|
| Alphabetical pseudonyms in order of conducted interviews to saturation point | Abraham | Bernanrdo | Charles | Daniel | Elias | Fred | Godfrey | Henry | xxxx |
| Age | 70 | 62 | 70 | 47 | 50 | 54 | 51 | 53 | |
| Cultural-ethnic background | Jewish American | Italian American | German American | Puerto Rican (Hispanic) raised in U.S. | Denied any: "Neither" (German & Swiss Parents) | African American | Scottish English | Irish American | |
| Highest level of formal education | Ph. D in Psychology | One year of college | Grade 12, 7 years navy training | College Graduate | Some college | Ph. D. student (clinical psychology) | Two years in college | Law school (Ph. D.) | |
| Religion | None | Roman Catholic | Roman Catholic | Roman Catholic | No religious affiliate | Roman Catholic | Episcopalian | Roman Catholic | |
| Age at firts marriage; and duration of first marriage | 20,40 | 20,20 | 22,25 | 21,15 | 23,7 | 24,15 | 21,7 | 32,11 | |
| Children from firts marriage and from second marriage | 1,0 | 2,0 | 4,0 | 3,0 | 3,2 | 1,1 | 1,2 | 2,1 | |
| Time in years between 1st. and 2nd. marriages; and time in remarriage to present | 28 | 2,19 | 2.5,21 | 2,8 | 3.5,16 | 2,10 | 4,21 | 11,8 | |
| Number of step-children | 1 | 1 | 0 | 2 | 0 | 1 | 0 | 0 | |
| Current residential neighborhood | Suburban | Suburban | Suburban | Urban | Suburban | Inner city | Urban | Suburban | |
| Annual family income in remarriage (U.S. dollars in thousands) | Over 130 | 90-130 | 75-90 | 45-55 | 55-65 | 75-90 | 75-90 | Over 130 | |

Figure 3. Demographic summary for the male participants.

## My experience

1. Which of the participants in this study most impacted me and why?
2. Which of the participants in this study do I most identify myself with and why?
3. How has the description of results in this study helped me to explore the different areas in my life that might have a significant impact on my stability and satisfaction in remarriage?
4. What lessons have I learned from the results of each female participant in this study?
5. What lessons have I learned from the results of the each male participant in this study?
6. What lessons have I learned from each participant's cultural background in this study?
7. Which gender differences manifested in this study have helped me to think deeply about the impact of my gender in regard to being a custodial parent?
8. How is my story different from the mentioned descriptions of the participants?
9. If I had been asked to be a participant in this study, what factors do I consider need to be added to the developed theory in order to reinforce stability and satisfaction in remarriage?

## *Description of the Female Participants*

### *Alicia*

Alicia is a 58-year-old woman of Italian descent, who migrated to the United States with her parents from Italy when she was 8 years old. She spoke Italian and English fluently. She was raised as a practicing Pentecostal. She completed a few college classes before she was married at the age of 21, for the first time to her husband (Paul) of Italian descent (second generation). The marriage lasted for 17 years. Paul was an only child and was raised by his single mother, who was a non-practicing Pentecostal. Paul and Alicia had one biological son (Bob), who is currently 29 years old and is in his first marriage.

At the time of the interview, Alicia had been remarried to Alex for 8 years. Alex was previously married and has a 35-year-old son (Samuel) from his first marriage. Samuel lives about 10 miles from Alicia and Alex's home and they visit each other regularly. Alicia and Alex live in a suburban neighborhood and have an annual income of over $130,000.

Alicia and Paul were married for 17 years when Alicia filed for divorce. Before the legal divorce was finalized, the couple sought marital counseling. The main reason for seeking help was an attempt to make the marriage work after Paul's use of cocaine and an on-going marital infidelity with a woman who was 10 years younger than Paul. After signing the divorce papers, the court granted custody of Bob to Alicia, and Paul was allowed monthly visits to see him. Alicia reported that 6 months after the court's approval of the divorce, Paul stopped using cocaine and married "that same younger girl" (Rose).

Immediately after the court approved the divorce, Alicia and Bob moved into an apartment. Six months later she started dating Alex, a Jewish American male, who had a Ph.D. and was 12 years older than Alicia. She described Alex as very respectful of her. During the first 6 months of dating, Alex and Alicia dialogued in detail about their finances, and in the 7th month they decided to get married. They put all their money into a joint account, bought a house in a suburban neighborhood, and Alicia and her son moved into the new house with Alex. In retrospect, Alicia reported her admiration of Alex's involvement in Bob's education and disciplining her son. According to Alicia, such involvement has helped her son to succeed in school and she feels very happy that her son has gained the trust of his stepfather without losing contact with his biological father. During the first half of the interview, Alicia spoke of the emotional abuse she experienced in her first marriage. However, after taking a break, she related how she has managed to find happiness and feel respected as a wife in her second marriage.

Currently, Alicia and Paul are in their second marriages. Based on Alicia's narrative, Bob seems to be a very significant person in the lives of nuclear and extended family members. Above all, it was interesting to hear Alicia narrate the joy she felt at Bob's marriage to Jane, because Alicia, Alex, Paul, and Rose had an opportunity to interact with one another in an extremely friendly and mutually respectful manner. Alicia even managed to dance with Paul. Alex had a good conversation with Rose. And Alex danced with Rose!

### Beatrice

Beatrice is a 64-year-old woman born and raised in Puerto Rico. Both her parents were Puerto Rican, devout Catholics, and they raised her as a Catholic, too. She attended college for 3 years, and at the age of 20 was married for the first time to Ricardo, a Puerto Rican man, during an official ceremony within the Catholic Church. After 10 years of marriage, they divorced. Eight years later, she married Antonio, who was also divorced, and has been married to him for 10 years. Beatrice and Antonio have not had any children together, although Beatrice has five children and Antonio has two children from their previous marriages. They now live in an urban neighborhood on an annual income of $45,000 to $55,000. According to Beatrice, being a Catholic contributed to her prolonged perseverance in her first marriage that she described as being "unhappy, abusive, and miserable."

After those 10 years, she felt that she could not bear the verbal, physical, and emotional abuses any longer. Consequently, she decided to divorce her husband and left the house immediately. After the divorce Beatrice suffered a lot of humiliation from her family members for having divorced. She experienced financial difficulties and could not meet her own needs and those of her children. Two years after the divorce, she moved to the United States with her five children and remained a single mother for the next 6 years. During this period she experienced a lot of loneliness and lack of support in raising the children.

In the meantime, Beatrice met Antonio, who had just migrated to the United States from South America. She first cohabited with him and later they married civilly. Her primary motivation for remarriage was the need for a com panion, someone who would help her with the financial needs of her five children. Antonio left his two children from his first marriage in his country of origin with their mother. Beatrice described Antonio as "a warm, respectful, mature, loving and religious person."

These values in Antonio helped Beatrice to regain her self-esteem, because she felt that he treated her with dignity, listened to her, went to church with her, and was always available to her children. Even if Beatrice did not enter the second marriage for reasons of love, she advocated that remarrying partners need to love one another and to seek counseling, especially about forgiveness for those who feel wounded from the previous marriage. In her opinion, mutual love is the key to stability and satisfaction in remarriage. She felt that the two partners have to be in love with each other because this helps them to understand each other and communicate about their problems with concern and seek solutions that benefit them and their significant other.

According to Beatrice, being a Roman Catholic has positively and negatively affected her marriage life. She described in positive terms that belonging to the Catholic Church has helped her to keep the faith in the midst of suffering, especially by praying the Rosary. However, being refused reception of the Eucharist has brought her a lot of self-blame and anger toward the Catholic leaders' insensitivity to the pain of people going through divorce. By the same token, as a remarried Catholic and churchgoer, she feels condemned for having remarried instead of being supported by the Church to which she belongs.

Beatrice expressed the pain in her first marriage and in being a single mother. Above all, she mentioned that being both a mom and a dad to her children was very draining. Now as a remarried divorced person she finds it hard not to receive the Eucharist in the Catholic Church. When the researcher asked her about the annulment process, Beatrice almost broke into tears, and spoke only after a 2-minute silence and sobbing. She said that she and her husband have tried for the past 5 years, but all their efforts have been in vain. At the same time she finds it difficult to start putting into writing what happened to her in the first marriage because the more she writes, as required by the Church officials working on the annulment process, the more she suffers the pain and humiliation experienced in the first marriage.

It is impressive that Beatrice had kept her faith and continues going to the Catholic Church even without being allowed to receive the Eucharist! Beatrice's holding on to the faith reminded me of the phrase my Grandmother used to say to me growing up: "Faith in God keeps those who keep the faith."

### *Catherine*

Catherine is a 54-year-old woman of Italian and Polish background, but she identifies herself as Italian, and as a non-practicing Roman Catholic. She graduated from college as a teacher. She was married for the first time to Andrew when she was 22 years old. The marriage lasted 8 years and during that time they had a baby girl (Eileen) first, and then a boy (Eric). After her divorce she spent 4 years taking care of her two children in a rented apartment. During the 4th year, she started dating Michael, who is of German and Italian background and they married. Catherine and Michael have been married for 22 years. They have not had any children together. Michael, also divorced, did not have any children from his first marriage. They currently live in an urban neighborhood and have an annual family income of $75,000 to $90,000.

In elaborating on her background, Catherine mentioned that she was the youngest in her family and that all three of her siblings were still in their first marriages. Consequently, she revealed, with a lot of pain, that it was hard for her siblings and parents to accept her after her divorce and to understand the circumstances that contributed to it. However, some of the extended family members who had divorced before her came to her rescue and she had a number of friends with whom she associated as she was mourning the loss of her first marriage.

One of the reasons that hindered Catherine's family members from sympathizing with her immediately after her divorce was the fact that they did not know about the tensions which the couple was experiencing, especially because, whenever Catherine and Andrew appeared in public, they seemed to be very friendly. They showed no expressed marital conflicts and misunderstandings, which would have made others suspect any tension between the couple. According to Catherine, 3 years before the divorce occurred, she had already made a decision that this was not the marriage she wanted to be in for the rest of her life. However, she did not want to be the one to initiate the divorce. To her advantage, on one occasion the couple got into a slight argument, and Andrew asked that they separate. With no further delay, Catherine took those words as a pretext to justify that Andrew was the one who initiated the divorce, and she separated from him immediately.

After the divorce, Catherine tried her best to keep in contact with her former in-laws, whom she described as very good people, and she wanted her children to maintain close contact with them as the children grew up. As mentioned before, in the 4th year after her divorce, Catherine started dating Michael, and during a 6month process of courtship Catherine realized, "This is the man [Michael] I was meant to marry. I mean, I thought I wanted to spend the rest of my life with him."

Elaborating on Michael's cultural background, Catherine mentioned that he described himself as Italian, but according to her he was "an ex-German." When asked to explain what she meant by "ex-German," she started by identifying herself as Italian. " We [Italians] are very emotional. We just go with our emotions and let them run, while he will think things out before he reacts to anything. So he does not let his feelings show, but you know they are there."

Catherine elaborated on why a person like her could stay in a marriage in which she was not feeling happy. She said: "It was the day before Mother's Day, we were driving to the grocery store because we were having everyone over for Mother's Day dinner, and he [Andrew] said to me: 'You seem so unhappy most of the time. Why do you stay?' And I said to him: 'I stay because of the children.' And he said: 'Well, we should separate.' And that was it. And that was the end of it. He gave me what I wanted because I didn't want to be the one to say: 'I want out.' So he helped me get out of it. But otherwise I probably would have stayed married to him [but unhappy]."

### *Dora*

Dora is a 50-year-old woman born and raised Roman Catholic in Peru. She speaks Spanish fluently and is able to express herself in English, though with some difficulty. She completed college in Peru as a nurse. She married for the first time at the age of 20 and her marriage to Pablo lasted for 5 years, during which time she had two children. Nine years after her divorce she married Alex. The two of them have been married for 18 years. They have not had any children together and Alex did not have any children. Alex and Dora live in an urban neighborhood, and their annual income is between $75 and $90 thousand. At the time of the interview, Dora said that although she does not attend Mass and other services at the Catholic Church, she still considers herself Catholic.

Dora grew up in a low-income family of five siblings and eight stepsiblings. While growing up, Dora stayed with her biological parents until she was four and then her parents separated. She went to stay with her mother until she was 11 and afterward she started staying with her father who was then remarried to Laura. Dora emphasized that the way she knew her second husband was primarily through cohabitation with him. When asked about her motivations to remarry, Dora said: " I decided to choose my second husband (Alex) because he was a man without children. I want in my house no other kids than mine because I had a negative experience with my divorced father who married a lady with too many kids."

Based on the experience of being a stepchild and the pain that it brought her, Dora resolved not to marry any man who had children. At the time of the interview, Dora mentioned that she was very happy in her second marriage and had already spent 18 years with Alex. Together they have co-parented her two daughters. Dora highlighted that she has done her best to provide "guidance" to these children because that is what she did not receive from her father, mother and stepmother while growing up. In addition, when asked whether she had concerns about becoming a stepmother by virtue of getting married to a man who had children, she responded: "No, no. It was not that. I think I could have been a real good stepmom, but I always have the idea that it's always a problem. Like if he could have had kids and I have kids, he always wants something for his kids and I will always want something for my kids and there is going to be trouble, not even over money, probably it is everything."

Dora's story emphasizes the need to think about children who grow up having witnessed the divorce of their parents. Later on these children may end up marrying for different motives and their marriages may also end up in divorce. Then they remarry and the cycle of divorce is repeated in their children. On the other hand, Dora's experiences of her parents' divorce, living in a stepfamily, her painful first marriage, her struggle as a single mother to raise her children and finally her stability and satisfaction in remarriage indicates that some people can be resilient through divorce and succeed in a remarriage.

### Elizabeth

Elizabeth is a 60-year-old woman. Her mother was of English and German background, and her father of German and Italian descent. However, she identified herself as Italian. When asked what makes her feel Italian, Elizabeth replied: "I associate Italian people with family, stable home, together-type people. They have parties. They are family-oriented. That is why, I guess, I feel Italian. I want to be like that."

Elizabeth's highest level of formal education was 1 year and 6 months in college. She was raised Roman Catholic and identified herself as a practicing Catholic. Elizabeth first married Sandro at the age of 18, and the marriage lasted 5 years. The couple had one son, Robert. After 2 years of separation, she then married Peter. They have been together for thirty-one years in the second marriage and they have one son (John). She lives in an urban neighborhood and has an annual family income of $35,000 to $45,000.

One of the experiences that Elizabeth emphatically mentioned during the interview was the way she came to terms with the resentment she felt toward her mother in regard to money. By the time of the interview, she had forgiven her for the poverty in which they had lived. This happened after her experience of being a single mother because that is when she realized that single mothers have stressful financial situations.

During the interview Elizabeth spoke also with notable enthusiasm about the wisdom of looking back at her experiences of love in her first marriage and her second marriage. She said that in the case of her second marriage, love was different from that in the first marriage. Elizabeth said:

> I remember myself thinking I was madly in love at 18 years old, and the word love meant sexual intimacy, nothing else. [In] the second marriage, there is a lot more than love. There is love [in the second marriage], but there is a lot of other stuff too. There is a commitment to one another, caring about someone. You think at 18 you love somebody, [but] you don't know the meaning of love. When you get older, when you go through that second marriage, you are seeing the care and the patience that all comes under love. Love isn't just a word or only for sex.

Elizabeth was willing to share her experiences about herself and other remarried parents. She mentioned that some divorced parents remarry for reasons related to security and love. She explained: "They don't want to be alone anymore. They don't want to struggle by themselves. [This does not mean] … that they would pick up anybody on the street. It is good if they find someone with whom they are compatible."

## Felicia

Felicia is a 53-year-old Hispanic American woman, born in Puerto Rico and raised in the United States. She speaks Spanish and English fluently.

She completed her second year of college and is currently remarried. She is Catholic and attends church services one or more times a week.

Felicia married for the first time at the age of 18, stayed for less than 1 year in her first marriage, and divorced her husband (Roberto) due to "humiliation above and beyond physical abuse." She and Roberto had one child, José. She waited about 1 year, and then married Fausto, whom she has now been married to for 33 years. Together they have a daughter, Ana. They live in the inner city on an annual income of $75,000 to $90,000.

After her divorce, Felicia had custody of her son. She spent the time before remarriage in an apartment within a housing complex. In the same complex there was a man, Fausto, who had also gone through a divorce and was staying in one of the apartments. After taking the bus together for 3 months without talking, Fausto initiated a conversation with her. For 3 consecutive weeks, every morning Fausto used to wait for Felicia so that they could go together to the bus stop and in the evening he made an effort to walk with her to her apartment. When the conversation became personal, Felicia started to withdraw from Fausto. However, Fausto remained persistent.

One of the reasons that Felicia stated for her withdrawal was related to her ongoing pain from the abuse from the previous marriage. Because of this, she had resolved not to date any man at all. Two months later, out of respect for her, Fausto decided to give Felicia her space. A month later Felicia felt a strong urge to ask Fausto out for a date. She started making plans as to how to meet him and how to invite him to her apartment! To make a long story short, in 6 months they decided to get married and at the time of the interview, they had been married for 33 years.

Felicia narrated her story of running away from home from her abusive mother and getting pregnant after her first sexual experience with a man who also abused her. She told of Fausto's expression of fatherly love toward José. Felicia described herself as a person whose decision to get married to Fausto has brought meaning, happiness, spiritual growth, and economic prosperity into the lives of her children, José and Ana, and her husband, Fausto.

### Grace

Grace is a 65-year-old African American woman raised in a Baptist Church. She attended college for half a year after her first marriage, which was at age 21, and lasted for 25 years. During this marriage she had two sets of twins (four girls) and one son who is the youngest. She did not have any children in her second marriage. She has been married to her second husband for 16 years, waiting 2 years after her divorce to remarry. She was born in the inner city in a poor neighborhood and her parents died when she was 11 or 12 years old. Her first marriage was very painful. She experienced problems with the

IRS because her husband used to spend a lot of money, which they did not have, and never filed income tax returns. Currently, she lives in the inner city and has an annual family income of $75,000 to $90,000.

Grace's first marriage involved a lot of marital infidelities on the part of her husband. While she was still married to him, he had a child with another woman. That became the "last blow" which influenced her to file for divorce immediately after she knew about that child. She left the house and started to care for her five children on a limited income. While still a single mother, she went back to school and also took on two jobs. Grace emphasized: "We were poor, but we were happy."

After 2 years of being a single mother, Grace married one of her best friends whom she had known when she was still in her first marriage. Her son is very proud of this man because he saved his mother from a lot of pain, humiliation, and shame. In reference to marriage and remarriage, Grace observed a major difference between most traditional Caucasians and many people of African American background in the United States. Grace said, "It seems in our community [African American], we do things backwards; the child first, then live together, and then somewhere along the line, for whatever reason, you get married."

When asked what advice she would give to African American boys and girls in order to prepare themselves for a happy marriage, Grace emphatically said:

> "Finish school, stay motivated, go to college, get a good education, do some traveling, get your own apartment, do not live with anybody and save yourself for that special person. It will be worth it. ... Save yourself. Abstain from sex. I mean, sex is wonderful, the best thing in the world, but with the right person, and only the right person. It can be the most out of this world. It will be well worth it."

Elaborating on the notion of marital stability and satisfaction in a post-interview note, Grace wrote: "People should be intent on looking for what works. What use is stability without satisfaction or vice versa?"

### Hilda

Hilda is a 58-year-old woman of German and Welsh background. She was a licensed professional with a postmasters degree in marriage and family therapy. She attended Presbyterian and Methodist churches when she was growing up. Her first husband was Jewish, and she learned a lot about the Jewish culture during her marriage to him for 12 years. She was only 19 when she married him and they had one child together. Hilda's first husband was physically abusive to her and after the birth of their first child (Damian), he became even more abusive and even mistreated his mother-in-law. She waited 13 years before remarrying and has spent 25 years in her second marriage. She currently belongs to the Quaker religion with her spouse and children. They live in a suburban neighborhood and have an annual family income of $45,000 to $55,000. She had experienced a number of miscarriages in her second marriage before she gave birth to a boy (Robert) and a girl (Jane). When asked what divorced parents need to know and to be prepared to encounter after remarriage, Hilda said:

> Remarriage is messy because whatever you do, you please one and you hurt the other. For instance, if you please the spouse, you may end up hurting the children or the ex-spouse or yourself.

Hilda highlighted that remarriage involves a lot of shame and fear of the unknown future and that is why remarried people need to be supported, rather than judged, for their mistakes. One of the mistakes Hilda admitted making, as a remarried woman, was to allow her son to continue making decisions in front of her spouse. This was a habit she had developed when she was a single mother. Hilda was proud of her German background. Hilda stated:

> We Germans, we don't make decisions lightly. We won't pack our bags at the first fight. You know we are going to stick with it.... We don't make a mountain out of a mere hill.

Therefore, it seems that for Hilda, divorce was the last option after bearing ten years of physical and verbal abuse from her first husband.

## Description of the Male Participants

### Abraham

Abraham is a 70-year-old Jewish American man with a doctorate in clinical psychology. However he is not a practicing Jew. He emphasized that he does not identify himself with any religion. He married his first wife (Hannah) when he was 20 years old. The couple had one child (Thomas), who was born with mental problems. Thomas' mental status created a lot of stress for Abraham and Hannah because of the extra care that he needed.

Abraham stated that this child contributed to the couples' divorce. He spent 40 years in his first marriage and it was 2 years before he remarried.

At the time of the interviews for this study, he had spent eight years in his second marriage to Joyce, who was also divorced. Joyce came to the second marriage with her 17-year-old son (John) from her first marriage. At the time of the interview Abraham and Joyce were living in a suburban neighborhood and had an annual income of over $130,000.

Abraham and his first wife, Hannah, had experienced a great deal of emotional stress as a couple while taking care of Thomas. During their courtship, Abraham and Hannah talked about their shared dream of having a normal child that they were going to cherish and educate. However, when their son Thomas was born handicapped, their dream was shattered.

According to Abraham, Thomas's physical and mental conditions were a big blow to their dream and they brought enormous stresses on the couple's relationship, which eventually led to their divorce. In spite of his unrealized dream in his son Thomas, Abraham experienced the joy that his stepchild (John) has brought into his life.

### Bernardo

Bernardo is a 62-year-old Italian American male. He has been a Roman Catholic for all his life. He completed 1 year of college. At the age of 20, he married Rose, to whom he was married for 22 years. The couple had two children, Alice and Tom. Bernardo's father, Robert, was also divorced. According to Bernardo, Robert's marriage failed because he put money first. Bernardo learned from his father to value money first. He became a workaholic at the expense of his marriage, the controller of money in the house, and the decision maker, which caused his first marriage to fail. Two years after Bernardo got divorced, he married a woman named Jessica, with one son, and they have been married for 19 years. Bernardo and Jessica live in a suburban neighborhood with an annual family income of $90,000 to $130,000.

Bernardo spent the two years after his divorce living in the same house with his daughter, Alice, who was 19 years old at the time of her parents' divorce. During that time Alice took on the responsibility of housekeeper and she considered herself the female owner of the house. When Bernardo remarried Jessica, Alice was highly upset with her father and her stepmother. Jessica was a widow who had one child (John), a situation that made Bernardo a stepfather to John. Based on the experience Bernardo had with Alice and Jessica, he had learned the hard way that remarried couples should sell their old houses and buy a new one to reduce the risk of a sense of entitlement, especially if children are involved.

Bernardo was against joint custody, which includes weekends and any other short periods of less than 3 months. His rationale was that the parents have their permanent homes, but the children have no place to call home. He supported this idea based on the experience of his grandchildren who are caught in the middle of the weekend visits to their mother Alice and her former husband. Bernardo and Jessica are currently preparing for their 20th anniversary, and they anticipate it to be a big family reunion. Although they had no children together, Bernardo and Jessica consider the children from each partner's first marriage as their biological children.

Bernardo emphasized that remarried parents should try to avoid "a selfish attitude [me, myself, and I] in a marriage, with a special emphasis on money." He compared the emotions related to divorce with the stages of grief. Bernardo highlighted that it was hard for him as a man to initially accept his responsibility in the divorce. Even after the divorce had occurred, he spent a lot of time in denial, blaming his former spouse. He experienced depression and kept going back and forth over these emotions. Bernardo emphasized that people should not rush into remarriage before removing the emotional baggage from a previous marriage.

### Charles

Charles is a 70-year-old veteran and semiretired. His parents came from Europe. He is of Hungarian and Polish descent. Although he did not go to college, he did have 7 years of training in the Navy. He is an insurance salesperson, involved in financial planning, who is taking care of his existing clients without looking for new cases. He was raised Catholic and continues to be an active member of the Catholic Church in his parish. He married his first wife at the age of 22 and their marriage lasted for 25 years, during which time they had four children. After 25 years Jenny, his wife, divorced him, and 2 ½ years later he married Julia, to whom he has been married for 21 years. Charles and Julia live in a suburban neighborhood on an annual income of $75,000 to $90,000.

Charles revealed that he dated his first girlfriend (Rose) for 4 years, but they never got married because of his mother's disapproval that the woman was not Catholic. Consequently, his mother set up for him a new possibility (Jenny). Charles' mother and Jenny's mother were friends and together they worked "to get us going together and later I realized that it was a mistake, but at that time it looked good."

Charles married Jenny when he was 22 years old. By then, he was in the Navy, and he would come home only on weekends. Charles elaborated:

> Nine months after meeting my wife [Jenny], we married, and I realized later that it was a mistake, [because] both of us were not ready for it. It was just a party every weekend and once we

had the baby machine going, we had four kids in 49 months [4 years and 1 month]… After about 18 years she (Jenny) wanted to go to college, which she did not do before we got married.

Charles stated that both his grandfathers were alcoholics and both his parents had only a grammar school education. He said:

> So when I got a high-school education there was no encouragement to go for further education. You know, get a job, get married, and have kids. [Charles did not obtain a college education because] I started having kids when I was 22, had three of them while I was in the Navy, and one when I got out. And I was living with my mother-in-law, who was a widow, just trying to support the family. When I started working as a mechanic, I had no time for the family. All the time was dedicated to work.

Additionally, Charles said that after 18 years of marriage with Jenny, the two of them agreed that Jenny would go back to finish her college education and if possible go for a Master's degree. Jenny dedicated herself to study until she completed her master's degree. Immediately after her graduation, she started working in New York, commuting from New Jersey. Three months after starting her job, she informed Charles that she had rented an apartment in New York from which she could commute to work. Charles was upset by all of these ready-made decisions, and, above all, after he became aware of this, by the fact that Jenny was having an affair with a married man from Japan.

After 25 years of marriage, Jenny divorced Charles for the Japanese man, who abandoned her because he did not want to divorce his wife and leave his teenage daughter. Charles added that, ever since Jenny divorced him, she has not been able to reestablish herself in another marriage. All the men who have come into her life stay with her for only a little while and then they separate. That has probably contributed to her frustration and jealousy toward Charles' second wife (Julia).

Charles expressed determination and commitment to his second wife and the clear boundaries he has developed with his first wife and 4 children. He reported feeling happy for taking his stand because he had won out over all their attempts to tear his remarriage apart. Surprisingly, irrespective of their negative attitude toward him and his second wife, he said that he still loves them and considers them part of his family.

### *Daniel*

Daniel is a 47-year-old man, born in Puerto Rico and raised in the United States. A college graduate, he grew up as a Catholic and at the time of the interview he attended church services once a week, usually the Sunday Mass. He married his first wife (Paulina) when he was 21 years old. They had 3 children (Evelyn, Ana, and Tomas). Daniel reported that his marriage to Paulina lasted 15 years, but within that period he separated from her five times, each time for 3 to 6 weeks. He would go to stay with his friends and on one occasion he went and stayed with his mother-in-law.

After trying different means of making the marriage work, including going for couple therapy, Daniel finally filed for divorce and left the house to Paulina. He stayed for 6 months with a friendly family. Then he rented an apartment, where he stayed with his 17-year-old daughter (Evelyn) for 1 year. During that year, he made arrangements to marry Maggie, who was also divorced with two sons from her first marriage. Daniel had known Maggie for 7 years at his work where he was her boss. By the time of the interview, Daniel and Maggie had been married for almost 9 years, were living in an urban neighborhood, and had an annual family income of $45,000 to $55,000.

During the interview, Daniel was very outgoing and detailed in his responses. For instance, his responses to some of the questions asked him may help the reader to get a better sense of some of his marital experiences and contributions to this study. Daniel clarified:

> There were a number of things that contributed to the end of the first marriage; there were a lot of things. Before my first daughter was born, my wife Paulina basically insulted my family and my parents… and my grandmother. She was very immature. I was blind, you know, I loved her, but she was from the street. She didn't have a father, and she did things in the beginning that just hurt me. But I dealt with it because my daughter was coming, and I wasn't the type of person to leave a person for that. I thought that in time things would get better, and it didn't. I was unhappy… I was just fed up with it already. She did so many things that hurt me and I lost my love for her little by little. It was 15 years, and we had a third child. I wasn't even looking for a third child. I'm not saying I'm not happy about it, but I wasn't ecstatic about the fact I was going to have a third child, because I already knew that our marriage wasn't what I was looking for.
>
> I was motivated to remarry because I found it difficult to be by myself. I always lived with somebody my entire life. I was either with my parents or I was with my first marriage. I never

lived alone and it was very hard for me. It was very difficult for me the first time that I was by myself and I just needed to be with somebody. It was very hard… I got separated a number of times. There were incidents that happened and I would leave the house and go live with a friend, or at one time I even stayed with her mom. For a few days, a week, I stayed with some friends of mine.

One friend that helped me out, I stayed in his house for a couple of months … But I never stayed by myself entirely until like I felt I was imposing myself on my friend because he had his family. He had his wife and his children and I needed to find a place on my own, which I did. I found a small room in [another place], and the first night was very difficult for me. I felt extremely lonely and sad, and I could hardly sleep that night. I was very depressed. I was very depressed, but as time went on, I adjusted.

Listening to Daniel's narratives about his remarriage experiences was profoundly moving as he referred to what he called: "one of the most horrible days in my life." He narrated the following story after being asked what was the impact of his children on his remarriage stability? Daniel responded:

That has been very tough, very tough. Because my children always thought that I left their mother for Maggie. The little ones didn't understand because they were younger at the time. But my older daughter [21 years old] knew what I had gone through. Even my first wife's mother understood why I stopped, why I left. Because she knew what I had gone through, but for the children, it was tough.

We had a lot of problems between my current wife and my children. My oldest daughter came to live with me at one point when I first got married, when I first got the house. She was living with me because she couldn't live with her mom. She [Evelyn] was having trouble because she felt Paulina was intolerable. They did not get along; I wasn't going to leave her in the street. So … my daughter came to live with me. Before I got married, she was still living with me. We got our house a month before we got married. First we got the house, then, when we got married, my daughter came to live with me. After the first 2 weeks, there was an incident in my house between my wife and my daughter, and there was fists thrown, there was a fight. That was very devastating for me. That was one of the most horrible days in my life. I had just got into the house with my new wife. My daughter didn't like her from the beginning. I spoke to my daughter that she could come live with us, that everything was going to be fine, that she would have her own room, which she did. It was OK the first 2 weeks; then an incident happened.

When asked: "What do you think your daughter might have felt that contributed to the misunderstanding with your wife?" Daniel replied:

They felt I guess, you know, that I shouldn't have gotten remarried, that it was my fault. That's the way they saw it. I think they were blaming her for taking me away from their mother.

After that fight, the oldest daughter (Evelyn) left Daniel's house and started living in an apartment alone at the age of 21. According to Daniel, "I think, for me it was best thing that my daughter left because that certainly wasn't going to work out." However, after the daughter left, Daniel expressed the following profound regret: "To this day, what I regret totally is that my daughter comes to my house, but she stays outside, and she speaks to my wife not for long."

By the end of the interviews, Daniel said that the reconciliation process had started between his second wife and his oldest daughter. That process made him feel happier in his remarriage. He used phrases which seemed to indicate that, although it was very difficult for him to act as a judge between his second wife and his children, he managed to put the events within a context that helped him to avoid taking sides. Daniel clarified:

All three of my children were there when the incident happened. So that was horrible. It took a few months before they started coming back slowly to come to the house and try and understand what happened. They accepted it and little by little. But it was tough. It was very tough for me. I'm not trying to discourage a person who wants to remarry and bring their children because my incident was a little unique … My new wife now, she worked for me. So right away they think that caused the problem, you know.

Consequently, Daniel cautioned remarrying parents as follows:

> Don't leave your children out. It is very important even in the tough situations and you have to try. It is very hard to be a referee or a judge when you have your children on this side, and you love them and you have your wife on the other side and you love her, and you're stuck in the middle with a problem. If you lean toward them, then you are prejudiced toward them, and vice versa. It's tough; it was tough. But I'm still with her, and I'm happy and work at it. You work at each situation you came up with and you try and resolve it without damaging either person, you know. And it's hard on the children because they're still growing up.

Daniel also used phrases of appreciation because of the role played by his second wife in reinforcing his remarriage stability, satisfaction, and relationships with his children from the previous marriage. Daniel elaborated:

> My wife has been very patient, you know. She has been supportive, and she has spoken to my children from time to time, you know, even though there are moments when she seems like [she] doesn't want anything to do with them. But she still tolerates it, you know, and she is an understanding person. My children were 7, 11 and 18 when I remarried. It seems, the younger the children, the easier it may be because they grow up with new wife. If they're older already at the time of remarriage and they have been together with the mother for a while, it may be more difficult for them to understand what's going on, and to adapt to the new wife.

Based on Daniel's descriptions and the whole interview process, it seems, that in order to understand the dynamics behind Daniel's stability and satisfaction in remarriage, it is important to understand the role played by his three children, especially the oldest daughter, and his second wife's patience. No wonder then that he finally suggested strongly that remarried parents should try their best to balance the time they dedicate to their children and second wives.

### Elías

Elías is a 50-year-old man, who refrained from identifying his cultural background and denied affiliation to any formalized religion. However, he admitted that his parents were of German and Swiss descent. Elías married his first wife, Bernadette, when he was 23 years old, and their marriage lasted 7 years. They had three children, whom Elías had custody of after their divorce. After the divorce, he waited 3½ years before he married Veronica, with whom he had two children. They have been married for 16 years. Veronica was also divorced at the time of her remarriage to Elías. The two of them had become romantically involved while both of them were still in their first marriages. Veronica and Elías live in a suburban neighborhood on an annual income of $55,000 to $65,000. Elaborating on the causes of his divorce, Elías mentioned: "My first wife had a psychological profile to only express things in anger."

In part, Elías attributed this profile of his wife to his involvement in an extramarital relationship with the woman he later married, "I became unfaithful because I felt tired of being blamed all the time by my first wife for everything that went wrong at home."

Elías seemed honest and willing to accept his mistakes in regard to the divorce. He expressed himself so calmly, without a defensive attitude, as he expressed his responsibility for the extramarital affair and the circumstances around it. In addition, he sustained a relationship in which his first spouse would only in anger hold conversations with him.

Throughout the interview, Elías' responses were very precise, direct and to the point whenever asked questions, and with little expressed emotion. Elías expressed concern for the children of remarried parents in that parents should be attentive to the children's pain and needs. Elías suggested that stability and satisfaction in remarriage primarily depend on the personalities of the partners, their compatibilities, shared values, the neighborhood, sex, parenting skills, and how they manage their finances.

### Fred

Fred is a 54-year-old African American male. At the time of the interview, he was a doctoral student in a department of clinical psychology. He was raised Roman Catholic and is actively involved in the Catholic Church. He married for the first time at 24 years of age and stayed in that marriage for 15 years. His first wife, Rosie, was a Caucasian. According to Fred, his motivation for marrying a Caucasian woman had to be understood within the context of how life was in the 1960s in the United States. It was a time when many young people wanted to test everything and to explore unknown territory. They were highly curious and rebellious. Fred stated: "I was a rebel, not to overthrow the Government ... but no one could tell me who to sleep with, what to do, experiment with and what I should not experiment with."

Fred and Rosie had one child, Bob. When the couple's marriage was going through a very tough time, Bob became a reason for the two parents to stay together. The contributing factors to their divorce included the lack of fulfilling their expectations and the lack of negotiating their racial differences.

Fred remarried Sarah 2 years after his first divorce and they have been together for 10 years. Sarah is an African Caribbean woman who emigrated to the United States in 1990.

Sarah was also divorced, had one girl from her first marriage, and together they have a son (Jason). They live in the inner city. Fred's annual family income is $75,000 to $90,000. Fred and Sarah belong to different religions. According to Fred, Sarah's religious background was not an issue when they were dating. However, after marriage, for reasons not clearly known to Fred, Sarah started to withdraw from some of Fred's sexual advances and ways of expressing intimacy, particularly oral sex and watching sexual movies.

After the interviews, I do not know what happened between Fred and Sarah. During the interviews they were having strong disagreements related to religious differences. Those differences had affected their sexual satisfaction. The couple also had financial difficulties and discomfort due to differences in their levels of formal education. Sarah completed elementary school and Fred was a Ph.D. student.

Fred complained that he had lost a lot of friends because when they came to his home it was difficult to hold academically focused conversations without Sarah feeling excluded. At the same time Fred mentioned that Sarah was complaining that Fred, with all his education, was not making enough money. In the meantime, Jason was the one whom Fred thought was making him stay longer in this marriage. Otherwise he was ready to move out. Fred was determined to seek professional help in order to make his remarriage work.

### Geoffrey

Geoffrey is a 51-year-old male of Scotch and English background who attended college for 2 years. Geoffrey was raised Episcopalian and during the interview period he was a very active member in his church. His first marriage was to Nora at the age of 21. Their marriage lasted 7 years and they had a daughter (Lucy). Four years after he divorced Nora he married again and has been remarried for 21 years. They have two children together. He was living in an urban neighborhood, and his annual family income was $75,000 to $90,000 at the time of the interview.

Geoffrey and Nora were both peaceful in their marriage in the beginning. However, after the first 6 months their personality differences started affecting their relationship. Geoffrey described himself as very sociable, friendly, interested in family dinners and church activities. This kind of sociability was the complete opposite of what Nora was interested in.

According to Geoffrey, Nora was more of a homebody, one-on-one conversationalist, who had no interest in social gatherings and events. This incompatibility influenced Geoffrey to socialize with friends outside the home and to return late in the evenings. At the same time, he bonded with his daughter and the two spent time together at home. This, however, made the situation more difficult for Nora because her daughter began to distance herself from her. In the final analysis, Nora decided to end the marriage.

After the divorce, Geoffrey spent 4 years before he remarried. Reflecting back on the 3 years after his divorce, he revealed: " I guess I went through a depression time. You know, where I was not doing the right things, and I started to drink a little more than I used to because I was going out with some friends and my mother had helped out. She was watching the baby for a while; however, that got old real fast."

Geoffrey's description of his sociability in relationship to the choice of mates was challenging if the common adage "opposites attract" is true. Geoffrey's first marriage failed primarily because his wife was extremely less social than he was, whereas he attributed the success of his second marriage to having a wife who was almost as sociable as he was. In fact, by the time of the interview, they had been married for 21 years, while the first marriage had lasted only 7 years.

Geoffrey was supportive of his second wife when she was making the transition from the Catholic Church to the Episcopalian Church to which he belonged. Geoffrey described his second wife as a woman who is very spiritual and who wanted to get her remarriage blessed by a church minister. However, she could not receive that blessing within the Catholic Church without getting an annulment. Consequently, she decided to get remarried with Geoffrey in his church.

### Henry

Henry is a 53-year-old male who identified himself as Irish American. He has a Ph.D. in Civil Law and did some preparation in Family Law. He is a devout Roman Catholic who goes to church every Sunday. He first married Anne, when he was 32 years old, and their marriage lasted 11 years. They had two children in that marriage, a boy and a girl. When they divorced, he got joint custody of the children. Eleven years later he married Sally and they have been married for 8 years and have had one child together. He lives in a suburban neighborhood and has an annual family income of over $130,000.

When asked about the reasons for getting married a bit late, Henry said: "My priorities were my studies and I did not want to marry before establishing myself financially." He mentioned that it was not only his studies that delayed him. He admitted that he was shy and felt uncomfortable around women, primarily because he was overweight.

When asked about the cause of his divorce, Henry stated:

"Every family member was surprised about it because there was no domestic violence, no alcohol abuse, no emotional cruelty and no infidelity. I admit the real problem was that I was overworking and bringing work home. While I was physically at home, I was absent-minded because I was primarily thinking of the cases I was currently working on, and the next ones. Consequently, this brought a lot of loneliness to my wife and children, a situation that led my wife to divorce me."

Questioned about finances in the second marriage, Henry said:

It is very important to discuss finances before remarriage. In my case, I admire my second wife [Sally] because she accepted to have a joint account with me, out of which I pay alimony to my first wife. Secondly, I admire the way my wife spends money for the well-being of my children from my first marriage and the way she treats them with due respect and love. I really advocate for joint accounts in every marriage.

Henry described his journey of growth. He was very elaborative in describing how he overcame his shyness, confronted himself, became aware of how work had affected his first marriage, and the amicable divorce he handled with his wife. At the time of the interview, Henry acknowledged that for him now home time is home time and work time is work time. Likewise, even if on certain occasions he was bringing work home, Sally had learned a way of reminding him prudently. In this regard, Henry considered her a buffer for him and he spoke about her with great admiration.

Henry expressed his pain of not being allowed to receive the Eucharist in the Catholic Church after his divorce. In pain and hope, Henry stated:

I long for the day the church officials will become more pastorally minded to administer to the divorced persons, encouraging them to experience God's love. I think it is also important to extend the pre-remarriage preparations to divorced Catholics who have not received annulments.

# Demographics of the Participants and Other Variables

*Age Range and Age Differences at First and Second Marriages*
*Contributing Factors to the Participants' First Divorce Experiences*
*Gender Differences and Similarities*
*Cultural Backgrounds and Differences*
*Religious Backgrounds*
*Impact of the Participants' Residential Neighborhoods*
*Levels of Formal Education*
*Description of Resilience before Discussing the Research Results*
*Overall Observations about the Participants' Resilience*

Before discussing the identified primary and secondary factors for both stability and satisfaction in remarriage, it is important to articulate the participants' demographics and other variables, because they seem to facilitate the conceptualization and contextualization of the dynamics within the remarriage triad. These include the participants' age range and age differences at first and second marriages, factors contributing to their first divorces, gender differences, cultural backgrounds, religious backgrounds, the impact of their residential neighborhoods, and levels of formal education. In the following discussion some of the participants repeatedly emphasized several points as important considerations for stability and satisfaction in remarriage. This is similar to the adage: "Repetition is the mother of learning."

## Age Range and Age Differences at First and Second Marriages

The chronological age range of the participants was 45 to 70 years. They were all very generous in sharing their stories, which seemed to be the fruits of longterm experiences, and their responses reflected a broad knowledge base. Most of their resourceful contributions were based on each participant's life experiences and the wisdom that comes only with age. Their input and feedback were far more advanced in comparison to the knowledge acquired through formal education about remarriage.

A typical example of such experience-based wisdom was communicated to me in a post-interview discussion with Abraham, a 70-year-old participant, in which he elaborated on his insightful observation:

> I have a Ph.D. in clinical psychology, but I have realized that there are some things that I could not easily learn from books in comparison to reallife experiences. After turning 70 years a month ago, I made a review of my life, and one of the things that struck me was the realization that every one of my resources had played a double role, as well as my constraints.
>
> Since we are talking about remarriage, let me take one example I have learned from my remarriage. One of my resources in remarriage is the ability to make right decisions, because I take time to think the pros and cons before I carry it out. The trade-off that my wife helped me to acknowledge was the dominion that I had over my first wife, and over my second wife, especially in the first 3 years of remarriage. My sense of always making the right decisions made me to think of myself as the sole decision-maker and was exaggerated to the point of dictating things to my family members, wives, and coworkers. I give sincere thanks to my [second] wife who one day confronted me about the lack of consulting her before making the decisions regarding where to spend vacations. After that I felt humbled and regretted having excluded her, and especially my first wife, from many family decisions that I had taken without consulting them.

When asked to elaborate on how a specific constraint turned out to be a resource in his life, Abraham answered:

> If constraints are looked at from a positive perspective, they can also be turned into instances of growth and positive change. For instance, one of my main struggles I experienced in my first marriage was the fear of being perceived as a failure as a result of divorce. On one hand, that fear helped me to maintain a stable marriage for 20 years, but I was unhappy, till it reached a point when I could not bear any longer the pain of staying in my first marriage. The pain I experienced helped me to start thinking of other alternatives in life. The alternative I chose was to file for divorce. Afterward, I met my [second] wife whom I adore and love to death. However, I would not have married her if I had not overcome my fear and pain that I suffered in my first

marriage. So, you can now see how I turned my lemons into lemonade.

## Contributing Factors to the Participants' First Divorce Experiences

A brief exploration of the factors that contributed to the participants' divorces was included in this study partly because the failure to identify and resolve the factors contributing to divorce in first marriages creates serious consequences in remarriage (Minuchin & Nichols, 1993). Two participants who remarried before resolving some of those issues reported their reenactments of the dynamics of their first marriages in their second marriages (Ganong & Coleman, 1989; Gottman, 1994b) until their second spouses confronted them.

Incongruent with the literature, which focused on the lack of communication as one of the principal causes of divorce (Berger, 1998; Gottman, Notarius, Gonso & Markman, 1976), the participants frequently reported marital infidelity, prioritizing of work at the expense of marriage, domestic violence, incompatibility between spouses, money used as a power source to control one's partner, and lack of premarital preparation.

Other contributing factors that were reported by the participants included unrealistic expectations about marriage and/or unrealistic idealization of one's partner (especially during courtship), constant social pressures that create stress, lack of open communication and negotiation about money, use of drugs and alcohol addiction. These observations are consistent with the literature (Carter & McGoldrick, 1998; Gottman, 1994a; Kaslow, 1996; Rutter, 1998; Treadway, 1989).

## Gender Differences and Similarities

Marked gender differences were noticed in recruiting participants. These included the differential changes men and women experienced in their finances after divorce, in who became stepparents, in the lengths of time between divorce and remarriage, in the levels of formal education, in the levels of social support during and/or after divorce.

For this study it was easier to recruit female participants than it was to recruit males. A likely explanation for this difficulty may be that more women than men tend to be the custodial parents after divorce (Davidson, 2003) and one of the criteria for this study was that all participants had to be custodial parents. However, every individual who volunteered to participate in the study was very generous in sharing his or her personal information and in making significant suggestions for the study.

Gender differences were also noticed in regard to finances. Seven out of eight female participants reported that their finances dropped drastically, especially in the first 2 years after divorce and before remarriage. Seven out of eight male participants reported a significant increase in their finances. This observation is consistent with the literature (Cox, 2002; Kelley & Burg, 2000). All seven female participants whose finances dropped remained with all the care-giving responsibilities of their children, and they were not wellsupported financially by their ex-husbands (Ahrons, 2004; Davidson, 2003). The eighth female, who reported that her finances improved, was the primary breadwinner in the family before the divorce and she continued in her profession after the divorce.

The seven males whose finances improved were those who had been the sole breadwinners in their previous marriages. The eighth male participant attributed the drop in his finances to losing his job during the proceedings of a bitter divorce with his ex-wife. Female participants reported getting more social support than males. This may also have contributed to the longer period most of the women spent before remarrying than did the men, whose self-reported loneliness was more frequent than that of women. More divorced males spend shorter lengths of time between divorce and remarriage than divorced females (Figures 2 & 3). This observation was supported by the existing literature (Baum, 2003; Kelley & Burg, 2000; Lofas & Sova, 1985; Reis et al., 1985).

In elaborating on finances as a primary factor within the theory developed, both males and females reported that each couple is unique in addressing finances. However, they suggested that clinicians and financial advisers should help to understand the three alternative models of how to handle finances in remarriage (joint account, independent account, or joint and independent), so that the partners can be able to consciously choose the best model for them. In general, the male and female participants who had joint accounts with their partners seemed to be more trusting of their partners and seemed to have almost similar spending habits as their partners, and more open communications about money, investments, and retirement plans in comparison to those who had independent or joint and separate accounts.

Gender differences were also noticed in relation to being a stepparent. Seven women participants had children from a first marriage and were married to men without children. On the other hand, four male participants had children from a first marriage and were remarried to women with children. In this sample, there were more men who were stepfathers than women who were stepmothers, and this observation was also congruent with the literature about stepfamilies (Kelley, 1995; Kelley & Burg, 2000). A possible explanation for this is that more women than men have been granted the custody of their children. Thus, if they decide to remarry, their husbands become stepfathers to their children. Both men and women participants seemed to collaborate with their partners in the parenting of each participant's child(ren) from the first marriage.

An overall view of the differences and similarities regarding the male and female participants' experiences seemed to be a shared vision with minor differences. As indicated later in Study Sessions 1 and 2, all the participants (eight males and eight females) perceived the application of a multidimensional view of committed love and integral maturity as the foundation and constant point of reference for the satisfaction and stability of their remarriages.

Minor, but important, gender differences were found in each of the identified factors of stability and satisfaction in remarriage. For example, in regard to the motivation for remarriage, more males than females reported that they remarried in order to have a companion who would be helpful in overcoming intense feelings of loneliness. The males had less social support after divorce than most of female participants, and this observation is consistent with the literature (Baum, 2003; Ganong & Coleman, 1989; James & Johnson, 2001).

## Cultural Backgrounds and Differences

Although attempts were made to obtain participants from different cultural backgrounds, the volunteers who finally participated were mostly of European descent (10), two were African Americans, and four were Latinos from different parts of the Americas. All of them were either first, second, or third generation immigrants to the United States. Given their diversity in terms of all their demographics, each one of them made a significant contribution to the study. There were no participants of Asian or Australian descent. Therefore, further studies are needed to explore their cultural input to such a study.

## Religious Backgrounds

Eleven of sixteen participants identified themselves as members of the Roman Catholic Church. The remaining participants belonged to the following denominations: Pentecostal (1), Quaker (1), and Episcopalian (1). Two participants said that they do not belong to any formalized religious denomination, but expressed their profound belief in a Supernatural Being that they referred to as God. One participant had converted to membership in the Catholic Church from the Baptist Church after remarriage to a Catholic partner.

All 10 participants who had been raised as Catholics had celebrated their first marriages in the Catholic Church. During the interviews, they all expressed their pain as they struggled to obtain annulments of their first marriages. Four of them reported their frustration and failure to get their annulments before they remarried and decided to get married in other religious denominations. The greatest number of participants were Catholics and all of them expressed painful experiences and rejection from their church leaders.

One of the non-Catholic participants reacted with emotion as to why the Catholic Church lawmakers had made it so difficult for divorced Catholics to remarry in the church.

Geoffrey stated:

> I have read the same Bible that Catholics read and I have found in it that the only sin that cannot be forgiven is the sin against the Holy Spirit. So, even if divorce may be a sin according to the Catholic Church teachings, it can be forgiven. So, can the Catholic officials use a more Bible-centered theology, so that they can stop punishing and excluding the divorced and remarried Catholics?
>
> My second wife was Catholic and she decided to get remarried with me in my church because she did not like to be perceived in her church as a sinner, and go to church on Sunday without be allowed to receive the Eucharist. I encourage you to do some study about theology, and you will realize that God does not blame people who divorce and/or remarry. I am not a Catholic, neither a religious minister, but think that the Catholic Church leaders should make some changes in their attitudes, Church laws, and traditions in order to offer better pastoral care to divorced and remarried Catholics.

## Impact of the Participants' Residential Neighborhoods

Eight participants reported that their residential neighborhoods were having an impact in one way or another on their marital stability and satisfaction. When asked about his experience of stability and satisfaction in remarriage in a suburban neighborhood, Elías stated that although the suburbs have most of the resources (e.g., excellent schools, swimming pools, shopping malls, and other facilities), they also have the potential to influence financial competition among residents.

Such competitiveness creates a lot of stress on many marriages, and many marriages break up in the suburbs because they cannot keep up with the demands of higher standards of living. Elías, however, attributed the survival of his marriage in a suburban neighborhood partly to the joint decision he made with his wife to stop competing and to teach his children about the need to be satisfied with what they have.

## Levels of Formal Education

Before elaborating on the formal education of the participants, it is important to keep in mind the social context in which most of the participants were raised (late 1930s to 1980s). Men were more encouraged to pursue higher education than were women. In light of the same trend, this may explain why seven female participants entered their first marriage before completing college (Figure 2).

One of the female participants completed her college education after divorce, and another earned her Master's degree after her divorce. Four female participants took on two jobs after divorce, started earning money, and opened personal bank accounts—opportunities that they did not have in their first marriages. Eventually, when the women started working and/or remarried, their finances improved. As they earned more funds, some went to school to complete college and/or pursue professional studies.

Two of the male participants held Ph.D.s, another was working on the completion of his Ph.D. in clinical psychology, and the other five males had completed college (Figure 3). The impact of the participants' formal education on their marital experiences was not studied in depth. In this study, only one participant (Fred) mentioned (without being asked) that his academic friends stopped coming to his home for academic conversations because his wife was always excluded from those conversations and that had started to affect the couple's relationships. Therefore, further studies may be needed to explore the impact that a partner's levels of formal education may have on their stability and satisfaction in remarriage.

## Description of Resilience before Discussing the Research Results

Before presenting a detailed discussion of the results of the research study on which this book is based, it is important to clarify that the stories of all participants implicitly included the notion of resilience. Beatrice, as well as six other participants, described the love that contributes to remarriage success as an act that involves self-sacrifice, perseverance, endurance, making tough choices and decisions, as well as daily dying to one's own selfish ambitions.

## Overall Observations about the Participants' Resilience

Although only one participant (Hilda) used the word "resilience," all the other participants used different phrases to describe the same concept. All of them, including Hilda, spoke about what had helped them to recover from the wounds of divorce and its painful repercussions as they worked toward the establishment of their stability and satisfaction in remarriage. Their expressions of resilience were congruent with Walsh's (1998) description of resilience. The participants identified some of the interpersonal processes and learned coping skills that enabled them to make meaning of their adversities and how they handled effectively the divorce, post-divorce, and remarriage challenges.

During the course of remarriage, the participants also developed a process of conflict resolution that helped them to express their points of view and communicate with their second spouses better than they used to do with their former spouses. Others managed to reconnect and reconcile with their former spouses. All of them managed to adapt themselves to the changes that come about with divorce, single-parenting and remarriage, step-parenting, and learned to establish clear boundaries with their multiple extended family members.

One of the main belief systems or the "heart and soul of resilience" (Walsh, 1998) that 15 participants manifested throughout the interviews was their belief in the success of their second marriages. Only one participant expressed concerns about the future of his remarriage, but he seemed determined to make it work. Some of the phrases that the participants used in expressing their resilience included the following:

> Grace: Based on personal experience, I have realized that remarriage is not easy. It is not an event, and it is not about how colorful the wedding was or not. My remarriage has been a process of hard work; a job to be done daily and it is an unfinished business. I will do whatever it takes to make it succeed.

> Felicia: Since my divorce process started, I do not know how I have reached where I am today. I do not even know where I got the energy and courage to overcome all the obstacles in my married life.

> Charles: Now I am able to function normally because I have learned to withstand the pressure from my ex-wife and my three daughters. Ever since we divorced, my ex-wife has

used these three children to mess up my second marriage, but I have managed to resist them, and I am happy that my son has not joined his sisters and mother, because he is on my side.

Irrespective of the hardships that Charles had experienced in his second marriage because of his first wife's intrusion and tension with his three children, Charles stated:

I have made a commitment to my second wife for life. If it ever happens, she will be the only one to walk away from me, but I will never walk away from her.

Additionally, Charles mentioned that, although he grew up in a very poor family, he now enjoys a very luxurious life in a suburban neighborhood and has a comfortable annual family income of over $130,000. In retrospect, Charles clarified that growing up in a poor family helped him to learn that there are some experiences that money cannot buy (e.g., friendship, love, and faith in God), and he still cherishes these experiences very highly.

Beatrice elaborated: Some inner strength within has helped me to survive my divorce and all the financial challenges I went through as a single mother while struggling to support my five children and myself. Now, I am happy because my second marriage is stable and my second husband is very supportive of my children.

The experiences of eight of the participants and the literature reviewed in this study concurred in affirming that remarriage is difficult and that there are more re-divorces than first divorces in the United States (McGoldrick & Carter, 1998; Nichols, 1996; Rutter, 1998). Likewise, programs on public television channels tend to affirm the participants' experiences that there is more publicity in the media about the remarriages that fail than about those that succeed. Yet, there are successful remarriages of couples who do work through the challenges of remarriage, as evidenced by the participants in this study.

The same eight participants suggested that there is a greater need for church ministers and other professionals to reinforce hope rather that pessimism about remarriage success. Fred mentioned implicitly the theme of resilience while referring to the challenges that were surrounding his remarriage during the time of the interview for this study. He and his wife were going through a very difficult time and Fred was concerned about the future of his remarriage.

When asked what is helping him to stay in his remarriage, Fred replied:

> Stick-to-it-ness. By stick-to-it-ness, I am referring to my inner resources that are keeping me hopeful, persistent, and persevering for the sake of my child whom I had with my second wife. [Fred added:] Yes, some people marry, divorce, remarry, and may re-divorce or stay in their second marriages. The problem is we hear very little about successful remarried couples. That is why we should not limit ourselves to the statistics of remarriages that end in divorce. There are many others that flourish, but they are not mentioned in the media!

# My History and Personal Reflections

This demographic sheet was created by the Author during the research project and has been modified to help custodial parents in remarriage situations to make an in-depth exploration of their contextual realities. You are encouraged to take note of any feelings, thoughts and/or memories that may come up as you fill-in the blank spaces or after the exercise.

My gender:   o  Male     o  Female

Date of birth:      /      /

Age:

Religion:
    Denomination:
    o   Nondenominational
    o   Atheist

My current attendance of religious services:
    o   Once or more times a week
    o   Once a month
    o   Less than five times a year
    o   Not attending

Gender of my first spouse:   o  Male     o  Female

Date of birth:      /      /

Age:

His or Her Religion:
    Denomination:
    o   Nondenominational
    o   Atheist

His or her attendance of religious services during your first marriage:
- o   Once or more times a week
- o   Once a month
- o   Less than five times a year
- o   Not attending

Gender of my second spouse/cohabitating partner:   o  Male     o  Female

Date of birth:     /      /

Age:

His or Her Religion:
Denomination:
- o   Nondenominational
- o   Atheist

His or her current attendance of religious services during your first marriage:
- o   Once or more times a week
- o   Once a month
- o   Less than five times a year
- o   Not attending

Cultural / ethnic background of my biological mother:

_____

Cultural / ethnic background of my biological father:

_____

Cultural / ethnic background with which I identify myself:

_____

Highest level of my formal education:

_____

My sexual orientation:
- o  Heterosexual
- o  Homosexual
- o  Bisexual
- o  Other

Cultural / ethnic background of my first spouse's mother:

_____

Cultural / ethnic background of my first spouse's father:

_____

Cultural / ethnic background with which my first spouse identified himself / herself:

_____

Highest level of formal education of my first spouse:

_____

Sexual orientation of my first spouse:
- o  Heterosexual
- o  Homosexual
- o  Bisexual
- o  Other

Cultural / ethnic background of my second spouse's (or cohabitating partner's) mother:

_____

Cultural / ethnic background of my second spouse's (or cohabitating partner's) father:

_____

Cultural / ethnic background with which my second spouse/cohabitating partner identifies himself / herself:

_____

Highest level of formal education of my second spouse / cohabitating partner:

_____

_____

Sexual orientation of my second spouse / cohabitating partner:

- o  Heterosexual
- o  Homosexual
- o  Bisexual
- o  Other

**Family of origin**
(Fill in all the spaces below with either Yes or No)

My biological mother:

- o  Alive
- o  Deceased
- o  Married
- o  Divorced
- o  Remarried
- o  Remarried more than once
- o  Never lived together with my father

My biological father:

- o  Alive
- o  Deceased
- o  Married
- o  Divorced
- o  Remarried
- o  Remarried more than once
- o  Never lived together with my mother

Biological mother of my first spouse:

- o  Alive
- o  Deceased
- o  Married

- o Divorced
- o Remarried
- o Remarried more than once
- o Never lived together with my first spouse's father

Biological father of my first spouse:
- o Alive
- o Deceased
- o Married
- o Divorced
- o Remarried
- o Remarried more than once
- o Never lived together with my first spouse's mother

Biological mother of my second spouse:
- o Alive
- o Deceased
- o Married
- o Divorced
- o Remarried
- o Remarried more than once
- o Never lived together with my first spouse's father

Biological father of my second spouse:
- o Alive
- o Deceased
- o Married
- o Divorced
- o Remarried
- o Remarried more than once
- o Never lived together with my first spouse's mother

**Biological siblings: numbers, birth order and marital status**

Number of my older brothers:

Number of my younger brothers:

Number of my older sisters:

Number of my younger sisters:

Number of my single brothers
(over eighteen years of age and never married):

Number of my brothers in their first marriages:

Number of my currently divorced brothers:

Number of my currently remarried brothers:

Number of my single sisters
(over eighteen years of age and never married):

Number of my sisters in their first marriages :

Number of my currently divorced sisters:

Number of my currently remarried sisters:

I grew up with:
- o   Both biological parents
- o   Single mother
- o   Single father
- o   Adoptive parents
- o   In a stepfamily
- o   With a stepmother
- o   With a stepfather
- o   With another relative

Number of my first spouse's older brothers:

Number of younger brothers:

Number of older sisters:

Number of younger sisters:

Number of my first spouse's single brothers
    (over eighteen years of age and never married):

Number of brothers in their first marriages:

Number of currently divorced brothers:

Number of currently remarried brothers:

Number of my first spouse's single sisters
    (over eighteen years of age and never married):

Number of sisters in their first marriages:

Number of currently divorced sisters:

Number of currently remarried sisters:

My first spouse grew up with:
- o  Both biological parents
- o  Single mother
- o  Single father
- o  Adoptive parents
- o  In a stepfamily
- o  With a stepmother
- o  With a stepfather
- o  With another relative

Number of my second spouse's older brothers:

Number of younger brothers:

Number of older sisters:

Number of younger sisters:

Number of my second spouse's single brothers
(over eighteen years of age and never married):

Number of brothers in their first marriages:

Number of currently divorced brothers:

Number of currently remarried brothers:

Number of my second spouse's single sisters
(over eighteen years of age and never married):

Number of sisters in their first marriages:

Number of currently divorced sisters:

Number of currently remarried sisters:

My second spouse grew up with:
- o   Both biological parents
- o   Single mother
- o   Single father
- o   Adoptive parents
- o   In a stepfamily
- o   With a stepmother
- o   With a stepfather
- o   With another relative

## Custodial parent's first marriage, divorce, and remarriage

My age at first marriage:

Duration of my first marriage:

Time between my first divorce and second marriage:

Duration since my second marriage to present day:

Number of my biological children in first marriage:

Age(s) of my biological child(ren) at time of second marriage

——————     ——————

——————     ——————

——————     ——————

Gender and current age of my biological children from my first marriage living or having lived with me in my second marriage
Females

——————     ——————

——————     ——————

——————     ——————

Males

——————     ——————

——————     ——————

——————     ——————

Number and ages of my biological children born in my second marriage:

——————     ——————

——————     ——————

——————     ——————

Age of my ex-spouse at time of my first marriage:

Age of my current spouse at time of my remarriage:

Gender and current ages of my stepchildren (current spouse's children) living with me at present in my second marriage

Females

_____  _____

_____  _____

_____  _____

Males

_____  _____

_____  _____

_____  _____

--------------------------⟡--------------------------

**Custodial parent's first spouse: Marriage, divorce, and remarriage**

Age of my first spouse at his/her first marriage:

His or her number of prior marriage:

Duration of his or her prior marriage(s):

Time between his / her first divorce and second marriage:

Number of biological children in his or her prior marriage(s):

Age(s) of his or her biological child(ren) at time of his or her marriage to me:

_____  _____

_____  _____

_____  _____

Gender and current age of his or her biological children from prior marriages who lived with me in my first marriage
Females

_____    _____

_____    _____

_____    _____

Males

_____    _____

_____    _____

_____    _____

Age of my ex-spouse at time of his or her marriage with me:

Gender and current ages of his or her stepchildren who lived with me in my first marriage
Females

_____    _____

_____    _____

_____    _____

Males

_____    _____

_____    _____

_____    _____

---

**Custodial parent's second spouse / partner: Marriage, divorce, and remarriage**

Age of my second spouse at his / her first marriage:

His or her number of prior marriage:

Duration of his or her prior marriage(s):

Time between his / her first divorce and second marriage:

Number of biological children in his or her prior marriage(s):

Age(s) of his or her biological child(ren) at time of his or her marriage to me:

———————   ———————

———————   ———————

———————   ———————

Gender and current age of his or her biological children from prior marriages living with me in my second marriage
Females

———————   ———————

———————   ———————

———————   ———————

Males

———————   ———————

———————   ———————

———————   ———————

Age of my current spouse at time of his or her marriage to me:

Gender and current ages of his or her stepchildren who lived with me in my second marriage
Females

———————   ———————

———————   ———————

———————   ———————

Males

———————   ———————

———————   ———————

———————   ———————

Current marriage

Is there something unique about the structure of my current marriage I think needs to be considered in my remarriage? Circle Yes or No. If yes, identity it and describe it clearly as follows:

_____

_____

_____

_____

_____

_____

_____

_____

_____

_____

_____

_____

_____

_____

_____

_____

_____

# Keys for Unlocking One's Past in the Present to Improve the Future

Everyone has a story and a history to tell. If there is no one to tell and/or to listen to your story, write it down and read it to yourself. Our stories have significant ways in which they can influence how we perceive ourselves, others and God. More often than not, we tend to project our past experiences into the future.

Becoming aware of your past and present, of unhealed wounds, dreams, failures, successes, joys, challenges and your innermost needs may help you in the future.

What should you be doing more of and what needs to be changed for a stable and satisfactory remarriage?

# Part II

## Study Sessions for Each Identified Factor of Stability and Satisfaction in Remarriage

# Description of the Identified Factors of Stability and Satisfaction in Remarriage

The identified factors of stability and satisfaction in remarriage have been divided into sessions in order to allow the reader and/or any discussion group to focus on one factor at a time, to explore it in depth, and to be able to reflect on its interconnectedness with committed love as well as the other factors.

Figure 4 below is a summary of the identified factors that contribute to both stability and satisfaction in remarriage. These factors were identified after a progressive and step-by-step analysis of the information gathered from the participants. The analysis was made by making use of three sequentially interrelated stages of data analyses, namely, open, axial, and selective coding (Strauss & Corbin, 1998). Nine primary factors and eight secondary ones were systemically selected from the data as factors influencing both stability and satisfaction in remarriage for remarrying parents.

The primary factors of stability and satisfaction in remarriage were categorized as follows: committed love, integral maturity, knowledge of the complexity of remarriage, finances, collaborative parenting, sexuality, communication, spirituality, and professional help. The secondary factors were marital history, remarriage motivations, dating, clear boundaries, conflict resolution, cohabitation, house rules and roles, and permanent sites for professional remarriage services. It is important to note that these terms, selected from the participants' input and feedback, are based on the participants' connotations. Therefore, the goal in these study sessions is to capture the participants' experiences and conceptualizations of each theme or category (e.g., love) and how each influences both stability and satisfaction in remarriage.

All in all, committed love was the most mentioned and most emphasized factor among all the primary factors and seems clearly connected to all the other factors, primary and secondary. In Figure 4 the darkly outlined circle in the center represents the central theme (committed love) and the darkly outlined rectangle represents the second primary factor to committed love. The other rectangles represent additional primary factors and all the ovals indicate secondary factors.

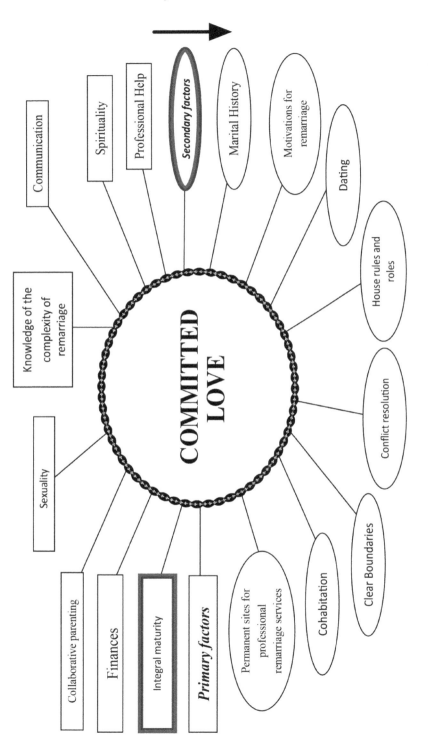

*Figure 4:* Influencing factors for both remarriage stability and satisfaction. Central theme is in a bolded circle ◯ , primary factor contributing most significanty to the central theme in a bolded rectangle ▭ , other primary factors are in the light rectangles ▭ , and secondary factors are in light ellipse ◯ .

# Study Session 1.

---

Committed Love:
Central Factor in Stability and Satisfaction in Remarriage

*Description of Committed Love Experience of Others*
*My Experience*
*Keys to Committed Love*

*Description of Committed Love*

In this book, committed love is described as a permanent decision each partner makes to offer one's self to the other and to accept the other partner unconditionally. This type of love is an act of the will, a choice not an obligation, mutually given and received. It reflects God's unconditional love for human beings beyond our imperfections. It involves self-sacrifice, sharing ordinary life together, as well as loving the partner beyond his or her physical appearance. Committed love is grounded in kindness, loyalty, fidelity, sacred trust, forgiveness and reconciliation, and caring for the partner's loved ones (e.g., children from his/her previous marriage). Committed love is manifested in specific actions, including nonromantic ones (e.g., putting out the garbage and doing chores). It involves seeking mutual satisfaction and growing in holiness.

It is also important to clarify what committed love is not. It is not a mere feeling. It is not selfish, temporary, stagnant, exclusively romantic, boring, nor rooted in lust, jealousy, unrealistic expectations, possessiveness, fantasies, wishes, and lack of knowledge about self and/or the partner. It is not a love one falls in or out of, but a love which each partner breathes in and out till death do them part.

*Experience of Others*

The findings of the research study on which this book is based started with what the participants mentioned during the interviews. All the participants expressed their convictions in similar words and related phrases: that committed love is the most important influencing factor for both stability and satisfaction in remarriage. However, the participants did not speak about love in generic terms. Instead, they focused on describing it based on their perceptions and experiencing it to be a complex reality, consisting of different components.

Focusing on the participants' responses, the word "love" reflected a complexity of meanings or connotations. Two examples of such meanings emerged when the participants were asked to describe what each of them meant by love. Four female participants said that love is a question of chemistry between the partners.

> Elizabeth: I think people love one another because of their chemistry makeup. That is why, I guess, some people are compatible, and others are not. In my case, on the very day I met my second husband for the first time, I felt something deep within myself that strongly attracted me to him.

Three other women and two men highlighted that love is a mysterious experience. For instance, Felicia said:

> Love is a mysterious experience and I don't find the exact words to explain to myself what turned me on to love my second husband. I really do not know because I resented him immediately when I noticed his manifestations of getting interested in me.

Even if the participants described love in many different ways, all of their descriptions fell within the following categories: love of self, love of the partner, mutual love between the partners, love of children and attentiveness to their needs and love toward the multiple extended family members. For the purposes of facilitating the conceptualization of these multiple categories of committed love, each category will be described separately.

### Love of Self

All the participants mentioned that they had come to the realization that committed love starts with love of self. For instance, Grace expressed:

> I have realized that the more I love myself, the more love I am able to give and share with others. Otherwise, without loving myself, I feel like my love for others is insincere. I am pretending to give to others what I do not have. Whenever I

do not love myself, I start to desperately demand my husband for attention and if he ignores me, I feel angry at him because [I start to think that] he is mean.

According to Elías:

I learned to love myself by paying attention to my own woundedness as a divorced person. It was hard for me to confront myself, and to admit that I was in pain. I knew that I needed healing before I could proceed with my plans for the next marriage. However, I told myself that "I had to learn to love myself by focusing on how to address and resolve my painful past."

Based on a biblical passage, Fred stated that it is not bad to love oneself. Otherwise, why would Jesus have commanded his followers to love God and others as they love themselves! Fred emphasized:

Jesus said: 'Love others as you love yourself.' Therefore, I have also learned to love myself. Love of self after divorce and before remarriage does not mean becoming narcissistic. It is about establishing a good foundation for feeling good about who you are as a person, developing your personal identity, exploring the unique person you are, your talents, limitations, dreams, needs, likes, dislikes, making priorities, fears, and accepting your uniqueness.

Henry emphasized:

Love of self goes hand-in-hand with the knowledge of self because the more you know about yourself and love yourself, the more you are able to learn to love and know about other people. This makes it possible to establish harmonious relationships with others without dominating them. Likewise, you don't allow yourself to be dominated by others. It is a winwin situation for people who individually have a conscious, mature, honest, positive, realistic and unconditional love of themselves.

Elaborating on love of self, Alicia stated:

I felt a real need for a man in my life. I could not imagine myself remaining unmarried for the rest of my entire life. I remained a single mother until the age of thirty-eight years. However, I was convinced that I would not get married with any man from the street. So, I started setting some of the things I would look for in a man before getting married with him. I had a chance this time to choose a man and I used it.

[Alicia added:] After my first divorce, I realized that there is no perfect man and no perfect woman in the world. So, I started to look for a man whom I would at least tell myself that his personality was matching the basics of what I wanted in a man to get remarried with. Fortunately, I got him and he is the one with whom I currently share a very happy marriage. I give myself credit for doing whatever it took me to love myself. I set up the qualities I wanted to look for in a man and I abided with them until I got the right one for me.

### Love for the Partner

Fifteen participants out of sixteen highlighted that it is important to develop a love for the person you want to marry. Dora stated:

After two months of dating my current husband, I realized that he had some of the qualities that I wanted in my spouse-to-be. However, I also realized that he was not a perfect man. He was a good man but I could not stand his smell of cigarettes. It was not easy for me to accommodate all his limitations. I realized that I was not perfect either. In the final analysis, after some negotiations about our differences of opinion and dislikes, I made a decision to love him and we have been married for 18 years.

Ten participants also mentioned that love for the other involves, among other things, knowing the other's cultural background, religious affiliation, likes and dislikes, hobbies, favorite food, and fears. The person has to be loved irrespective of the stepchildren.

In regard to the other's religious affiliation and likes, Geoffrey stated:

Even if my second wife agreed to have our marriage celebrated in my Episcopalian Church, I have realized that she is still attached to the Catholic Church, and I encourage her to continue praying at home the Catholic prayers she likes a lot, especially the Rosary. I love her and respect the teachings of her religion even if I do not agree with all of them. Secondly, because of the love I have toward her, I let her go to socialize with her friends. Sometimes I accompany her to visit her friends just to make her feel supported because she likes to socialize and network with other people to help the people in need. She also likes to go shopping with her friends and my daughter from the previous marriage. They love one another and that makes me have a greater love for her. My second wife also likes to cook and invite her friends at home. I entertain her friends and help her with the washing of the dishes. I do all this because of the love I have for her.

### Mutual Love

Based on the descriptions of mutual love by all the participants, it can be deduced that mutual love is a complex concept with different connotations. However, all of them agreed on describing it as a bond of trust and caring for one another. Abraham clarified:

> Immediately after my first divorce, but before I married my second wife, I dated a number of women. The lesson I learned during those series of dates was that marital love is a two-way street. Later on, I realized that some of those women I had sex with did not actually love me. They were only interested in having a nice time, yet I had felt that I had fallen in love with them.

> [Abraham added:] Well, after some time, I started to realize that some of them seemed to have fallen in love with me, but I cannot certainly say that I really loved any of them. I was primarily seeking them out for sex and to hide away for some time from my loneliness.

Fourteen participants considered mutual love not to be an overnight product. It is a process that involves a journey of growth, self-giving to the other and a give-and-take experience. It involves mutual fidelity, loyalty, unconditional commitment to one another and the ability to be there for one another in joyful and painful moments of life.

In a special way, when asked to describe how mutual love between partners in second marriages differs from that of the partners in first marriages, all the participants pointed out that the uniqueness is based on each partner's conscious decision not only to love his or her spouse, but also the partner's children from the previous marriage. Eleven participants mentioned that love involves the ability to grow together beyond conflict, the ability to love the person, without focusing too much on the person's possessions, but who he or she is as a person.

Thirteen participants stated that mutual love involves peace, companionship, feeling secure, trust, tranquility, and above all the ability to enter into a nonjudgmental and constructive dialogue with one's spouse. They also agreed that the ability to laugh and to eat together are also very important in reinforcing mutual love. Likewise, 12 participants expressed that mutual love is based on mutual respect for one another, honesty, and transparent communication.

Fifteen participants considered sexual intimacy to be their greatest expression of mutual love. Grace expressed:

> Sex is wonderful, the best thing in the world, but with the right person, and only the right person, it can be the most out-of-this-world experience.

Elaborating on the notion of mutual love, Beatrice emphasized that men and women lack the knowledge and practice of how to treat one another. No wonder then, Beatrice stated:

> Every woman should learn about how to treat a man and vice versa. This requires preparation and self-challenge because people always run the risk of getting remarried primarily by instinct and/or physical needs.

Mutual love was described by all participants as a decision, based on commitment, to be there for the person "no matter what" [added Catherine], and the ability to enter marriage by prioritizing love before anything else.

### *Love of Children and Attentiveness to Their Needs*
All the participants highlighted that whatever happens to the children affects the parents. Grace emphasized:

> Once a parent, you remain a parent for life; even grown up children turn to their parents for advice and support.

These participants, by virtue of being parents when entering remarriage as custodial parents, expressed that the love for their children and their attentiveness to the needs of the children have highly contributed to the couple's stability and satisfaction in remarriage.

All sixteen participants stated that, for at least the first three years of remarriage, none of them paid sufficient attention to the needs of his or her child(ren) for two main reasons: (1). the remarried parent's lack of knowledge regarding the unique needs and challenges faced by children of remarried parents (2). the remarried parent's emotional investment in pleasing the partner. Such pleasing was prioritized because the custodial parents were struggling to make the second marriage work in order to reduce the risk of another divorce.

As all the participants later realized, the parents' lack of identifying and paying attention to their children needs not only affected the children but also affected the stability and satisfaction of their marriages in a negative way. This was particularly applicable to remarried parents with adolescent children from a first marriage. The following paragraphs highlight some of the children's needs and challenges which the participants identified and suggested that remarrying and remarried parents should pay a lot of attention to them. For instance, Fred suggested:

> Parents should be attentive to children who blame themselves
> for their parents' divorce.

Fred made this suggestion after realizing that his first son from the previous marriage had taken onto himself the responsibility of having failed to save the marriage of his parents. Four other participants also mentioned a similar story about their children. However, they acknowledged that the failure of the first marriages was not their children's fault. Additionally, five female and four male participants reported that, after remarriage, their children struggled for more than a year while grieving over the lost fantasy for their biological parents to remarry. These nine participants also reported that their adolescent children rejected disciplinary rules from their respective stepparents.

Remarriage ceremonies also have an impact on the significant others of custodial parents. For instance, twelve participants reported that it took them more than a year to realize how their adolescent children experienced conflict of loyalties and guilty feelings for having attended the wedding ceremony of a biological parent with a non-biological parent. Some children, as reported by nine participants, struggled with feelings of resentment and anger with themselves for having failed to forgive the biological parent for remarrying.

Ten participants mentioned that their children had difficulty in handling feelings due to the loss of privilege and of being the center of attention as a result of passing from being the only child to living with other stepsiblings and/ or half-siblings. These feelings were also reported by two male participants as still a problem for their adult children, already in their thirties, because it involves sharing the inheritance from their parents with their stepsiblings.

Without referring to their children, nine participants mentioned that they have witnessed the children of their friends in second marriages having profound concerns and fears that their parent's new marriage might also end in another divorce. Unfortunately, the participants reported that those concerns and fears have started to have negative effects on those children because some of them seemed very preoccupied about the risk of experiencing another divorce and another adaptation situation.

All the participants highlighted that parents contemplating remarriage should pay attention to the children's developmental needs and introduce their prospective spouses at the right time. This involves prudent dating, whereby the parent ought not to introduce his or her biological children to everybody he or she starts to date before making a commitment to live together. Otherwise, breaking up with a particular person might also affect one's children.

After acknowledging that it might not be easy to date a compatible partner the first time after divorce, 14 participants cautioned that parents contemplating remarriage should avoid the risk of playing out their romantic experiments with different partners in front of their children. According to Henry, "It is heartbreaking for the children to see their parents with a different stranger every now and then."

### Loving Attitude toward Multiple Extended-Family Members

Fifteen participants mentioned that they had found it very helpful, within their remarriages, to extend their love to different members of their extended families. Catherine discussed this further in the following interchange:

> Ever since I knew that I could not change my fate, I resolved to change my attitude. I had to accept the bitter truth that, even if signing the divorce papers officially indicated the legal ending of my first marriage with my first spouse, those signatures did not terminate our family. My exspouse and I continued to be significant others to one another because we had children who needed to be in contact with both of us after the divorce. By the same token, for the sake of the children, I sought family therapy for myself and the children in order to learn how to handle the conflict of loyalties between me and their father. They needed him and they needed me and they still need both of us.

Daniel stated that he did whatever was possible to keep in contact with his former spouse for the sake of the children:

> Every attempt was in vain. That woman has a lot of psychological issues and they are really affecting the children I had with her. Nevertheless, I managed to reconnect with my ex-in-laws and they are very understanding, friendly with me, have compassion for my children and me. This is because they know that my ex-spouse is a trouble-maker. Fortunately, keeping a healthy relationship with my ex-in-laws (especially my motherin-law, father-in-law and brother-in-law) has relieved me of the stress and guilt I have been feeling for my children to grow up while disconnected from their maternal relatives. I have realized that, ever since I reconnected positively with my ex-in-laws, the relationship with my second wife has also improved. For instance, if I want to have a good time with my wife for a weekend or have another honeymoon experience, we can leave my children in the safe hands of their maternal grandparents.

Grace commented on her experiences as follows:

> My love toward significant others included making a conscious decision to embrace a positive attitude of forgiving my ex-spouse. I did this after realizing that the more I held on to blaming my ex-spouse and keeping the grudges we had ten years ago, the more I suffered from the resultant anger of recalling the events that surrounded my divorce. I realized that my lack of forgiving him was negatively affecting my relationship with my current husband. Given these observations, I felt challenged to decide between holding on to blaming him or forgiving him. Four years later after the divorce, with the help of a religious minister, I made the decision to forgive my ex-spouse for whatever he did to me. Ever since, I started to feel better. However, I admit that was difficult for me to let that anger go because I still think that I was faithful to him and he is the one to blame for cheating on me. Nevertheless, I had to let go of holding on to my sense of self-righteousness because the emotional price I was paying for it was draining all my emotional resources and integrity.

All in all, based on the results of this study and after a step-by-step and systematic analysis of the data (Strauss & Corbin, 1998), the selected central theme from this data is committed love. All the other selected themes seem to be coherently interrelated with this central theme. The criteria for choosing this theme to be the central theme is based on the unanimous consensus and experience of all the participants that love is the most influencing factor for both stability and satisfaction in remarriage.

All the participants' contributions were a synthesis of their short-term and long-term experiences that go beyond what each knew, did not know, did and/or did not do at the time of entering their second marriages. Unless otherwise stated, whatever was reported in this study reflected the participants' views at the time the interviews were conducted and during follow-up sessions.

## My experience

Based on what you have read in this session, reflect on your own personal experience.

1. What do I know about myself in terms of personality, talents, weaknesses, likes, dislikes, desires (interests) and goals that I want to achieve in my lifetime?

2. Which of the following were my primary motivations for the first marriage?
   o I thought I was in love
   o Companionship: needed somebody to be with
   o Female spouse was pregnant
   o Wanted to have children
   o Wanted to get out of parent's house
   o It was time to get married
   o Wanted to have on-going sexual expressiveness with the same partner
   o Curiosity and rebelliousness: wanted to experiment with a person of another race
   o Other:

3. Which of the following summarizes the my major attitude in my current marriage?
   o Love of self

- o Love for your partner
- o Mutual love
- o Love of children and attentiveness to their needs o Love toward multiple extended-family members
- o Other:

## Keys to committed love

As keys are important to open doors, consider the following keys to committed love.

- Having the right motivations for marriage
- Focusing on realistic expectations about remarriage and prospective spouse
- Compatibility, involving the picking of the right partner or chemistry match
- Love involves making a decision and a commitment to marriage
- Love of children and attentiveness to their needs
- Intelligent and emotional maturity
- Unconditional love
- Self-identity and personality qualities (e.g., reliable, responsible, sociable, easy going, kind, reasonable spending habits, perseverance, joyful, spiritual, independent and dependent)
- Mutual love between partners
- Love toward the multiple extended-family members
- Maturity based on one's experience
- Ability to handle and resolve conflicts to arrive at mutually acceptable decisions
- Children's mental status
- Wisdom that focuses on knowing your position and roles in the marriage
- Forgiveness is part and parcel of maturity
- Love of self and love of the partner
- Sense of order, structure, and flexibility with self and others
- Awareness that all marriages are difficult and the need to work hard for the relationship to succeed
- Perception of remarriage as an iceberg

- Compatibility: described as enjoying some of the same things and values
- Keeping up with the lessons learned by from one's past mistakes that contributed to the end of the first marriage (e.g., marital infidelity and overfocus on work at the expense of marriage and family life) in order to avoid the risk of making the same mistakes again
- Parent's realization of the pain and losses suffered by the children as a result of parental conflict and divorce and resolve to make the second marriage work so that the children do not face the same fate again

# Primary Factors of Stability and Satisfaction in Remarriage: Study Sessions 2-9

As mentioned before, the following results are categorized as primary factors because they were referred to by more than eight of the 16 participants. There are eight primary factors which emerged: integral maturity, knowledge of the complexity of remarriage, finances, collaborative parenting, sexuality, communication, spirituality, and professional help.

# Study Session 2.

## Integral Maturity in Remarriage

*Description of Integral Maturity*
*Experience of Others*
*My Experience*
*Keys to Integral Maturity*

### *Description of Integral Maturity*

In an effort to establish a sense of priority among all the factors identified as influencing stability and satisfaction in remarriage, it was determined from the research results that all the participants described committed love as possible because of each partner's integral maturity. In metaphorical terms, as sunlight is important to chlorophyll during photosynthesis, so is integral maturity important to committed love for stability and satisfaction in remarriage.

It seems that the communication that reinforces stability and satisfaction in remarriage is not a matter of communicating or dialoguing about any topic, at any time, in any place, with any other person, but communication that is geared at building relationships, solving problems, and communicating maturely instead of a mere venting of one's emotions without due consideration for the recipient(s) of the communication.

The same rationale could be applied to the other primary and secondary factors that were identified. A typical example is in reference to maturity and finances in remarriage. Based on the collected data, 10 participants stated that intelligent decisions have to be made before spending the money, and other decisions that go along with money (e.g., deciding whether to have a joint account or separate accounts).

Whenever the participants applied maturity to stability and satisfaction in remarriage, most of them were describing it as a fruit of perseverance, earned through hard work and through overcoming hardships. Six participants spoke of maturity as the ability that had helped them to maintain self-control in emotionally charged moments in their remarriages.

At the time of the interview, all the participants seemed to have what Kerr and Bowen (1988) referred to as a high "differentiation of self." They expressed themselves with clarity of feelings and thoughts, yet, while listening to their stories about their first marriages, they seemed to have been in these earlier marriages more driven by their emotions (e.g., love perceived as being "head over heels" or limited to romance) than a balance of thought and feelings. Based on what was learned from all the participants, stability and satisfaction in remarriage appear to require individuals with an above-average level of differentiation of self.

Analyzing how the participants presented the details about their first marriages, most of them had a differentiation of self that was below average. It seems that each participant's acquired higher differentiation of self may have played a significant role in positively influencing his or her stability and satisfaction in remarriage.

In elaborating on the importance of hardships and maturity, Fred highlighted: "Whatever does not kill you makes you to grow." From the participants' descriptions that however tough their divorce process and its consequences were for most of them, all the participants reported having grown in one way or another through their divorces. Examples of related areas of growth included forgiveness, compassion, patience, and ability to take risks, as well as self-improvement through education, spiritual growth, and the courage to seek help. Maturity is a core domain in stability and satisfaction in remarriage because it helps the individual to be in control of his or her life, to make coherent decisions, and to assume responsibility for his or her actions.

## Experience of Others

All the participants highlighted that maturity is one of the most important influencing factors in stability and satisfaction in remarriage. However, based on how each participant described how he or she conceptualized maturity, it was not a mere notion of one's chronological age that determined his or her level of maturity. Accordingly, Catherine exclaimed:

> My second husband is ten years younger than me, but mentally he is above me!

Based on the participants' descriptions of maturity and how they applied it to remarriage, maturity is a complex concept. For instance, six female and five male participants described maturity as an individual's ability to independently make coherent decisions and that individual's ability to put into action the decisions made. On the other hand, Geoffrey mentioned:

> A mature divorced parent should be capable of assuming responsibility for his or her past, present, and future actions. One of the greatest lessons I learned, as I was struggling to come to terms with my divorce, was to stop blaming other people for all my actions and wrong choices in life. This included learning to confront myself by reflecting upon my personal contribution to the previous divorce.

Likewise, Bernardo stated:

> Now, when I look back at my divorce, however difficult it may be for me to admit, the truth is that I was responsible, in one way or another, for my previous divorce. It takes two to make the marriage work and it takes two to break it.

Elaborating on the importance of integral maturity and self-love, Hilda stated:

> At the time of remarriage I was more focused on finding a companion to overcome my loneliness. What I have learned along the way is that I lacked the appropriate degree of maturity to love myself better. Integral maturity is indispensable for every partner contemplating remarriage. This implies maturity at different levels (e.g., emotional, spiritual, moral, interpersonal, and ability to handle conflict with prudence). Maturity is also based on the ability to slow down, think things through, not rush into another marriage before resolving one's baggage.

Furthermore, ten participants stated that seeking professional help after divorce is also an expression of maturity. This includes a willingness to make an effort to work through his or her frustration and guilt from the first marriage. This requires honesty and self-love. Charles said:

> Maturity embraces the ability to hold on to realistic expectations in a second marriage. One should be able to decide when it is the right time for him or her to enter a second marriage.

Nine participants mentioned that they felt seriously hurt by their former spouses because all the events that surrounded the divorce and ultimately the divorce itself marked an irreversible change in their lives. This was based on the intensity of the pain, suffering, humiliation, and shame related to their divorce experiences. Four participants mentioned that they experienced thoughts of retaliation toward their former spouses, but they did not carry out any imagined act of revenge. However, according to the nine participants, their pain and related losses from the divorce persisted until each discovered a real solution that they referred to as forgiveness based on maturity.

Grace clarified:

> Real forgiveness is a manifestation of maturity, especially when people acknowledge their own contributions to actions that have brought pain, humiliation, or loss of any kind.

Bernardo stated:

> I did not experience comfort in my heart and the ability to move on with my life after divorce until I took a decision as a mature person to forgive my ex-spouse. I also had to make another tough decision of forgiving the family friend whom my ex-spouse went to bed with while we were still married. As I look back now, I guess becoming more mature and understanding my contribution to her marital infidelity helped me to forgive my ex-spouse and that family friend. I guess, if I had not forgiven them, I would still feel very hurt.

Ten participants stated that recovering one's integral health is an act of maturity and it has a significant influence on stability and satisfaction in remarriage. Henry remarked:

> Being healthy in terms of mind, body, spirit, and emotionally helped me to enter my second marriage with a sober mind and helped me to discuss tough issues with my current wife before remarriage. Good health also helps me to relate with my significant others without becoming extremely dependent on them, but rather relate with them maturely and interpersonally.

Along the same trend, Beatrice cautioned divorced parents who are still single:

> Do not stuff somebody into your life before feeling whole about yourself. You need to be independent in order to establish an intimate relationship, without feeling the exaggerated urge to have someone into your life nor looking for others to fill into the hurt parts of yourself.

Additionally, Grace spoke of compassion and forgiveness as integral parts of maturity.

> Even though my first husband had cheated on me, had a child with another woman while we were still married, and I was very angry with him when we divorced, I managed to forgive him before he died.

> [Grace added:] After divorce, I converted to the Catholic Church, and during Lent, a priest at my new parish encouraged us during the homily to visit the sick, especially those who were lonely. Surprisingly, the priest gave us that homily during the very moment when my ex-husband was sick and lonely. I don't know how to say this. Anyway, I had vowed never to forgive my husband. However, that homily really turned my life upside down. After Mass, I felt a strong urge to talk with my ex-husband but I did not know how my second husband would react about my going to care for my ex-husband. After some serious thought, I acted maturely by letting my husband know about my ex-husband's illness and I asked him to accompany me to go and visit him. He [second husband] welcomed the idea and … and was happy because I had included him in the visit. He even suggested that I could stay more days alone with my ex-husband in his final days. It was a very powerful experience. We talked a lot, he asked me for forgiveness, and I forgave him. After his death, I arranged for his funeral and I really feel happy that I had the opportunity of reconnecting with him before he died. I have realized that life is too short to go around not talking to your family and in-laws. I really believe in forgiveness with everybody, including the people who had seriously hurt me.

Elías also considered himself to have become more mature in his second marriage in comparison to his first marriage. When asked about what he thought had contributed to his great sense of maturity, Elías said:

> I perceive myself wiser in the second marriage because I no longer put all the blame for my divorce on my ex-spouse. I have learned to assume responsibility for my actions. I have learned to be realistic and not to expect everything to be wonderful in remarriage, because life is not that way and people are not that way either.

Elaborating on this acquired wisdom and maturity, Elías suggested that divorced male parents preparing for remarriage should primarily look at what is their part in the marriage, what they each might not be doing, how one's faults might have contributed to the first divorce.

Twelve participants mentioned that counseling and psychotherapy were part and parcel of maturity insofar as they contributed to those participants healing from the wounds of divorce. Those participants considered counseling and psychotherapy to be very helpful in setting the tone for establishing stability and satisfaction in second marriages. Accordingly, in a post-interview note, Hilda wrote:

> I think the whole key to marriage and remarriage is counseling! I can't stress this enough. I think I should have gone through this process the first time I got married.

Eight participants highlighted that maturity involves the way remarried people strategize working with their family members in order to avoid family tensions. In this regard, Elizabeth clarified how her second husband's business with his brothers has strained her marriage as follows:

> In the last few years, the relationships have strained a lot. I resent not having the closeness of family. Even though we are older, and thank God, my sons both grew up with their uncles and that was fine, but now everything is kind of strained. In the business, the guys have different views. One has one view and another has another view. They clash.

Eleven participants mentioned that maturity included their ability to discern how to apply the knowledge gathered from daily life events or information to strengthen their second marriages. A typical example was that of Elizabeth, who prudently applied to her marriage a technique that she had overheard on a television channel. She overheard that technique at the moment when the stability and happiness in her marriage had started to be affected negatively by her husband's demanding and stressful work. The television message that Elizabeth recalled was: Giving a strong hug to a loved one reduces his or her stress.

Consequently, Elizabeth started to give a strong hug to her husband as soon as he entered the home door from work. Elaborating on the impact of that hug on her marriage Elizabeth said:

> Whenever my husband comes home from work, I give him a big greeting because that changes his mood. Always I have learned to stop whatever I'm doing, and come out and say: 'Hi, how are you? How was your day?' If I greet him like that, he becomes a better person. If I just say: 'Hi, how are you, hey, how you doing?' he comes in miserable. Now, I truly believe in that hug. I heard it on the TV one day, and I applied it to my husband, and it really works.

Emphasizing the notion of forgiving one's former spouse as an expression of love by the one who forgives, Alicia stated:

> Currently, I do not care whether my ex-spouse acknowledged his mistake or not. The most important thing for me is that forgiving him has made me feel better about myself and improved the love I have for my second spouse. This is because I am no longer wasting my energy ruminating about the past abuses. Instead, I am more focused in the present and how to keep my second marriage successful. So, you see, forgiveness of the ex-spouse has had many benefits for me. Therefore, I recommend that those who find it harder to forgive should do it at least for personal reasons if they cannot for other motives. I have experienced that forgiveness heals the one who forgives, and it is based on love.

## My Experience

Based on what you have read in this session, reflect on your own personal experience.

1. How am I preparing myself to live without what I greatly miss from the first marriage?

   _____

   _____

_____
_____
_____

2.  Who are the people I consider to be significant in my life as I prepare to remarry?

_____
_____
_____
_____
_____

3.  What unique role does each of these people play in my life and why do I perceive that person to be uniquely important?

_____
_____
_____
_____
_____

4.  Who are the people in my life that I can turn to when I need various kinds of help (e.g., emotional, spiritual, financial, social, parenting and/or finding meaning in life)?

_____
_____
_____
_____
_____

5.  Which of the following affected me the most in-between my first and second marriage?
    o   Single mother's finances dropped significantly
    o   Perception of divorce as an iceberg
    o   Single father's finances and standard of living increased
    o   Suffering and rejection from family members and friends
    o   Felt very, very lonely
    o   Single mothers who had never done paying jobs entered the job market
    o   Took on two jobs to handle financial demands

- o Went for further education
- o Some single fathers started overdrinking
- o Change in interactions between custodial single parents and their children

## Keys to integral maturity

As keys are important to open doors, consider the following keys to integral maturity.

- Ability to set realistic expectations about oneself and others
- Having the right motivations for marriage
- Practice of unconditional love
- Companionship in order to overcome loneliness
- Ability to give and receive emotional support
- Fidelity to God's plan for humanity: man was not created to live alone
- Tenderness toward self and significant others
- Patience and wisdom to search for the right and compatible partner
- Getting financial support from future spouse
- Need for a parenting partner and real model for children
- Being in love with the partner
- Getting away from pain in the first marriage
- Search for meaning and happiness in life with a partner
- Ability to start over again, praying and trusting in God so that this time it (marriage) would work
- Taking responsibility for one's actions without projecting blame to other(s). For example: Each adult should take responsibility for their role in the divorce. Children are not to be blamed for the divorce. Note: Before, during and/or after divorce, there is a high risk of finger-pointing and projecting blame. More often than not, the person blamed may not be the perpetuator but rather a victim. It is worth noting that whenever a problem arises in a stepfamily, divorce is not usually the child's fault (Satir & Baldwin, 1983; Tessman, 1978; Walsh, 1992).

# Study Session 3.

## Knowledge of the Complexity of Remarriage

*Description of the Knowledge of the Complexity of Remarriage*
*Experience of Others*
*My Experience*
*Keys to the Knowledge of the Complexity of Remarriage*

*Description of the Knowledge of the Complexity of Remarriage*

The description of the complexity of remarriage is based on the various responses from the participants when asked: What factors contribute to stability and satisfaction in remarriage? Based on their responses, remarriage is complex because there are many components that have be taken into account for it to work successfully. Establishing a stable and satisfactory remarriage may be compared to creating a symphony, whereby you have to pay a lot of attention to the many different notes and the many musicians. Examples of such components include (but not limited to) all the identified factors in this book that contribute to stability and satisfaction in remarriage: namely, committed love, integral maturity, knowledge of the complexity of remarriage, finances, collaborative parenting, sexuality, communication, spirituality, professional help, marital history, remarriage motivations, dating, clear boundaries, conflict resolution, cohabitation, house rules and roles, and permanent sites for professional remarriage services.

The art of knowing how to pay attention to each factor and how to integrate all these factors and others as well makes remarriage complex. The lack or misuse of any of these factors or other factors that are not mentioned in this book is likely to have a significant impact on stability and satisfaction in remarriage. It is not easy to obliterate completely one's experience from a prior marriage. Carrying past experiences into remarriage may have both positive and negative consequences. Bringing two families together may not be easy.

Imagine a situation that is already complex being further complicated by new challenges. Some of the challenges that add to the complexity of remarriage include: not accepting one's stepchildren and/or not being accepted by them, the increase in number of biological children and stepchildren (for example, from three to seven), caring for children with severe physical and/or mental disorders, caring for aging parents, especially if they live far away and have limited financial resources. Additional challenges include: the loss of a job and lack of child support from the ex-spouse, involvement in addictive substances or behaviors, involvement in criminal or illegal activities by any member within the remarriage nuclear family, including the ex-spouse, the parent's and/or children's lack of processing the grief and other losses associated with the previous divorce and current remarriage.

## Experience of Others

All the participants admitted that they did not know much about remarriage at the time of their second marriages. They did not know what they were entering into, especially the challenges that they have faced, yet such knowledge could have prevented some of these challenges. A typical challenge that 12 participants were not prepared for, at all, was how to handle the constant interference of their former spouses and/or those of their current spouses. Accordingly, Alicia stated:

> The ex-spouse of my husband has given us a lot of headache in our remarriage. She does call on a regular basis, almost daily, with the excuse of the child, you know, to ask questions about the child. But, and she is a … sort of a lonely person, has no one to reach out to and so she still continues to reach out to her ex-husband for support and some of her own things, like you know if she is sick or whatever, and he has continued to support her. Fortunately, I feel very secure in my relationship with my husband. If he wanted that relationship, he would have stayed with her. He chose to leave her, so I don't feel threatened by her in any way.

Daniel cautioned divorced parents contemplating remarriage that they should know about its complexity before they enter it. Daniel's advice: " Know what you are getting into before you enter it [remarriage]."

Likewise, eleven other participants indicated that making the right decision (e.g., in regard to who to marry) presupposes the need to have the right information. This information involves knowledge about oneself (self-knowledge), the prospective spouse and about how to resolve the specific issues in remarriage. According to Henry, such awareness matches the adage: Prevention is better than cure.

[Henry added:] That is why I like very much the Book of Proverbs in the Bible. It speaks of knowledge as a source of life for those who possess it. In fact, the knowledge I have now about remarriage helped me to understand my wife's concerns better and avoid many potential problems. Now, I have a better knowledge of how to handle the sensitive topics with my wife. I have a better practice of self-control than I did at the beginning of my remarriage.

Seven male participants out of eight and six females out of eight revealed that they entered their second marriages with very little awareness about the complexity and challenges of remarriage. Based on a marital experience of at least 8 years or more in their second marriages, all the participants revealed their realization that remarriage is complex, especially if it involves children from the previous marriage that ended in divorce and if the previous spouse is still alive.

Elaborating on the value of awareness, thirteen participants highlighted that rushing into remarriage, particularly when children are involved from the first marriage and before resolving the "baggage" associated with divorce, may be very dangerous. Therefore, the emphasis of putting into practice what they have learned is helpful in remarriage because awareness alone about its complexity and challenges is not enough. Additionally, Hilda indicated that awareness of the resources and practices that reinforce both stability and satisfaction in remarriage go beyond guesswork.

To make sure that knowledge about remarriage complexity gets better disseminated, 14 participants suggested that qualified personnel with different professional backgrounds are needed to form a joint team. Examples of such professionals will be mentioned later. However, according to those fourteen participants, such professionals are the ones who might play a significant role in helping divorced parents learn about the complexity of remarriage and its challenges before and/or after remarriage.

Eight participants (four men and four women) highlighted that, in order to reinforce stability and satisfaction in remarriage, it is important to know the factors that influence remarriage instability and unhappiness. Elaborating on re-divorce prevention, Bernardo observed:

One of the main reasons why my first divorce occurred was because my first wife and I contracted a marriage that did not have a good foundation. We married young because my girlfriend was pregnant. She wanted to get out of the house, and our marriage was just focused on the business of raising children… She [Rose] became pregnant, we claimed to have loved one another, and we wanted to go forward, anyway. Each of us wanted to get out of our homes and go to our own home that we thought would be better, "the grass is greener" [on the other side],something like that. Therefore, based on the lessons I learned from my first marriage and from the re-divorces of my loved ones, I think re-divorces could also be reduced if every remarriage begins on a good foundation.

Regarding the notion of how to establish a good foundation for remarriage, various participants identified the following factors as effective because they had used them and/or they had proven effective for their significant others. Seven participants mentioned the absence of unkind and continuous aggressive behaviors from the former spouse. Five participants spoke about the partners' responsibilities to become more aware of and to avoid repeating the factors that contributed to the first divorce. Four participants mentioned the need for the remarrying partners to work toward considering and resolving the parts they played in the first divorces.

In order to prevent the risk of re-divorce, fourteen participants emphasized that remarried couples should try individually and as a couple to avoid all the conditions that could lead one or both spouses to extramarital sex. Marital infidelity was reported by 14 participants to be one of the most significant factors contributing to remarriage instability and unhappiness. An honest act of introspection inspired Bernardo to reveal:

> I acknowledge that I share part of the blame in my first wife's extramarital affair because I have left her on her own. I had separated myself emotionally from her as I was so much immersed in my work. However, whatever the case, the truth is that I cannot tolerate a wife who cheats on me.

By making use of a metaphor of owning a new motor vehicle, Elías, a mechanic by profession, said it is not enough for remarrying parents to focus exclusively on the factors that contributed to establishing a good foundation for remarriage. Elías clarified:

> Focusing on the factors for a good remarriage foundation is like having a new Toyota. For the first few years, you drive your Toyota without the need for immediate service. However, for the proper functioning of that car, it has to be serviced every now and then. Almost the same thing happens to remarriage. In order to keep it stable and a source of happiness for the

spouses involved and their significant others, the spouses have to keep working on their remarriage, and that work never stops. The parts of the car that wear out and need to be replaced may represent the changes that the spouses have to make in their lives and the adaptations they have to make as they go through the different transitions of their remarriage cycle. In a special way, this refers to when their children leave home for college, get married, move to other states, a new grandchild is born, when one of them retires [or both of them], or changes a career, or when death occurs in the family. All these changes and adjustments can radically affect the stability and happiness of a remarriage even if it had a good foundation.

## My experience

Based on what you have read in this session, reflect on your own personal experience.

1. What self-help books, DVDs and/or CDs have I found helpful during any of the following periods:
   o Preparation for first marriage
   o First marriage enrichment
   o Parenting in first marriage
   o Divorce process
   o Healing from divorce
   o Life after divorce
   o Single parenthood
   o Preparation for remarriage
   o Remarriage after divorce
   o Step-parenting
   o Stability and satisfaction in remarriage?

2. What are the main ideas that have impacted me in each of the books, DVDs and/or CDs that I have identified in question 1?

_____

_____

_____

_____

_____

3. Which of the ideas in each the books, DVDs and/or CDs have I found least helpful and why?

_____
_____
_____
_____
_____

4. Which of the books, DVDs and/or CDs would I recommend to somebody based on his or her situation?

_____
_____
_____
_____
_____

5. Based on past, current and/or projected challenges within the remarriage triad, what kind of topics, books and/or research studies do I consider beneficial in influencing stability and satisfaction in remarriage?

_____
_____
_____
_____
_____

## Keys to the knowledge of the complexity of remarriage

As keys are important to open doors, consider the following keys regarding the knowledge of the complexity of remarriage.

- Handling the complexity of remarriage
- Awareness and acceptance of one's contribution to the failure of the first marriage (e.g., without putting all the blame on the ex-spouse or on oneself)
- In-depth communication that is reinforced by trust
- Gradual introduction of the prospective spouse to one's biological children

- Parental satisfaction: reinforced by peaceful and well-behaved biological children and stepchildren, e.g., those who do not get into trouble, not out of control, able to receive correction, without raising their voices, and are self-motivated
- Taking courage to trust again
- Caring for mentally and emotionally challenged children
- Friendly relationship with stepchildren
- Ability to ask for help from trusted loved ones and/or professionals
- Accepting support from trusted relative and friends
- Humor and optimism, especially in hard times
- Doing things together with spouse
- Equality and equity in remarriage
- Acknowledging whatever each partner brings and takes from the relationship
- Consistent and mutual respect for one another
- Personal attributes beyond animal magnetism of sheer desire: kindness, generosity, shared view that the relationship is built on equal effort
- Ability to share with others and overcoming a deeply rooted selfish attitude, that makes constant focus on: "Me," "My," and "I"
- Better spending habits by both spouses
- Integral maturity that encompasses the whole life of the individuals
- Ability to forgive as a manifestation of maturity and personal growth
- Overcoming transference issues in second marriage based on unresolved issues from first marriage (e.g., an erroneous projection on the second spouse of one's suspicion of marital infidelity on the basis of unresolved feelings that are related the infidelity of the first spouse)
- Making use of accumulated knowledge through experience
- Appropriate response to the unkind and continuous aggressive behaviors of the ex-spouse
- Maturity based on ability to slow down to think things through, accept one's personal limitations, seek professional help, and if necessary to resolve them, and start to implement the adage: "prevention is better than cure"
- Overcoming frustration, anger, and/or guilt from first marriage
- Kindness to self and consideration for others
- Know what you are getting into

Kelley and Burg (2000) compared entering a remarriage to walking into a movie set long after the film has begun. While the other cast members have to adjust to a new presence and to the fact that the script may have been rewritten, the one who enters has to find a way to fit into a story line and mood that has already been established. Based on this metaphor, Kelly and Burg emphasized that it is important for remarrying partners to be aware of the changes that will occur between marriages (the first marriage that ended through divorce and the next marriage, i.e., remarriage).

Consequently, Kelley and Burg (2000) cautioned remarrying parents to prepare their biological children for their plans to remarry. These authors' observation is that "Most people do not seem to spend enough time preparing children for a remarriage and the many changes that will occur" (p. 113).

Additionally, Kelley and Burg noted that children of divorce, regardless of their age, almost always cling to the magical hope that their parents will reunite. Therefore, it is understandable why many of them have trouble accepting anyone whose presence will necessarily put an end to this fantasy. Kelley and Burg also observed that remarriage adjustments are difficult for everyone because people are resistant to change, even when change is for the better. In other words, change is often associated with loss (Berry, 1998; Bowlby, 1980).

Kelley and Burg (2000) suggested that divorced parents contemplating remarriage should not rush into too much togetherness with the prospective stepparent of their children nor surprise the children about their plans to remarry. Several authors have recommended that, instead of rushing into remarriage, dating should begin with brief, get-acquainted visits in a relaxed, causal setting before planning any significant time together, including weekends (Black, 1998; Brehm, 1992; Nichols, 1996). Therefore, divorced parents should give their biological children time to get acquainted with their prospective stepparents before announcing any plans to remarry, and if possible, the announcement should be done in person (Kelley, 1995; Kelley & Burg, 2000; Wallerstein & Blakeslee; 1995).

# Study Session 4.

## Finances

### Description of Finances

Every participant presented a story that was quite unique as to how couples handle money. Therefore, professionals should help each couple to decide how to handle their money. Based on the interviews participants who had joint accounts with their spouses reported more trust in their partners, but joint accounts were not the ideal for all participants. Some of the participants were using both joint and separate accounts, while others had completely separate accounts from their spouses. Such account arrangements were congruent with Kelley and Burg's (2000) observations regarding remarried couples (Model #3).

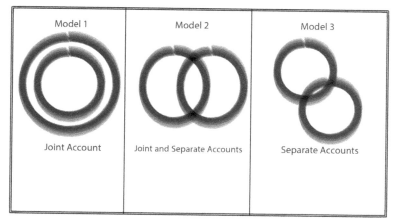

*Figure 5. Three models used by remarried couples in handling their finances.*

Based on personal experience in her first marriage, one participant emphatically warned partners preparing for marriage, whether in a first or second marriage, to be very careful about the use of credit cards. Grace highlighted that "partners have to train themselves to use the money that they have. Live within their means, and think economics."

## Experience of Others

All participants highlighted that finances are not easy to handle in stepfamilies if they are not negotiated before remarriage. Divorced parents who bring children to second marriages create a situation for the stepparents of their children that may affect the dynamics of the couple and bring about many emotional issues. Fourteen participants mentioned that finances become a difficult topic to handle, especially because there are many people involved within the stepfamily.

For instance, Felicia who entered the second marriage with her son reported:

> My second husband [Fausto] was uncomfortable in the first three years to spend money for the well-being of my son. However, I also noticed in him [Fausto] an attitude of ambivalence. This was because I had realized that he wanted to be with me alone [without my son], but how could he do that without paying attention to my dear son?

According to Felicia, once in a while, Fausto would resent spending his money on Felicia's son because Fausto clearly knew that he was not the biological father of her son. Felicia reported that Fausto used to complain to her about her first husband's failure to help her with money for her son. Nevertheless, when he realized that he could not love the mother without caring for her son, he changed his attitude toward the son and started spending money on him. During the interview, Felicia acknowledged with gratitude Fausto's helping her to pay for the college education of her son because her former spouse never spent a penny on her son.

Twelve participants mentioned that remarried parents, together with their spouses, should have better spending habits. In order to do this, these participants suggested that they needed to know about themselves and how to prioritize their expenses because there are many needs and many people to take care of within a stepfamily setting. Twelve participants highlighted that each couple is unique with regard to finances. Therefore, they suggested that remarrying partners should have better communication skills about money.

If left undiscussed and unclearly negotiated, finances can severely contribute to the disruption of marriage.

Likewise, Grace suggested:

> Remarrying parents should not spend all the money they have, nor spend the money they don't have, especially through use of credit cards.

Although none of the participants discussed finances with a professional accountant before remarriage, all the participants highlighted that parents contemplating remarriage, together with their prospective spouses, should consult a qualified financial accountant before remarriage. Bernardo mentioned that this kind of consultation is particularly important for remarrying parents who are very rich, have a lot of assets, and/or a lot of valuable inheritance.

In similar terms, nine participants mentioned that prenuptial written agreements are helpful in securing the financial benefits of the remarrying parent and his or her children, just in case the second marriage ends in another divorce or in the death of one of the spouses. Otherwise, the person bringing money into the marriage without a prenuptial agreement might feel insecure financially and not want to risk their money being shared by the children and/or relatives of the other spouse. By the same token, 10 participants perceived this kind of insecurity as a hindrance to stability and satisfaction in remarriage.

When asked how the participants were currently handling their financial arrangements with their spouses, the responses showed three models of accounts: one-pot method, one-pot and independent method, and independent method (Figure 5). Elaborating on these models of accounts, nine participants mentioned that they use the one-pot method. This involves two spouses putting together all their resources into an account and spending together from the same account.

Elías clarified: "The pot method has strengthened my marriage and it has helped me to learn that marriage is all about sharing." In specific terms, Bernardo highlighted: "Sharing money with the second spouse symbolizes a leap of trust that spouses put in one another, especially for the partner who invests more money and assets into the relationship." Grace emphasized:

> I grew up in poor family and that helped me to learn to value the little we had and to share the little with others. However, irrespective of our poverty, we survived, partly because my parents spent the little money they had prudently, and I used to

hear dialoguing about what item to spend money on. Therefore, I think that when spouses have a joint account, they should not make surprise purchases of more than a hundred dollars without consulting the other spouse, even if the purchase is for the well-being of the other spouse.

[Graced added:] I recall that my parents had to make tough choices of removing completely some items from the shopping list because … they did not have the money. They put those items on hold until they got the money for them. My parents also discouraged me and my siblings from borrowing money in order to offer very expensive gifts to one another during the Christmas season.

Five participants reported that they were using the one-pot and independent method. This consists of the two spouses putting together some of their financial resources, especially money, and putting some of their money into a separate account. Hilda was one of the participants who used this method of accounting. Hilda said:

In my second marriage, we have three accounts. I share one account with my husband, my husband has another one of his own, and I have another account that is mine alone.

When asked for her rationale for maintaining these two separate accounts in addition to the joint account, Hilda replied:

After divorce, I became a single-mother and I learned how to handle my own money. I started to make all the financial decisions by myself. So, after remarriage, it was not easy for me to give up that autonomy. As a woman, my husband in my first marriage kept me out of all the decisions regarding money. My [second] husband has a separate account also because it is specifically for his business and both of us contribute to the joint account.

Four other participants emphasized the usefulness of having some money that one can spend as he or she likes without the need to be on constant negotiations about money with one's spouse. Two participants out of these five had a separate account primarily because they were running businesses that needed different kinds of accounting.

Two participants out of 18 mentioned that they had independent accounts with their second spouses. When asked about the rationale for separate accounts, Fred mentioned that since his adolescence, he decided not to have a joint account with any future wife because he got tired of hearing fights his parents had over money because they had a joint account.

Another participant, Dora, resolved not to have a joint account based on her experience in her first marriage in which the other spouse spent a lot of money they had in a joint account a few months before their divorce. By the same token, listening to all these stories, it became evident that most of the participants made their financial decisions based on their histories and what they learned from their parents.

Thirteen participants clarified that most of the conflicts surrounding money in the early stages of their remarriages were focused on who pays for what, how much, and why me, as a stepparent, if the children are not mine. However, as the problems surfaced about money, these 13 participants reported that those conflicts helped them to start discussing openly the impact of money on their remarrying. They said it was difficult to speak about the topic of finances. The conversations were emotionally charged at the beginning, but they realized that silence about money would not resolve the problem.

These participants recommended that divorced parents contemplating remarriage should take the risk of discussing money and other financial assets that they bring to the marriage and define in concrete terms (e.g., who is going to pay for the expenses?) Along the same lines, Dora mentioned:

> Informing my second spouse about my elderly parents that I had to take care of has helped my second spouse to understand my financial needs and become supportive by providing more money from his separate account.

Charles narrated his experience as follows:

> I grew up in a poor family, whereby being on the breadline affected my attitude toward money. I learned that there are things that my rich neighbors had (for example, swimming pools, nice houses and new cars), and to my surprise the lack of those things influenced me to develop a deeper friendship with the children of our rich neighbors. Detailed conversations and interactions with some of these friends helped me to realize that, although their parents were rich, there were things that their parents could not buy for them, even with all the money that

they had. I kept that lesson all through my life and I have not let money take away from me those things that money cannot buy: love, friendship, respect, spirituality, common sense.

In concluding about finances, Charles emphatically cautioned:

Divorced parents should not focus all their attention on money because there are many important things in second marriages that cannot be bought with money, for instance, winning the trust of the stepchildren.

## My experience

Based on what you have read in this session, reflect on your own personal experience.

Indicate with an (x) in the table below the approximate annual income before taxes and explore how such an amount impacts my persona, life style and/or power dynamics in marital relationships:

| Annual family income | Annual family income in my family of origin (before my first marriage) | Annual family income in my first marriage | Annual income after my divorce and before my second marriage | Annual family income in my second marriage |
|---|---|---|---|---|
| Below $15,000 | | | | |
| $15,000 – 25,000 | | | | |
| $25,000 – 35,000 | | | | |
| $35,000 – 45,000 | | | | |
| $45,000 – 55,000 | | | | |
| $55,000 – 65,000 | | | | |

| | | | | |
|---|---|---|---|---|
| $65,000 – 75,000 | | | | |
| $75,000 – 90,000 | | | | |
| $90,000 – 130,000 | | | | |
| Over $130,000 | | | | |

Identify the number of all the people dependent on my annual income:
Before my first marriage:
In my first marriage:
In my second marriage:
Currently:

My current home neighborhood may be categorized as:
o   Inner-city
o   Urban
o   Suburban

What are our considerations and conclusions in regard establishing a pre-nuptial agreement or not?

_____
_____
_____
_____
_____

## Keys to financial security and management

As keys are important to open doors, consider the following keys to finance.

-   Each couple is unique in regard to finances. Although none of the participants and his or her current spouse discussed finances with the help of a professional accountant, all participants highlighted the need for parents contemplating remarriage and their prospective spouses to consult with an accountant before remarriage in order to choose their appropriate financial model(s) in remarriage. Three models were used by the participants:

One pot method – whereby both spouses have mutual trust and commitment that empower them to put all their financial resources together, hold transparent dialogues about how to invest their money and how to spend it. "Marriage is all about sharing."

Independent accounts – no sharing of financial resources, each spouse handles his or her personal account

One pot method and independent accounts – this method was reported by the participants who used it for the well-being of their children from a previous marriage, safety reasons and emergencies and/or for separate business accounts

- Lack of financial resources in a remarriage may contribute to strain on a marriage and on the individual's psychological well-being, thereby bringing about other kinds of mental problems, selfish attitudes, and behaviors. For instance, being on the breadline could affect people's mental health
- Separation of money should primarily be done for the benefit of the children from the first marriage
- Know the limits of money and be attentive to resources that money cannot buy
- Sharing money also symbolizes a leap of trust that spouses put in one another; especially the partner who invests more money and assets into the relationship
- On-going child support and whenever applicable, paying alimony for the ex-spouse
- Neighborhood (e.g., living in a suburban neighborhood due to the expected high standard of living, thus creating financial pressure on the couple and family struggling to fit in)

# Study Session 5.

## Collaborative Parenting

*Description of Collaborative Parenting*
*Experience of Others*
*My Experience*
*Keys to Collaborative Parenting*

### Description of Collaborative Parenting

Fourteen participants mentioned that children need the collaboration of both biological parents because each parent has something unique to offer to the children that cannot be given by the other parent. Therefore, even before the divorce occurs and after it takes place, the two parents should make an effort to make sure that their interpersonal relationships, especially if they are conflictive, do not hinder the children from interacting with either parent. Accordingly, by means of a metaphor, Henry emphasized: "Even if the two elephants [parents] are still fighting, they should protect the grass [children]."

### Experience of Others

Charles narrated a typical example of how the on-going conflicts between divorced parents affected his children and his second marriage. He clarified that before his first wife (Jenny) finished her education, she revealed in private to their youngest son (Paul) that, after her education, she would leave the marriage in order to get alimony. At first, Paul kept this information to himself because he thought that his mother was joking. However, when he saw his mother carrying out all of her hidden agendas, he was upset by his mother's actions, and he decided to inform his father about all the things she had told him.

This revelation impacted the whole family system, whereby Paul sided with his father and against his mother, while his three older siblings sided with their mother and became rebellious to their father's authority over them. As a result, Jenny started using these three children to the detriment of Charles' second marriage by soliciting them to hurt his wife and make his second marriage difficult for him.

Charles elaborated that, although he went through a very hard time after his divorce, he also felt relieved that his marriage with Jenny had ended because he could not endure any longer the sufferings he was experiencing when they were together. Four years after the divorce, he started dating Julia and they married after 6 months. They have been married for 21 years and he described his marriage with Julia as satisfying, fulfilling, spiritual, and stable.

Felicia's story illustrates how the fight between the parents prevented their son (José) from knowing his father. Felicia narrated that because of the way her first husband (Roberto) had mistreated her, she did whatever was within her powers to make sure that José should not have any contact with his biological father. She also decided not to inform José who his biological father was. However, at the age of 16, José wanted to meet his father but his mother would not give him any clue. Felicia's rationale was that she did not want her son to be in touch with the man who had abused her emotionally and physically during her pregnancy with José. Nevertheless, José desperately continued to contact other family members to help him find his father.

On one occasion, one of his aunts found Roberto in a certain restaurant and immediately went to call José, so that José could meet his father. They found him in that restaurant, but the meeting was very painful for José. After Roberto recognized who José was (because José introduced himself to his father), Roberto just gave a handshake and left José and his aunt in the restaurant. After that meeting, José's aunt told Felicia how both of them had gone to meet Roberto and the unhappiness that José felt because Roberto did not respond to him at all.

José did not know that his aunt had informed Felicia about that meeting. After that meeting, up to the time of the interview with Felicia, both José and Felicia had had no conversation at all about Roberto. Even when Roberto died, and Felicia was informed about it, she refused to tell José about it. Therefore, Felicia stated:

> If my son [José] happened to know about his father's death, somebody else might have told him, not me.

Felicia seemed to have taken a definitive decision not to initiate any conversation with José about her first husband. Felicia stated:

> I assume the responsibility of saying nothing to my son about his father, but also I rest assured that I have done whatever is

in my power to be there for him [José]. Fortunately, my second
husband has done his best to treat José almost like his biological
child.

Elaborating on the notion of collaborative parenting, 13 participants
emphasized that custodial parents, who remarry after divorce, should
understand the importance of the parenting role of the stepparent. It is very
difficult for an adult person who lives in the same house with the children to
have no impact on them at all and vice versa. Even if the stepparent plays a
parental role with the stepchildren, every child who reaches the age of reason
should be encouraged by the biological parent to address the stepparent,
directly or when making reference to them, by his/her first name or a title
that the child feels comfortable using.

Catherine made the following detailed clarifications. First of all, she said
that it is important to let the children from the first marriage find the right
title in regard to how to address a stepparent. Many children struggle with
how to address their stepparents without feeling disloyal to their biological
parents of the same gender as their stepparents. This became evident as
Catherine was narrating how her daughter, Eileen, felt comfortable addressing
Michael by his first name at all times, although Eileen perceives Michael as
a father figure, but without losing sight of her biological father. On the other
hand, although her sibling (Eric) addresses Michael by his first name when
talking to him or introducing him to others, in his absence, Eric refers to
Michael as his stepfather.

## *Stepparents' Collaboration with the Biological Parent*

Nine participants mentioned they experienced peace and happiness in their
remarriages whenever their second spouses collaborated with them regarding
the children from their first marriages. One of the typical examples of this
collaboration was that mentioned by Abraham, who had a son (Paul) from
the first marriage. Paul was 27 years old at the time of Abraham's remarriage
to Joyce. Abraham stated:

> Two months after remarriage, I experienced an inner struggle
> about how to learn to be a caring stepparent to John who was a
> physically and mentally normal child. Additionally, I keep on
> expressing my loving care toward Paul who was born physically
> and mentally handicapped. Indeed, it is not the same feeling
> to raise a normal child and a handicapped child. [However,
> with a smile in his face, Abraham added:] I have progressively
> established a close relationship with my stepson [John], because

he is very intelligent, respectful, responsible and outgoing, and his qualities have played a significant impact in my marriage.

## *Stepparents' Collaboration in Disciplining and Rewarding Children in Second Marriages*

Speaking about disciplining stepchildren, Bernardo emphasized that the biological parent should be the one to discipline one's own children. The stepparent may have the right answers and words, but they may be coming from the wrong person. However, the biological parent and stepparent should form a united front, together set rules for the children, which the biological parent should carry out. Henry stated that in his house, after he had consulted in private with his second wife about the adequate disciplinary measure to carry out on his two children from the first marriage, Henry (the biological parent) was their sole disciplinarian. However, together with his second wife, they were the disciplinarians of their biological child.

If the two children do something that he and his second wife think it is worth rewarding them for, his second wife does the rewarding. By the same token, Henry reported that his two children from the previous marriage were on good terms with their stepmother and vice versa. Henry was also feeling supported by his wife, and he recommended that other parents in similar situations exercise most of the disciplinarian role for their children instead of leaving all the responsibility to the stepparent. Otherwise, one risks creating an environment of resentment and anger between the stepparent and the stepchild.

## *Need for Parents to Avoid Loading Their Parental Roles onto Children*

Based on the data in this study, seven participants had biological children in both their first and second marriages. The reported minimum age difference between each participant's youngest child in first marriage and the participant's first child in the second marriage was 3 years and 6 months. The average age difference was 5 years, and the maximum age difference was 8 years.

During the interviews, six participants out of the seven parents who had children in both marriages regretted having loaded some of their parental roles onto their young children from the first marriages, for example, taking care of their younger half-siblings. Another participant, Elizabeth, who had biological children in both marriages and who had personally taken care of her half-sibling while growing up in a stepfamily discussed this:

My mother and her second husband [Jim] had a son together [José]. Unfortunately, Jim died 4 years after marrying my mother. I ended up taking on the responsibility of caring for my younger half-brother [José] because our mother was not available to us.

Elizabeth mentioned that it was very painful for her to take care of José. Later on, when Elizabeth was in her second marriage, she resolved that her older son, Robert, should not take care of his younger half-brother, John. Instead, she decided to take care of both of them because she was convinced that it was her role as a mother to parent her children.

When asked about her feelings toward Robert and John, Elizabeth said that she was trying her level best to express her love to both of them without showing any kind of preference. However, she clarified that, deep within her heart, she was feeling a stronger affection for her first son "because we [Elizabeth and Robert] went through so much there is more communication between us." Elizabeth added:

> I find myself feeling a little guilty knowing that my second child, you know, has two parents. [My] first child only had the one parent [me alone], and it was a little bit tougher. My first son and I [had] to go through a tough life, and we sacrificed a heck of a lot more than the second child.

When queried as to whether it seems as if her second son's needs are better taken care of than the first, Elizabeth replied:

> Yes. And, you know, you are growing up, and the second child gets all of this stuff; and not that the first child does not, but he is older now. I think, I just bent a little more to my first child knowing that the second one got so much more, and I felt a little guilty because the first one did not get as much.

During the interview, Elías acknowledged that he accepts part of the responsibility for the end of his first marriage. He added that he has become aware of his own faults and that maturity is a process that one goes through by learning from his or her mistakes. Elías also clarified that his father was a child of divorce, and his father used to relate to him the pain he suffered after the divorce of his parents. This trend of divorce and children suffering the consequences of their parents' divorces continued when Elías' parents also divorced. In that case Elías experienced a lot of pain as he witnessed the bitter divorce of his parents (Erera-Weatherley, 1996).

According to Elías, the lesson he learned from this series of divorces and the pain suffered by the children had helped him in making the decision to do whatever was within his powers to protect his children from suffering the consequences of his divorce. Consequently, Elías suggested that every remarried parent, after a first divorce, should make an effort not to subject his or her children to a second divorce, because "divorce pains the children."

The research results from Wallerstein and Blakeslee's (1989) longitudinal study were congruent with Elías' perception of the impact of divorce on children. However, in Ahrons (2004) later study, children of divorced parents were reported to have overcome the negative impact of their parents' divorce and to have become resilient and functional in life.

## My experience

Based on what you have read in this session, reflect on your own personal experience.

How am I preparing myself to become a good stepparent if my prospective spouse is a custodial parent to his/her children from the first marriage?

_____
_____
_____
_____
_____

## Keys to collaborative parenting

As keys are important to open doors, consider the following keys to collaborative parenting.

- Set house rules that state clearly how you want things to be (e.g., in this house, nobody has the right to badmouth one's ex-spouse in front of the children; table manners must be respected, including the positioning of the forks, knives, and saucers
- Keep clear boundaries with significant others, especially with your ex-spouse, children, and the impact of society on your life and remarriage
- Avoid unnecessary resentment of your prospective spouse by your biological children
- Develop and put into practice the guidelines for parenting and stepparenting
- Understand that divorce ends a marriage, not a family

- Reduce your children's risk of feeling responsible and/or guilty for your divorce by verbally informing them it was not their fault
- Overcome frustration and/or guilt from your first marriage, and if necessary, use professional help
- Be aware that joint physical custody that involves very short term alternations of residences (e.g., on a weekly, weekend or monthly basis) enables the children to be with both parents, but it leaves the children lacking a place to call home
- For the greater benefit of your children, avoid the risk of bringing anybody you are dating to your home until both of you really feel committed to one another
- Prevent and/or reduce the risk of another divorce by maintaining marital fidelity. Avoiding an extramarital affair is crucial to marital trust. It is not easy to forgive an affair. Even if one does, there will always remain a doubt in one's mind: "Can I trust my ex-spouse again? No."
- Seek counseling if necessary to address your unresolved issues related to the previous marriage (e.g., unresolved pain, anger, and/or frustration).

# Study Session 6.

## Sexuality in Remarriage

*Description of Sexuality*
*Experience of Others*
*My Experience*
*Keys to Satisfactory Sexuality in Remarriage*

### Description of Sexuality

All the participants highlighted that they entered their remarriages when they were chronologically older in comparison to when they entered their first marriages, and that that age difference had affected the frequency of their sexual expressiveness. Additionally, five participants above the age of 60 years indicated that they had started to struggle with the question of how to keep sexuality alive as a result of advancing in years.

### Experience of Others

All the participants emphasized that sexuality was one of the aspects that they wanted to continue to keep alive in their second marriages on the part of both partners. Some of the techniques used by the participants to maintain active sexual expressiveness with one another included the following:

Ten participants mentioned that they had developed a habit of dressing well. Accordingly, Elizabeth identified physical attraction as an integral part of marital stability and satisfaction. In fact, Elizabeth was the only participant out of the sixteen who mentioned physical attraction as a factor influencing both remarriage satisfaction and stability. Elizabeth said:

> If … you are not physically attracted [to him or her], then you
> shouldn't be with that person. There has to be a reason why you
> connected to begin with.

Fourteen participants mentioned that taking periodic honeymoons by going to a hotel (at least twice a year), and/or going to a different place by themselves as a couple were excellent ways to reinforce their stability and satisfaction in remarriage. Two participants highlighted that watching sexually seductive movies together with their spouses was an influencing experience for them to feel motivated to engage in romantic activities in the privacy of their bedroom.

In regard to maintaining sexual expressiveness, seven participants spoke of the practice of being tender with one another, doing activities together with their partners, eating together, sharing opinions, having sex for pleasure, and learning new techniques of how to position themselves during sexual intercourse.

According to Daniel, changing such positions was helpful in overcoming the routine of having sex in the same position. Likewise, changing positions was helping him and his partner to improve their communication about which positions were more suitable for their sexual satisfaction. Hilda elaborated:

> Scheduling the time for having intimacy with my spouse has proven very practical. Due to the many activities that go on in our life as a couple, by the time we go to bed, we are very exhausted and have less energy to engage in sex. In fact, it is my experience that without scheduling sexual intercourse, especially for working and aging spouses, it is possible to let it go without intending it. Yet, genital intercourse is a very important activity that you cannot leave to the fate of spontaneity.

Hilda emphasized that sexual intercourse is an expression of mutual love for one another and can serve as a buffer in bad times. Consequently, she referred to "good sex as good glue" in remarriage.

On the other hand, Charles made this statement:

> Good sexual life starts in the kitchen. Good sexuality begins by helping out with the cooking, with the clean-up of the dishes, and helping clean the house. [It involves] listening to each other's needs and trying to be open to taking care of her needs and what she wants out of the marriage, and by supporting her in her desires to grow as a human being. This kind of mutual collaboration keeps us together, and then we feel comfortable to relax in the same bed, with our arms wrapped around one another.

Felicia spoke of the willingness to engage in sexual intercourse as a means of caring for one's partner. She suggested that spouses should think not only about individual sexual satisfaction but also the satisfaction of their partners. Felicia clarified:

> Sometimes, I'm not in the mood to have sex, but when I think of my husband's needs, I motivate myself to have intimacy because, in the end, both of us benefit from the experience.

Felicia added that this kind of self-motivation had significantly contributed to her marriage stability and satisfaction. This was because, before developing this self-motivation, her history of low sexual desire was affecting the couple's sexual satisfaction in her second marriage. In her opinion, the low sexual desire was a result of the abuse she suffered from her first husband.

Seven participants reported having engaged in sexual liaisons during the divorce process while experiencing moments of high anxiety. While elaborating on their loneliness after divorce, the participants' stories included themes of anxiety and anger toward their former spouses, especially the stories of those who reported being involved with multiple partners after divorce, and those who started cohabiting with their partners before remarriage. This was congruent with the literature that reported individuals experiencing intense emotions of anxiety, frustration, anger and/or hatred were more likely to experience intense feelings of sexual attraction (Cox, 2002; Dulton & Aron, 1999).

Aging was another factor that ten participants expressed as one of the factors hindering their remarriage satisfaction. They reported that aging had negatively affected their frequencies of sexual expressiveness because of the reduced physical energy in their weakening bodies. These observations were congruent with the literature (Kelley & Burg, 2000). Some of the concrete examples that the participants had designed to keep sexuality alive included establishing a ritual or routine for couple time, and/or going periodically to a different place for honeymoon-like experiences to rejuvenate their remarriage experiences.

**My experience**

Based on what you have read in this session, reflect on your own personal experience.

1. What are my fears and negative experiences regarding sex and intimacy?

   _____
   _____
   _____
   _____
   _____

2. What contributes to a strong sexual relationship for me?

   _____
   _____
   _____
   _____
   _____

3. What are my positive attitudes and preferences about sexual intimacy?

   _____
   _____
   _____
   _____
   _____

4. What skills do I need to learn for a mutually satisfying sexual relationship?

   _____
   _____
   _____
   _____
   _____

5. What do I occasionally think and feel before, during and after a sexual relationship?

   _____
   _____
   _____

_____
_____

6. What past sexual experiences may negatively impact my remarriage experience?

_____
_____
_____
_____
_____

7. What sexual experiences may positively impact my remarriage experience?

_____
_____
_____
_____
_____

8. What sexual activities make me feel uncomfortable if demanded by my partner?

_____
_____
_____
_____
_____

9. What sexual activities help me enjoy sex and how do I let my partner know about them?

_____
_____
_____
_____
_____

10. What will help us as a couple to avoid the risk of using sex to control one another?

_____
_____
_____

_____
_____

11. What skills do I need to maintain sexual fidelity and yet interact with other people?

_____
_____
_____
_____
_____

12. What method of family planning are we going to use that protects life by natural means?

_____
_____
_____
_____
_____

13. How will we keep the marriage and sexual relationship alive beyond changes in desire, needs, moods, age, energy, fidelity, health and/or geographical locations?

_____
_____
_____
_____
_____

14. What am I going to do/not do as a parent to help my children and stepchildren develop a positive attitude toward sexual intimacy, marital fidelity and openness to procreation?

_____
_____
_____
_____
_____

## Keys to satisfactory sexuality in remarriage

As keys are important to open doors, consider the following keys regarding sexuality.

- Differences in sexual desire and in aging couples
- Scheduling time and space for intimacy
- More people are currently entering remarriage when they are chronologically older in comparison to those entering first marriages. Keeping sexuality alive by aging spouses in remarriage is vital, especially as partners advance in age. Participants suggested that they handled this by maintaining a youthful attitude that involved dressing well, staying mentally alert, taking periodic honeymoons, tenderness, doing things together, going places, eating together, sharing opinions, having sex for pleasure, learning techniques for igniting desire and intent in one's partner and/or watching sexually seductive movies together with their partner
- Take into account gender differences and remarriage

More divorced men spend shorter lengths of time between divorce and remarriage than divorced women (Baum, 2003). Rushing into remarriage before resolving the loss and grief associated with divorce is a great threat to stability and satisfaction in remarriage (Kelley & Burg, 2000; Lofas & Sova, 1985; Reis, Senchak & Solomon, 1985). Men generally differ from women by how they learn and practice rituals, attitudes and habits that hinder or facilitate the process of mourning a divorce as a result of having grown up in a given culture (Worden, 1991). Such learned practices may be reinforced by expectations and norms that a particular culture sets for people in reference to their gender, age, religious orientation, level of formal education, socio-economic status, and openness to seeking professional help during grief (McGoldrick, Giordano & Pearce, 1996; Miller, 1999; Parkes, Laungani & Young, 1997; Tatelbaum, 1980; Staudacher, 1987, 1991).

# Study Session 7.

## Communication

### Description of Communication

Fifteen participants mentioned that communication in remarriages is important because it facilitates relationship building, especially because of the diverse numbers of people involved in a stepfamily. These people include one's children, one's spouse, the former spouse, ex-in-laws, current in-laws, the ex-spouse of one's current spouse and stepchildren. Hilda stated that miscommunication of any kind of contributes to the emotional hurting of the people involved. The flow of information among these members of the extended family can get out of one's control. By the time it reaches the fourth or fifth person, a given message may not match the meaning of what the first speaker wanted to say.

Twelve participants emphasized that in order to avoid higher risks of miscommunication in stepfamily settings, remarried spouses should learn better communication skills and create time for themselves as a couple. In this way, they can dialogue about the diverse topics that need to be resolved.

### Experience of Others

According to Beatrice, some of those conversations may revolve around stepparenting and how to ask the current spouse to be supportive for the partner's children if their other biological parent does not respond to their emotional needs. Elaborating on the importance of the need for communication in regard to stability and satisfaction in remarriage, Felicia mentioned that learning when to keep her mouth shut and when to open it had helped her to improve the relationship with her second spouse.

Based on her experience, Felicia revealed that words can hurt people and affect the relationships of the people one cares about. She emphasized that even if one can offer an apology, what has been said cannot be taken back. Felicia described communication at length as follows:

> Communication involves trust and mutual respect because, even if both spouses see things differently, they can still communicate and influence each other's views. I think that, in a marriage, you learn a lot from your spouse, but at the end your spouse also learns a lot from you. So you learn to, I would say, adjust. And I would say that behind every good man there is a good woman, and behind every good woman there is a good man. And not being always the same, I think that is a good thing. Being flexible and being different is OK because my husband and I are like day and night. I never always see things the way he sees them. However, when we sit together and I tell him what I think and he tells me what he thinks, we negotiate our differences and come to conclusions.

When asked the following questions: Now, being different as you are and at the same time sharing a dream, what do you think has contributed to your marriage stability? Felicia replied:

> Sometimes I will hold back things just to keep the peace in the family. Sometimes I am not happy with decisions, but I hold back. At the end it works. At the end it is for the better because I am too quick at judgment. And I find that, if I hold back and think about things, I am better off.
> So you withhold your judgment, you think through things, and eventually things work out. For the sake of peace sometimes you just stay quiet. For the sake of peace sometimes you should swallow your pride and holds things back. Not always.

Elaborating on the theme of communication, all the participants' input could be put into two major categories, informal communication and in-depth communication. The informal communication is focused on the casual conversations that help people to start interacting with one another, and these conversations need to be maintained throughout the remarriage. Examples of these conversations include topics that are less emotionally charged and they do not tend to be personal. Catherine referred to these kinds of talks as ice breakers that might help in creating an environment of mutual trust so that people may feel comfortable to speak about their personal lives.

On the other hand, Beatrice highlighted:

> Even if casual conversations are important, remarrying spouses should go beyond the romantic talks, discussing their ex-spouses, discussing politics, or the weather, and focus on the topics that are more relevant to the establishment of successful remarriages for the partners and their significant others.

The other kind of communication, which encompassed the opinions of all the participants and their perceptions, is the need for in-depth communication between the partners. According to all the participants, in-depth communication consists of taking the risk to discuss emotionally charged conversations which most remarrying parents feel insecure to bring up into open discussions with their partners, and the issues remain unresolved. Examples of such issues that all the participants mentioned included money in second marriages, religion, sexuality, relationships with in-laws, unresolved issues from the previous marriage, step-parenting, relationship with their former spouses, pending credit debts, and death. Hilda added that it is also important for divorced parents contemplating remarriage to discuss any histories of mental illness, substance abuse, and domestic violence.

In agreement with the reviewed literature, the participants expressed the need for a validating and interactive process in contrast to avoidant and volatile communication (Burleson & Denton, 1997; Gottman, 1994b; Johnson & Greenberg, 1994). Communication is one the most important ingredients of marital success (Gottman, 1994a; Kiura, 2004; LeBey, 2004; Nichols, 1996). The participants identified communication as one of the primary factors of stability and satisfaction in remarriage.

According to Yalom (1985), communication is an on-going process in relationships because people keep on communicating (Kiura, 2004). Likewise, five participants who reported that they were still angry at their former spouses said that even if they tried their best to have no face-to-face interactions with their ex-spouses, the efforts they were making to maintain the silence had become for them like another means of keeping the communication in place with ex-spouses. In light of this, divorced parents contemplating remarriage and those who are already in remarriages should be aware of their constant communication with their significant others, with special regard to the risk of prolonged silences, especially if there are on-going conflicts and separations within their family systems (Papernow, 1998).

In order to reinforce communication between remarried spouses, and/or significant others, they need to know some of the major skills of effective communication and to be able to express themselves to their partners in at least one language. Additionally, Charles emphasized the perception of good communication requires:

> Every spouse's willingness to be a good listener and ability to learn how to communicate effectively, honestly, constructively, timely, in an appropriate space, in the right manner, with empathy and reduced risk of jumping to conclusions.

These observations are also mentioned in the literature about marital communication (Gottman et al., 1976; Kiura, 2004; LeBey, 2004).

## My experience

Based on what you have read in this session, reflect on your own personal experience.

1.  What communication skills have I been able to implement and which have helped me and others to get the needed win-win results?

    _____
    _____
    _____
    _____
    _____

2.  Which communication skills do I want to learn and implement in dialogues and/or conversations in order to improve my communication with the significant people in my life?

    _____
    _____
    _____
    _____
    _____

3. What are the advantages of communication in life and specifically in remarriage?

_____

_____

_____

_____

_____

4. Which factors of stability and satisfaction in remarriage identified in this book do I need to communicate about in greater detail with my partner and/or other significant people in my life?

_____

_____

_____

_____

_____

5. What are the specifics of each factor that need to be resolved?

_____

_____

_____

_____

6. How can I engage in difficult conversations and say what I mean without making enemies in the process?

_____

_____

_____

_____

_____

7. What benefits have I realized by asking more questions than making commands when communicating with others?

_____

_____

_____

_____

_____

8.  What strategies am I going to use in remarriage to maintain face-to-face communication other than relying primarily on technological means (e.g., e-mails, telephone and texting)?

    _____

    _____

    _____

    _____

    _____

9.  What do I need to do to help the other(s) hear clearly and understand what I am saying?

    _____

    _____

    _____

    _____

    _____

10. What are my set ways of listening, attitudes and/or behavior patterns that I portray to help the other person know that I am hearing and understanding what he/she is saying?

    _____

    _____

    _____

    _____

    _____

11. What makes me think/feel that I am communicating with my partner effectively?

    _____

    _____

    _____

    _____

    _____

12. How can I determine that my partner is showing mutual respect?

    _____

    _____

    _____

    _____

    _____

13. Am I more of a talker or a listener?

_____
_____
_____
_____
_____

14. What do I need to become more of?

_____
_____
_____
_____
_____

15. What areas mentioned in this book and/or occurring in our remarriage relationship do my partner and I need to discuss, resolve or negotiate before it is too late?

_____
_____
_____
_____
_____

16. How are we going to arrange our schedules in order to set aside quality time each day to speak with each other without other distractions (e.g., TV, cell phones, sports and computers)?

_____
_____
_____
_____
_____

## Keys to communication

As keys are important to open doors, consider the following keys to communication.

- Values and opportunities for informal and in-depth communication
- In case of on-going conflicts with ex-spouse, avoid the risk of getting children caught up in the midst of those conflicts

- Each should know that he or she may have the right answers or words, but may have to hold back to avoid the risk of speaking with anger
- Listen and learn from another person's point of view
- Be aware and accept that every marriage involves some level of conflict
- Learn some conflict resolution skills and practice them (e.g., be patient, give yourself time to think through the issues)
- Establish clear boundaries and guidelines with your children so that they do not break your remarriage in the dream of getting you together with your former spouse.
- Take into account the child's age while communicating about your remarriage arrangements
- Be aware of the challenges in remarriage related to children (e.g., children with special needs as they create a lot of stress on a marriage
- Avoid behaviors that influence your children to live in conflict of loyalty situations between you and your exspouse (e.g., putting children in the middle of your ongoing conflicts with your ex-spouse
- Timely communication of feelings (e.g., if one is hurt by the other spouse, the hurt party should let the other person know that he or she has been hurt in less than 48 hours). Likewise, each spouse should know that he or she may have the right answers or words, but may have to hold back to avoid the risk of speaking with anger
- Complexity of remarriage is important to know about before remarriage
- Dating while simultaneously parenting may be difficult and emotionally charged
- Difficulty in finding a name to address the stepparent, his or her title, and roles
- Communicate clearly with your spouse about how to discipline and reward children in second marriages
- Keeping in contact with the other biological parent and celebrating future events

Gottman et al. (1976) observed that communication between spouses was a very fundamental ingredient in marital stability. Its absence and the lack of communication skills created a real danger to marital stability, dialogue, and decision-making.

Gottman and collaborators drew a general hypothesis that couples who have poor communication may not be able to work collaboratively and they tend to send contradictory messages to their children (Richmond, 1995; Russell-Chapin et al., 2001).

Nondialoguing spouses are likely to find it more difficult to maintain harmonious relationships, to negotiate about money, friends, religion, sexual expression, work, relaxation time, and stepparenting roles than dialoguing spouses (Gottman et al., 1976; Nichols, 1996). Likewise, depressed individuals who know communication skills but lack motivation are inclined to communicate negative information (Burleson & Denton, 1997; Gottman & Silver, 1999).

- Usefulness of flexibility: Becoming attentive listeners

A typical example of a needed paradigm shift between custodial parents and other significant people in remarriage situations involves a consistent practice of empathic listening. Covey (1989) made this recommendation after realizing that most people typically seek first to be understood by the person or people they are talking to, but it is difficult for them to listen with an equivalent amount of intent to understand what the speaker is saying. That is, while the other person is speaking, most people listen with the intent to reply. Most often, during a conversa tion, these kinds of people are either speaking or preparing to speak. Hence, there is a need for learning and practicing basic communication skills.

Many people apparently seem to be listening, but in actuality they are filtering everything through their own paradigms and reading their autobiographies into other people's lives (Covey, 1989; Ferch, 2001). Therefore, exploring some of the realities and challenges experienced by currently remarried parents may provide some pathways to improve stability and satisfaction in remarriage. Such exploration offers a deeper understanding of the experiences for remarrying parents, children and significant others (Falicov, 1988).

- Design interventions that encourage verbal communication

It is hard for some grieving divorced persons to confide in someone else (Smoke, 1995). Many think that, by telling the stories of their losses, they will be exposing their failure to their listeners and/or burdening them with their troubles. Others feel ashamed to disclose their difficulties because they perceive them to be too personal and too intimate. The fear of unveiling too much about themselves overwhelms them. Many also find it harder to be honest while disclosing personal baggage and they usually put all the blame on their former spouses

# Study Session 8.

## Spirituality

*Description of Spirituality in Marital Situations*
*Experience of Others*
*My Experience*
*Keys to Establishing Spirituality in Remarriage*

### Description of Spirituality in Marital Situations

All sixteen participants reported that painful experiences in their divorce had brought them closer to God, especially during those moments when they had to make their hardest decisions as to whether or not to divorce. All the participants (including the two males who had denied belonging to any formalized religion) stated that spirituality played a great role in their stability and satisfaction in remarriage.

Elaborating on marital spirituality, Kiura (2004) noted: "Marriage is a relationship of love... The spirituality of marriage will therefore be as good as the personal spirituality of the individual spouses... The first neighbor in a marriage relationship is one's spouse... It is impossible to love God without loving the neighbor... Basic spirituality for a married couple consists in loving God through each other in the hustle and bustle of daily life. This includes forgiving each other here and now for past failures and mistakes.... [and] ending each day by praying together and reading the Scripture. This will provide the couple with resources to handle their human problems with greater insight and understanding."

### Experience of Others

Elías was a participant who did not identify himself with any religion. He shared his insights on spirituality and religion and how he expressed the influence of spirituality on his stability and satisfaction in remarriage. Elías stated:

> Whenever I have to make a decision in my marriage or any
> other major decision in life, I have to pray first. I give witness
> that God listens to my prayers whenever I pray.…. In my life, I
> consider spirituality a great inspiration for living an ethical life.
> I believe that that supernatural power blesses my marriage and
> family. I perceive this supernatural power to be compassionate,
> inclusive, transcendent, and infinite.

Even if Elías reported not belonging to any formalized religion, he made
the following remark:

> Having no church to go to is a bad thing. [Elías added]: Any
> religion, if well understood and practiced by its believers in the
> right way, can be a profound source of faith, solidarity, unity for
> its members, improvement of peoples' lives in their marriages
> and family life. Religions are good sources of hope and meaning
> to people, especially if they do not become breeding grounds
> for dirty politics. Religions are a means of transmitting God's
> mercy, love and forgiveness, compassion, and hope for eternal
> life with God.

Nine Catholics out of the eleven who participated in this study expressed
that faith in God had played a significant role in their remarriages. It had
empowered them in many ways, especially during the most painful moments
of their lives, during the process of divorce, and its aftermath. On the other
hand, to illustrate how spirituality was a significant factor in lives of the
Catholic participants, eight out of the eleven did not seek annulments from
the Catholic Church before they remarried. Consequently, they went to
ask for God's blessing for their marriages in front of a religious minister of
another religious denomination.

A typical example of a couple's remarriage celebrated by a minister of
another religion was that of Charles and his wife Julia. Charles stated that
God had a very profound place in his life. He described Julia as a very spiritual
woman. According to Charles, he and his wife did all that was possible to
have their marriage blessed by a Catholic minister before they started living
together. Both of them were divorced Catholics and it was very difficult for
them to remarry in the Catholic Church before receiving an annulment from
their previous marriages. They tried to get the annulments, but they could
not get them by the time of their anticipated marriage.

In pain and frustration of not being able to get married in the Catholic
Church, Charles agreed with his wife-to-be to seek God's blessing from an
Episcopalian minister. Five years later, they received the annulments. Their

marriage was then validated in the Catholic Church. This made them very happy, and since then they became actively involved in their Church and have conducted pre-remarriage talks for 10 years to divorced Catholics preparing for remarriage.

According to twelve participants, spirituality was described as a resource that had contributed in one way or another to their stability and satisfaction in remarriage. It has helped them to find meaning and purpose and has kept them in close connection with a Transcendent Being whom they identified as God. All 16 participants expressed their belief in the spirit of God empowering them to live by their marriage commitments, learning to love other people, and forgiving those who had hurt them in one way or another, especially their former spouses. Ten participants also described how spirituality had motivated them to improve their behavior in their everyday lives. Additionally, spirituality was a resource for them in their remarriages because it was helpful in motivating them to live morally better lives. By the same token, they were able to distinguish between good and bad ways of interpersonal relationships with their family members, community, and society at large.

All eight female participants and six males stated that God had a very special place in their remarriages. Some of the ways they had been able to strongly experience God's presence included holding onto prayer, hope, searching for forgiveness from God for the mistakes they felt they had committed as wives or husbands, and as parents against their children. Catherine remarked:

> I owe a lot of thanks to God for the success of my remarriage. I remember waking up at night and kneeling down to ask for God's guidance and strength when my remarriage was going through a very difficult financial situation. My husband started to have misunderstanding with his brothers and their business almost broke down, yet at that time I was not working. Surprisingly, a month later I got a job, and my husband's relationship with his brothers improved. Their business improved from loss to gain.

Ten participants mentioned that turning to God and to their church ministers, and/or to the faith community were also resources for them and were bringing them God's solace, particularly during the moments of discouragement and frustration in their second marriages. They also realized that spirituality was affecting them in their decision-making process. In fact, belonging to a religious denomination and being an active member within one's church were reported by 12 participants to be significant influences on stability and satisfaction in remarriage.

Nine participants reported that belonging to a church community was beneficial for them. Each one of them acknowledged the social support he or she received. In a special way, seven female participants appreciated the community support especially during the divorce process, mourning divorce, financial difficulties, strong feeling of ambiguity about dating again and remarriage.

One of the participants who elaborated on the importance of spirituality and belonging to a supportive religious community was Henry. After his divorce, he continued to go to Church and did a lot of volunteer work in the Catholic Church with other parishioners. Three years later, his parish priest and other committee members in the parish started making arrangements for him to work in close contact with a single woman interested in meeting someone to marry. As anticipated, the two of them started dating, got married, and by the time of the interview they had been together for eight years. All in all, Henry spoke with admiration about how a supportive religious community had helped him on his spiritual journey and helped him meet his second wife, whom he described as "very spiritual, community oriented, and very compassionate."

Dora elaborated on the quality of spirituality in remarriage. She was an active member in her Church and her faith was evident as she expressed herself during the interview. She stated:

> Spirituality and action are inseparable. That is why I think that any married man who believes in God should also treat his wife with respect. If he makes a mistake, he should learn to apologize. I feel men should learn to say "sorry" or at least should admit their mistakes and talk about them with their wives. I am concerned about the spirituality of

Furthermore, Dora stated that spirituality goes beyond the mere fact of belonging to a formalized religion and going to a religious building for prayers. Dora made this observation:

> Some people go to Church and just pray, and some of them are not as good as they are in the Church. Outside of the church building, they do the things they are not supposed to do as churchgoers. So I believe, if there is a God, I know He is happy with me because I try to help. I always try to do the best, do the correct thing, … I taught my kids too.

As noted in the reflections of Adams (1980) and Kiura (2004) on spirituality and marital life, all the participants mentioned that spirituality was a very significant factor influencing their stability and satisfaction in remarriage. Two participants clarified that, even if they did not belong to any formalized religion, spirituality was one of the greatest sources of empowerment in their remarriages. Based on the input of the other 14 participants who identified their religions as resources contributing to spirituality, as well as the input of the other two, it seems that that spirituality and religion are not mutually exclusive (Miller, 1999). Marital spirituality seemed to go beyond the boundaries and norms within the participants' religions.

The central message that could be derived from the way all the participants described their remarriages was as a covenant or bond with a Supernatural Power (whom they identified as God). The participants were doing their best to integrate some of their experiences of the characteristics they attributed to God into their remarriages and relationships with their significant others.

Two participants, Grace and Geoffrey expressed additional resounding statements based to their spiritual beliefs. Grace stated:

> "I believe in a God of love, forgiveness, and who wants us to love our neighbors, and to forgive those who have offended us. Inspired by this belief, I forgave my ex-husband." Geoffrey mentioned: "One of the reasons I remarried was because God said in the Bible that it is not good for man to be alone. So, after my divorce, I did not want to stay alone."

## My experience

Based on what you have read in this session, reflect on your own personal experience.

1.  How do I describe God in my own words?

_____

_____

_____

_____

_____

2. What is spirituality for me?

_____
_____
_____
_____
_____

3. What is spirituality for my partner?

_____
_____
_____
_____
_____

4. What is spirituality for my children?

_____
_____
_____
_____
_____

5. What is the usefulness of spirituality in my life, especially in regard to my divorce experience and/or remarriage?

_____
_____
_____
_____
_____

6. What key beliefs in my religion have helped me to develop a profound spirituality?

_____
_____
_____
_____
_____

7.  What are the impediments to my spiritual journey?

    _____

    _____

    _____

    _____

    _____

8.  What are my beliefs about the annulment process in the Catholic Church and in the sight of God?

    _____

    _____

    _____

    _____

    _____

9.  What resources do I have that empower me to grow spiritually together with the people in my household?

    _____

    _____

    _____

    _____

    _____

10. What are my beliefs about life after death?

    _____

    _____

    _____

    _____

    _____

**Keys to spirituality in remarriage**

As keys are important to open doors, consider the following keys to spirituality.

- Acknowledgment of the existence of God as Almighty, Creator, Loving and a Spiritual Being interested in the lives of all people as one family and as individuals
- Ability to enter freely into a relationship with God, especially through prayer and spiritual reading, hymns and songs of praise, spending time in adoration, contemplation and meditation
- Commitment to a communal and/or personal spiritual experience and journey of faith
- Acknowledging the religious traditions in family of origin, praying together as a family, participating in religious ceremonies and entrusting our lives to God
- Making use of spiritual values within the religion that one is affiliated with and passing those values on to the next generation
- Turning to God who heals the broken hearted and offers forgiveness
- Understanding the impact of divorce and remarriage on devout Catholics
- Searching for God's blessing on the couple's wedding date and asking for God's continued graces daily
- Giving thanks to God for small and big things in our lives

# Study Session 9.

## Professional Help

### *Description of Professional Help*

Professional help may be described as the services one receives from a competent person trained in a specific field in order to nurture one's growth, to get advice, assessment, and treatment, and/or to obtain guidelines for addressing a given problem(s). Some of the different types of professionals whose counsel may be sought in regard to divorce, remarriage and stepfamilies include: spiritual and religious leaders, marriage and family therapists, psychologists, psychiatrists, divorce mediators, lawyers, medical doctors, financial experts and/ or social workers.

### *Experience of Others*

Twelve participants stated that, even if they did not seek professional help before they remarried, they acknowledged that their remarriages would have been a little easier if they had received some guidance and counseling from competent personnel before remarriage. They indicated that, because of the complexity of remarriage and its challenges, pre-remarriage counseling is important. Henry stated:

> Looking back at my remarriage journey and what I have heard other remarried people experience in my profession as a family attorney, I would recommend that remarrying people, should consult religious ministers to understand the importance of the third Person, namely, God in the relationship. Consult social workers to impress upon you reasonable expectations. Um,

> you know, women don't wake up with make-up on every day. Sometimes they don't look attractive as others and the guys sometimes don't shave for 3 days in a row.

Five females and four male participants acknowledged that, if they had not received professional help from excellent marriage and family therapists after they remarried, their remarriages would most probably have ended in another divorce. Additionally, six female and five male participants attributed their stability and satisfaction in remarriage to having consulted their religious ministers after they remarried, but they emphasized that it would have been better if they had received this help before remarriage.

Seven males and four female participants suggested consulting financial accountants, especially to establish prenuptial agreements. Five females and three male participants suggested seeking help from social workers, especially those who are competent and interested in working with divorced persons, remarried parents, and children in stepfamilies. One of the participants (Abraham), a clinical psychologist and researcher expressed his appreciation of the work done by family therapists, psychologists, and social workers in their efforts to help parents and children in remarriage settings.

Accordingly, Abraham stated:

> Based on what I have gone through in my life as a married man in both marriages, I think there is need for specialized training of professionals working with the divorced and people living in remarriage contexts and stepfamilies. I say this because most of the traditional psychologists that I know, including myself, we were trained to work with individuals, not stepfamilies. Based on my literature reviews, I have realized that there are very few specialized remarriage professionals working with people in stepfamilies.
>
> Furthermore, I have realized that there are some similar things between my first marriage and remarriage but the two marriages are extremely different. Therefore, I suggest that pre-remarriage preparation programs for divorced parents have to be distinct from those of first marriages and vice versa.

Elaborating on the factors influencing stability and satisfaction in remarriage, eight female participants and seven males mentioned the need for effective step-parenting. According to Henry and Hilda, stepparents need to go slowly and have to be sensitive to the child's gender, age, developmental needs, and temperament. Grace suggested: "It is extremely important to begin relating as a friend to the children of a prospective spouse, instead of presenting oneself as disciplinarian or as a representative of the other biological parent."

Thirteen participants highlighted that remarrying parents need to be educated by competent personnel to evaluate their motivations and expectations before remarriage. According to Daniel, this is important because: "Setting realistic expectations and holding on to the right motivations for remarriage positively influence stability and satisfaction in remarriage."

One of Hilda's greatest convictions was that the key to marriage and remarriage is counseling. She emphasized, "I wish I had gone through this the first time." Hilda also acknowledged that remarriage is a real challenge. A success for remarriage requires first healing from the wounds of divorce before remarriage. Otherwise, one runs the risk of projecting onto the second spouse suspicion of marital infidelity, as was her case.

Based on his background as an African American, Fred offered the following suggestions for African American divorced men. He advocated that they should avoid remarriages of convenience. In preparing themselves for marriage, he stressed that the facilitators of preparation programs for remarriage should help highly educated black males to stop denying their pain, loss, anger, resentment and emotional baggage from the first marriage and families of origin. They should be encouraged to be custodial parents to their children because they need their fathers.

Before identifying the needed professionals for remarriage services, the reader is reminded about the phrase "remarriage triad" described previously in this book. Given the unique needs and challenges of remarrying and remarried parents, together with their significant others (Ahrons, 2004; LeBey, 2004), some of the professionals that may bring about a positive impact within the remarriage triangle include the clergy, marriage and family therapists, financial advisers, social workers, psychologists, divorce mediators, remarriage counselors, psychiatrists and medical personnel (Wallerstein & Blakeslee, 1989).

Because partners tend to idealize one another during courtship (McGoldrick & Carter, 1998), Dora (one of the participants) suggested that professionals should discern the right moment during the remarriage preparation phase to ask the partners some hypothetical questions to help them think more realistically than idealistically. According to Dora, professionals need to act like the devil's advocate by asking questions based on real life experiences and applying them to the partners' lives.

A typical example of such questions that Dora highlighted was the "What if ...question?" For instance, what if one should become ill and be unable to work? What if one's children should not accept his or her partner? What if one of you should get involved in an extramarital affair?

The professional may formulate other questions to help the partners become more reflective about the responsibilities ahead of them after the wedding. For example, engaged partners who are more invested in the remarriage wedding events than the remarriage itself may be asked by a remarriage facilitator: What is the difference between a wedding and a remarriage? If the partners say that a wedding is for one day but they are intending to stay together until death do them part, then the remarriage facilitator may ask them: Apart from the wedding preparations, what are the benefits of preparing for remarriage? By means of such questions, that is, hypothetical and reality-testing questions, the partners may start to think seriously about the complex responsibilities and remarriage commitments ahead of them.

## My experience

Based on what you have read in this session, reflect on your own personal experience.

1. Have I ever sought professional help related to my marriage, divorce and/or remarriage?

_____

_____

_____

_____

_____

2. If yes? What were the reasons for seeking help?

_____

_____

_____

_____

_____

3. If not, what hindered me from doing so?

_____

_____

_____

_____

_____

4. Other than for marriage, divorce and/or remarriage, what other type(s) of professional help have I ever sought and when?

_____

_____

_____

_____

_____

5. What were the reasons for seeking help (e.g., alcohol, drugs, gambling, promiscuous behavior, or mental health issues)?

_____

_____

_____

_____

_____

6. Which problems were resolved as a result of seeking professional help and which ones were not resolved?

_____

_____

_____

_____

_____

7. What has been my experience regarding each type of professional help I have sought?

_____

_____

_____

_____

_____

8. Did I seek professional help during my first marriage?

_____

_____

_____

_____

_____

9. Would I consider seeking professional help before I remarry or during my current remarriage?

_____
_____
_____
_____
_____

10. What types of resources do I need in order to seek professional help now or in the near future?

_____
_____
_____
_____
_____

11. Do I have the needed resources to seek professional help?

_____
_____
_____
_____
_____

12. If not, what am I going to do so as not to miss this opportunity?

_____
_____
_____
_____
_____

13. Has my partner ever sought professional help?

_____
_____
_____
_____
_____

14. If so, what were the reasons for seeking help?

_____

_____

_____

_____

_____

15. What was his/her experience regarding professional help?

_____

_____

_____

_____

_____

16. What are his/her attitudes and level of willingness to seek professional help in regard to our stability and satisfaction in remarriage?

_____

_____

_____

_____

_____

17. What are his/her attitudes and level of willingness to seek professional help in regard to other related problems?

_____

_____

_____

_____

_____

## Keys to seeking and making use of professional help

As keys are important to open doors, consider the following keys to professional help.

- Develop a positive attitude toward seeking professional help
- Be aware of the social stigmas and/or personal biases regarding the seeking of help for problems related to mental health
- Be humble and overcome the pride, stereotype and negative experiences attached to seeking professional help

- Determine and clarify the types of problems you want resolved
- Find a licensed and competent professional who specializes in the area of your interest (e.g., marriage enrichment, divorce mediation, remarriage preparation, conflict resolution skills, self-esteem, domestic violence, stepfamilies, taxes, marital spirituality, sexual abuse, financial management, pornography, setting clear boundaries, writing one's will, etc.)
- Be honest when speaking with a chosen professional
- Set realistic expectations about seeking professional help
- Seek professional help with the awareness that professionals provide guidelines not answers to your problems. They do not live your life for you. Therefore, take responsibility for your decisions and actions while seeking professional help and be consistently committed to making the needed changes
- Seek professional help before it is too late. Prevention is better than cure
- Admit your problems, take responsibility for them and stop blaming yourself by seeking the necessary professional help
- Seek professional help if, on your own, you cannot resolve your problems (e.g., perpetuation of unnecessary guilt, pathological jealousy and/or unresolved problems from the past
- Seek professional help if you have a tendency to blame yourself for other people's problems (including those of your current partner or former spouse). Know that nobody is perfect. It cannot always be your own fault or the other person's fault. Each person has some "dirty laundry" or unfinished business that may call for professional help
- If you do not have the money and/or the other necessary resources to receive the needed professional services, ask for help from charitable agencies. Ask a friend if you need help(e.g., for transportation or babysitting). Pursue all available means to get professional help.

# Secondary Factors of Stability and Satisfaction in Remarriage: Study Sessions 10-17

As mentioned previously, the following are categorized as secondary factors because they were referred to by at most eight out of the 16 participants. These eight secondary factors include: marital history, motivations for remarriage, dating, house rules and roles, conflict resolution, clear boundaries, cohabitation and permanent sites for professional remarriage services.

# Study Session 10.

## Marital History

*Description of Marital History*
*Experience of Others*
*My Experience*
*Keys to Exploring and Handling Marital History*

### Description of Marital History

Marital history refers to the experiences I have from my previous marriage. It involves the "who" the "how" the "where" the "why" the "how long" I was with him/her, as well as a multiplicity of feelings, thoughts, actions, and behaviors I experienced during my former marriage. It also includes the experiences I had as I observed the marriage of my parents and how I was influenced by the marriages of other significant people in my life. It is a history that I cannot change but one I can learn from by exploring the impact it has on me right now and as I move toward the future

### Experience of Others

Seven participants mentioned that they strongly attributed their stability and satisfaction in remarriage to the lessons they had learned from their families of origin and their past experiences of marriage. At the time of the interview, those seven participants reported that their parents were divorced, at least once. However, for the sake of illustrating the impact of marital history on remarriage, two detailed stories have been selected: one of a male participant, Bernardo, and another of a female participant, Elizabeth.

Bernardo stated:

> I do not blame my parents for having divorced when I was nine years old. They had their reasons for doing so. However, since I grew up without seeing my father and mother living together, expressing love for one another and love for us [their

children, my sister and I], all that had a negative impact on my life. Secondly, even when they got married with other people, their remarriages also ended in divorce. As a result, when my first marriage ended in divorce, I felt guilty because I saw myself repeating what my parents had done. Surprisingly, my daughter also had children in her first marriage, then divorced, and is now remarried. Therefore, for the success of my second marriage, I am putting into practice what I have learned from my past mistakes and those of my parents and my daughter. Now I believe that history tends to repeat itself unless lessons are learned from it and put into practice.

Elizabeth mentioned that her stability and satisfaction in remarriage were in one way or another influenced by the experiences she had gone through while growing up. While elaborating on her family of origin, Elizabeth stated that the divorce of her parents, when she was four years old, affected her very much because she ended up living with her mother, a woman whom she resented for many reasons. Some of these reasons included the way Elizabeth emphatically described her mother as an alcoholic, who spent most of the time away from home dating other men. Elizabeth stated:

My mother was never satisfied with one person. My mother needed recognition from a lot of people. I think that was her sickness. I didn't recognize that, of course, until I was older. But she did have a sickness. She drank a lot. She wasn't a fall-down drunk but her first priority was herself, not her children…I resented my mother very much; I resented her lifestyle. I resented the way she lived. We had nothing; I resented that and took my anger out on her because we had nothing.

[Elizabeth added:] We had no family life; she didn't keep in touch with her family. We didn't have cousins. We didn't have uncles; we didn't have aunts, so to speak. Once in a great while we would have family. You see other people, you go to school with bad clothes, people make fun of you, and you have no real friends, because nobody wants to be bothered with you because you are trash! That is what we were. We were trash. I mean, I look back now and say my mother tried. She was single, she went to work every day but my mother thought about herself. I needed a pair of shoes. I can remember this. I needed a pair of shoes really bad. I had holes in my shoes, and she wouldn't buy them because she had to go out to the bar that night. She had to have money for that bar, and that was more important to her. I did resent that.

Based on this resentment, when her mother remarried Jim, Elizabeth felt a strong attachment to Jim because she found in him a lot of compassion and understanding. Elizabeth elaborated on her relationship with her stepfather as follows:

> Very good from what I remember. I remember specifically one time he [Jim, my stepfather] came home for lunch. He had a cake in his lunch box or something and my mother gave all the cake to my younger halfbrother [José]. Then my stepfather took the cake and cut it in half and we got half and half. That I remember. I remember good things with him. He was a good man. Unfortunately he passed away just after four years of living together.

The seven participants reported that the lessons they had learned from their first marriages and/or from the experiences of their second spouses helped them to avoid many mistakes in their second marriages. A typical example was one that Daniel narrated in detail, illustrating the precautions he was taking to reduce the risk of transference issues that had started to affect his second marriage.

Among all the participants, Daniel provided a detailed description of marital history which is worthy citing because of his profound insights. It is important to note that Daniel used the colloquial phrase, "you know," several times simply as a connective between his ideas. When queried about his marital history, Daniel responded:

> We [my second wife and I] have spoken about our past marital experiences. Actually, she has spoken a lot more than I have about my divorce because I have always spoken about things that happened in my [first] marriage to her and she has told me everything basically that has happened to her in her [first] marriage. This helps us to understand what each one of us expects, OK. ... Her situation was a lot different because

her ex-spouse traveled a lot, and ... he was with other women. She found out that, afterward, he had children, you know, while they were still married, so that was a different situation than mine. I didn't have that problem ... but it did affect me somewhat because she went through so much with that situation. And her divorce, I think that, it kind of like it carried over to me because she was very, um, not pressure, she was very, not jealous either but she was very watchful of different things I did. You know, she was being careful that I wasn't doing anything. You know, because she already was so hurt so much before that, and she didn't want the same thing to happen to her. And I knew that; I know that.

*Daniel added:*

Sometimes we had situations where I would turn to her and say, you know what, you have been really hurt too bad with him that you are really starting to take it out on me. I told her a couple of times. Maybe I shouldn't have, but I wanted to tell her that, because I realized she was bringing up her past and bringing it on to me when really she shouldn't have. But that's part of learning, you know, that's part of the learning. If you don't say something to her, then how is she going to know? So I think one of the things to help us bond is to let each other know what we didn't like about the previous marriage. So, you know, and, by me telling her what I went through with my wife, with my first wife, she will be careful not to do those things. And the same thing for her, you know, I'm careful. You know, I don't try to, you know, give her any idea that something is going on.

Given such experiences of marital history, when Daniel was asked about what was contributing to his stability and satisfaction in remarriage, he replied:

> Yes, yes, because [now] I know what hurts her. I know what doesn't hurt her. ... and I try to keep it there. I keep it in that frame of mind, you know. I think that is important; you know you might make the same mistake.

Based on the experiences of the participants, some remarried spouses ran the risk of transference (Nichols, 1996) , that is, of projecting their negative experiences with the former spouse onto the current spouse. For instance, if a former spouse was involved in an extramarital affair, a spouse may become suspicious of the current marital partner's interactions with people of the opposite sex for fear of his or her being unfaithful. This situation may gravitate into the spouse's developing an over-controlling attitude toward the current spouse.

Hilda shared a narrative of how she overcame her transference issues with her second husband, a situation that almost contributed to the ruining of her second marriage. The following dialogue gives a clear sense of how previous marital experiences can negatively reinforce transference in a remarriage. Hilda emphasized:

> My first husband was physically and verbally abusive to me. I developed a lot of fear toward him. It even reached a point where the mere sight of him made me to become very anxious and lose track of whatever I was doing.
>
> Unfortunately, when my second husband and I got married, whenever he made a comment about something that I had done wrong or had forgotten to do, then I would withdraw from him, be silent for a day or two. This was because I imagined that, if I would respond to him, he would become more verbally and physically abusive to me and shout at my son as my first husband used to do.
>
> I recall a particular instance when I kept silence for almost three days without saying a word to him. That happened after he told me about his discomfort on the pretext that I had consulted my son, instead of him, about which restaurant we would go to for dinner. I was so terrified that was going to become a big issue and probably lead us to separation.

When asked how have the two of them resolved that, Hilda replied:

> On that same day, I decided to ask pardon from my husband and explained to him how my ex-husband used to beat me and shout at my son whenever we had an argument. So, my second husband, with a smile on his face, and with a great sense of humor said "I am not your ex. He then gave me a big kiss, and we started talking again.

When asked whether she had other arguments after that and how she reacted to him afterward, Hilda responded:

> Of course, yes. I am sure it is not uncommon to disagree once in a while for people who love and care about one another. Ever since, whenever my husband sees me withdrawing from him, he says "I am not going to do you harm. I am [mentioned his name) not _____ [mentioned her ex-spouses' name]. Then, the two of us start laughing and hug one another.

In addition to overcoming the risks of transference in remarriage, by the time of the interviews, all the participants had learned significant lessons from their past marital mistakes in both the first and second marriages. For instance, the participants who entered their first marriages thinking that they were in love acknowledged during the interviews that they were not motivated by love per se when they entered their first marriages. They had motives other than the love that bonds the spouses together. Catherine said that she no longer believed in the adage that "love is blind" because marrying for the wrong reasons is what makes people perceive love as blind.

Based on the lessons learned from past marital mistakes, Catherine and six other participants suggested that divorced parents should avoid the risk of marrying for the wrong reasons. Some examples included: sole interest of sexual expressiveness, begetting children and/or alimony, pregnancy of the female partner, impatience, that is, claiming that it is too long a time to wait or it is too late to get married, extreme dependence on others, feeling uncomfortable living alone, wanting to get out of one's parent's house or escape a bad marriage, or as Fred (an African American participant) said: "I married a Caucasian woman because I wanted to experiment with a person of another race."

Seven participants suggested that divorced parents contemplating remarriage make the best use of the time between the end of the first marriage and the beginning of the second marriage. Based on their retrospective experiences, those participants said that although they had not adequately utilized that duration constructively before they remarried, they considered it a golden opportunity for healing from the wounds of divorce, further education, introspection, spiritual growth, purifying one's motivations for remarriage, dating with a lot of prudence, and comprehensive preparation for remarriage with the help of competent professionals in providing remarriage services.

## My experience

Based on what you have read in this session, reflect on your own personal experience.

1. What motivated me and/or contributed to my getting married to my former spouse?

_____

_____

_____

_____

_____

2. What did I learn about myself based on my first marriage?

_____

_____

_____

_____

_____

3. What did I learn about my former spouse during my marriage and/
   or after divorce?

_____

_____

_____

_____

_____

4. What do I still miss from my first marriage?

_____

_____

_____

_____

_____

5. What factors contributed to my first divorce and what must I work
   through before entering a second marriage?

_____

_____

_____

_____

_____

## Keys to exploring and handling marital history

As keys are important to open doors, consider the following keys to marital
history.

- You and your partner must NOT be suffering from severe mental
  and/or biological disorders
  Mental and physical health play a significant role in all aspects
  of our lives. Personality disorders (e.g., narcissistic, antisocial,

schizoid, paranoid, dependent and avoidant) are likely to have a significant impact on stability and satisfaction in remarriage.

Remarriage is put at a great risk with an individual or between individuals with a severe mental disorder and/or physical dysfunction. These include: severe mood disorders, unresolved traumas, alcoholand other substance-related disorders, pathological jealousy, communication disorders, eating disorders, gender identity disorders, sexual disorders, sexual dysfunctions and/or other mental disorders due to medical conditions. The adage: "A healthy mind in a healthy body" applies also to stability and satisfaction in remarriage.

All in all, mental disorders and/or physical dysfunction need to be diagnosed because they play a significant role in every individual's relational life. Seeking professional help is highly recommended whenever there is any damage to the human brain (Amen, 2008) before and after remarriage.

Become aware of the contributing factors to divorce in first marriages and remarriages Minuchin and Nichols (1993) emphasized that the failure to identify and resolve the contributing factors (possible causes) of divorce in the first marriage creates serious consequences, because remarrying spouses usually reenact the dynamics of the first marriage in their second or subsequent marriages (Ganong & Coleman, 1989; Gottman, 1994b). Clinical findings in reference to some of the causes of divorce indicated 80 % of the clients reported the lack of in-depth communication as the main contributing factor to divorce (Berger, 1998; Gottman, Notarius, Gonso & Markman, 1976).

Other factors cited as contributing to divorce include personality incompatibility between spouses, unrealistic expectations about marriage and/or unrealistic idealization of one's partner (especially during courtship), marital infidelity, personality abnormality, constant social pressures that create stress, lack of mutual prayer and spiritual life, cultural values that condone violence, domestic violence, conflictive relationships with in-laws, pathological jealousy, money used as a power source to control one's partner, lack of open communication and negotiation about money, use of drugs and alcohol (Carter & McGoldrick, 1998; Gottman, 1994a; Kaslow, 1996; Rutter, 1998; Treadway, 1989).

- Working on past and present problems

Remarried spouses and people in stepfamilies are constrained not only by present problems but also by problems lingering from divorce and previous relationships. Therefore, each custodial parent is encouraged to seek professional advice if needed, so that a professional may help them to mourn the losses from a previous relationship. The professional may also be able to show the custodial parent how the new family structure is being affected by those feelings (Berger, 1998; McCulullough, Spence & Worthington, 1994). Similarly, seeking professional help before it is too late may serve as an excellent preventative approach. Consequently, remarrying partners may receive a comprehensive assessment of their integral lives before remarriage in order to explore, anticipate and address future problems before they occur (LeBey, 2004).

# Study Session 11.

## Motivations for Remarriage

*Description of the Motivations for Remarriage*
*Experience of Others*
*My Experience*
*Keys to Exploring the Motivations for Remarriage*

### *Description of the Motivations for Remarriage*

Individuals who have experienced divorce enter remarriage for various reasons. Some of those reasons are right and others are not. Therefore, it is important to do a self-evaluation to assess the appropriateness of one's reasons for remarrying and also to listen to other people's approvals, concerns, constructive criticisms and/or disagreements regarding the upcoming remarriage. More often than not, people who remarry for the wrong reasons then end up disappointed, frustrated, hurting themselves and/or their partner, or ultimately experiencing another divorce. Some feel they have "fallen in love again" even before they heal from the wounds and baggage from the prior marriage that ended in divorce. Others are not sure of what they really want, whereas others have hidden agendas and/or unrealistic expectations about the new partner and remarriage. Those who remarry for financial support from the new partner but without committed love may experience financial security, but sooner or later may realize they are lonely and miserable.

### *Experience of Others*

Six participants acknowledged in retrospect that they entered their second marriages with many unrealistic expectations. Daniel clarified:

> After two years of remarriage, I thought of divorcing my second wife because I was not happy and we had started to disagree on many things. On further analysis of what was going on, I found out that part of my frustration was related to my expectations.

At the same time, I started to feel ambiguous about myself. You know, on one part, I was having thoughts focused on divorce, and yet I was feeling insecure and fearful of experiencing a second divorce. I was very concerned about subjecting my children again to what they had just gone through. Four months later, I decided to let go some of my unrealistic motivations for remarriage and as a result, I felt happier and more loving of my second wife.

Based on Daniel's experiences and those of six other participants who had expressed their frustrations about remarriage because of their unmet and unrealistic expectations about remarriage, the participants were asked to mention what each of them had experienced as realistic motivations. In reply, five participants identified the search for companionship and friendship. Six others emphasized the need for mental, social and psychological support (three males and three females). Four participants mentioned the need for a co-parenting partner and a real model for their children.

Seven participants spoke of being in love with the partner, while six emphasized the need to share household expenses with the significant other. Eight participants highlighted the need to move on with their lives as they worked on resolving their pains from the first marriages. Eight highlighted the search for meaning and happiness in life with a partner. Five participants stated that they felt motivated, but at the same time, though unsure, they risked it to start over again, praying and trusting in God, so that their second marriages would be successful.

According to Geoffrey, his motivation for remarriage that had proved successful was what he referred to as his "fidelity to God's plan for humanity: man was not created to live alone." Eight participants said that their remarriages were successful because their motivations for remarriage were based on their convictions that they had found the right and compatible life partner.

Interviewing the participants about what motivated them to remarry seemed to be one of the most difficult areas to respond to spontaneously and immediately when asked the following question: "What motivated you to remarry?" Six participants acknowledged that they entered their second marriages with many unrealistic expectations.

Based on the participants' input, one of the greatest lessons learned from them is that the family environment in which children are raised and one's previous marital experiences are likely to have an effect on their future marital decisions and motivations for remarried life. A typical example was that of Dora. She was raised in a stepfamily, and she spoke about her stepmother with a lot of resentment. Dora suffered the pain of growing up lonely "because I had no family member to identify with." As a teenager Dora had a friend who introduced her to a young man. Dora added: "Although I did not love that young man, I decided to get married with him in order to escape my stepmother and my never available father."

Looking back, Dora regretted her marital relationship with that man (Jorge). Speaking about her marriage to Jorge, she described Jorge as "very dominating."

Above all, Dora expressed her feelings of resentment related to her first sexual experience and one of the main motivations for her remarriage as follows:

> I had never slept with any man until I was 20 years old. He [Jorge] forced me to have sex with him without my consent. So, [started shedding tears, then a brief silence, then added:] I lost my innocence, that is, my virginity with a man I did not love. Unfortunately, I had to give in to his demands for sex because by then he was the only one who would help me to escape from my stepmother. So, one of the main reasons that motivated me to get married with my second husband was because he did not have children. I didn't want and I still don't want to be a stepmother to anybody's child.

## My experience

Based on what you have read in this session, reflect on your own personal experience. Answer as honestly as possible the following questions regarding remarriage

1. What is motivating me to remarry?

_____

_____

_____

_____

_____

2. What motivated me to get married the first time?

_____
_____
_____
_____
_____

3. How am I planning for remarriage?

_____
_____
_____
_____
_____

4. What do I have to do to avoid my past mistakes?

_____
_____
_____
_____
_____

5. What should I do better in my second marriage?

_____
_____
_____
_____
_____

6. How am I preparing my children and the other significant people in my life in regard to my plans for remarriage?

_____
_____
_____
_____
_____

7. What are my expectations in remarriage? Are they realistic and/or unrealistic?

_____

_____

_____

_____

_____

8. What factors do I think influence stability and satisfaction in remarriage?

_____

_____

_____

_____

_____

9. What kind of a spouse do I need to establish a stable and satisfactory remarriage?

_____

_____

_____

_____

_____

## Keys to exploring the motivations for remarriage

As keys are important to open doors, consider the following keys to motivation for remarriage.

- Explore and identify your needs in specific and concrete words More often than not, human behavior is needs driven. Be interested in remarriage without being desperate and impatient to remarry. Desperate people tend to make desperate decisions and actions.

# Study Session 12.

## Dating and Remarriage Preparation

*Description of Dating after Divorce and Remarriage*
*Preparation*
*Experience of Others*
*My Experience*
*Keys to Dating after Divorce and Remarriage*
*Preparation*

### *Description of Dating after Divorce and Remarriage Preparation*

Traditionally, courtship or dating refers to the time partners spend getting to know one another and discussing a number of topics that are geared at helping each of the partners make up his/her mind whether to proceed with the relationship or to part in peace before they become engaged. The duration of courtship varies from couple to couple. Some people just spend weeks or months dating another, while others spend years. In regard to dating after divorce, custodial parents have a number of considerations to take into account in comparison to those dating without children from a prior marriage/relationship.

Once a person becomes a parent, the children become a top priority. Consequently, custodial parents ought to date with extra caution in order to reduce the risk of exposing children to one's dating partner. Because dating partners have the potential for separating, this not only hurts the partners but also the children if the children have formed a relationship with the partner. Therefore, time for dating or courtship has its values and limitations. Getting to know one another is important, but some people do not express their real motives for marriage whereas others have a significant set of unrealistic expectations.

*Experience of Others*

Six participants highlighted that dating after divorce may be difficult, especially for divorced parents. Part of this difficulty may be related to the unresolved pain, anger, frustration, guilt related to the previous marriage, on-going social stigma attached to divorce, fear of experiencing another divorce and being hurt again, and/or because of the challenges that may surface from dating while having a parental role to play. By the same token, Bernardo emphasized:

> Dating parents need to be very careful, learn to take the risk of trusting again in their partners, but they should start as friends and companions. This is because friends do things together, share hobbies, communicate with honesty, understand each other's views and even if they hurt one another, they let the other person know, explore the cause of conflict, analyze stuff within 48 hours and are flexible with one another. And all this lays a foundation for mutual love and sexual satisfaction.

Beatrice also mentioned the need for family reunions for divorced parents who are dating their prospective spouses. She described such reunions as less intimidating and it lets the two people get to know one another and to interact with each other's children. By the same token, the children are likely to start seeing the stranger as a family friend with no strings attached. Parents should take seriously their children's needs to feel comfortable with people whom they date. Beatrice added: "If the children don't feel comfortable with their stepparents, they can make their parent's remarriage miserable."

Grace suggested that, if a parent senses that his or her children are not receptive to his or her prospective spouse, then that parent should make a decision to seek family counseling before proceeding with the remarriage arrangements. Likewise, six participants suggested that remarrying parents should slow down before starting to date and give themselves sufficient time to heal from the wounds of divorce. Four participants added that prudent dating involves exploring and addressing the likely problems in remarriage, more than paying attention to the color of the wedding gown.

Elaborating on the notion of dating, Abraham, a 70-year-old participant, cautioned parents, especially those with teenagers and/or young adults to be very conscious and moderate about their dating styles and behaviors. Otherwise, if they exaggerate by becoming very persuasive in their seeking or take on mannerisms that put their dignity into jeopardy, they may embarrass their children and/or give or set a bad example for them. Abraham suggested:

> They [partners contemplating remarriage] should date with dignity and prudence, without forgetting that they are parents. For that matter, they should be very careful about how they dress, the dances they go to, the time they come back from their dates and, if possible, never spend the whole night with their dating partners outside or inside their residential homes without informing their children.

Bernardo said that when his divorced daughter starting dating again, he told her: "Date again as a mature adult without manifesting behaviors that seem as if you are in competition with your teenage children."

Seven participants, with large extended-family backgrounds, suggested that remarriage tends to be harder and more complex. This is especially true if it involves children from the previous marriage. Therefore, remarrying parents should include the in-laws in the remarriage arrangements, because they are constantly present in one's marriage. Three participants clarified that remarriage involves a lot of work because you marry a family, not just a person, and that is outside of your control. Five participants highlighted that dating again after divorce ought to start by developing friendship first, mutual respect between companions, and holding in-depth talks about children, expectations, money, sex, personal history, family of origin, parenting skills, and disciplining of children. Given Geoffrey's deteriorating health as a result of overdrinking and unresolved grief that was associated with his divorce, his mother and friends advised him about the overdrinking and encouraged him to seek therapy to better handle and resolve depression instead of trying to escape from it by drinking.

He took their advice, sought professional help, became more sober, and started to date some women, including Melissa, whom he eventually married.

Elaborating on the value of dating after divorce, Geoffrey, one of the participants emphasized:

> I started to meet some women around, and actually I got introduced to my second wife through friends. And, you know, we had a nice time and we saw each other once in a while, and then we just stepped it up. It was a natural progression, you know? So I guess, the motivating factor was just the fact that we hit it off real well, and it was enjoyable being together, and she was very good with my daughter, and then so it all came together.

Catherine cautioned dating parents with the intention of establishing happy and lasting remarriages to avoid the risk of believing that remarriage changes people's behaviors. She learned that lesson from her first marriage. Catherine described her first husband as a good man, a good father, and hardworking. Nevertheless, his problem of gambling, which she knew about before they got married, contributed to a lot of financial battles in the family and consequently to the end of the marriage.

In retrospect, Catherine suggested that whoever is dating someone whose behavioral problem he or she knows and is not happy about (e.g., smoking, alcoholism, and flirting), that problem should be brought up, thoroughly discussed and resolved before marriage. Catherine arrived at this conclusion:

> Marriage doesn't automatically change people from their habitual behaviors. If there is any behavior of one's partner that one does not want or cannot stand, it should be completely resolved before remarriage takes place.

The participants related that each divorced parent contemplating remarriage or involved in any romantic relationship should be extra prudent and think thoroughly before dating. He or she should plan diligently how to verbally introduce his or her prospective spouse to the child(ren) in a nonthreatening setting. Ahrons (2004) elaborated on the dangers involved if dating parents do not take into account how their dating behaviors impact their children.

It is also important for dating parents to make the best use of the courtship period by risking to have detailed dialogues about sensitive topics in comparison to focusing on the idealization of their relationship (McGoldrick, 1998). Such sensitive topics may include discussions about money, children, and motivations for remarriage expectations, and marital compatibility.

Given the current advances in technology, dating on-line is also increasingly common. The same recommendations for those dating on-line with the goal of entering a second marriage apply and they should be extra careful because of the real life dangers associated with on-line dating (Oyebade, 2005).

**My experience**

Based on what you have read in this session, reflect on your own personal experience.

1.   What are the resources I already have (e.g., relatives, friends, spiritual and material) that I can rely on as I enter remarriage with all its benefits and challenges?

_____
_____
_____
_____
_____

**Keys to dating after divorce and remarriage preparation**

As keys are important to open doors, consider the following keys to dating and remarriage preparation.

Dating after divorce: Participants' suggestions for parents preparing for remarriage

-   Slow down before you start dating and behaving romantically after divorce
-   Date appropriately and make a profound preparation for remarriage with your partner
-   Inform the children involved when the right time comes
-   Give yourself time to heal from the wounds of divorce
-   Dating ought to start by developing friendship first, mutual respect between companions
-   Hold in-depth talks about children, expectations, money, sex, personal history, family of origin, parenting skills and disciplining of children
-   Anticipate that your teenage child might react with a negative attitude toward your prospective spouse, especially if the teenager still has hopes that you and his or her other biological parent will reconcile and remarry
-   Be aware of your marital history, interpersonal dynamics in your family of origin, in your first marriage

- Be clear about your motivations for remarriage, develop right and realistic expectations, know the consequences of your actions and be flexible in order to adjust well to changes in remarriage
- Prenuptial agreements are extremely necessary especially between very rich partners
- Let each partner sell his or her residential house or apartment so that the two partners (and custodial children) can move into a new house. If one of the two partners has to move into the other's house or apartment, that move must be on a temporary basis
- Focus on exploring and addressing the likely problems in remarriage rather than paying more attention to the color of the wedding gown
- Acknowledge that remarriage is hard, complex, especially if it involves children from the previous marriage. Remarriage involves a lot of work because you marry a family, not just a person, and that is outside of your control. Therefore, include the in-laws in the remarriage arrangements because they are constantly present in your marriage
- Take advanced studies because that might also help you to get a better paying job
- Be extra prudent in regard to dating, know the challenges involved, and keep up with your parenting roles while dating
- Establish and maintain consistent house rules and roles
- Know that conflict is inevitable in all human relationships
- Be aware of the potential areas of conflict in remarriage, learn the skills of conflict resolution and practice them
- Understand that cohabitation has its advantages and disadvantages, and it is still not encouraged in all religions, societies, and/or individuals close to you may not approve of it
- Look primarily at what your part will be in the remarriage, what you might not be doing now, and how your faults might affect the remarriage
- Maintain chastity during courtship and be careful with other people's money

    Let me explain this key with the words of my Grandmother. As mentioned before, my Grandmother was a great teacher. I recall the way she coached one of my sisters to be very careful while dating and to watch the dating habits of other people. Above all, I remember almost every word I overheard while Grandmother cautioned my sister who had started dating a rich man after her first divorce as follows:

> Be careful with him. Know what you need out of the new relationship. Don't rush into remarriage. It is true he has a lot of money but you should marry the person not his money. I understand money is very important in marriage but he may or may not give you the money. Secondly, maintain your chastity throughout the courtship. Some people do not buy the cow if they can get the milk free. Don't fall into the trap of thinking that you need to sleep with him before marriage in order to assure him that you love him. If he threatens to leave you because you are not generous with him in that sense, let him go. That is a clear sign that he cares less about you than that he wants to instantly gratify himself. Care about him too. Don't pick the oranges prematurely from the orange tree. Training yourself to wait from being intimate with him will bring mutual benefits and you will maintain you dignify if things don't work out with him. Don't change the rules of the game [Grandma added with a raised voice]. Remember: all behavior is need-driven. You may call me old-fashioned and now that I am over 80 years old, I care less about what people think of me. I am saying this to help you and your partner to spend the quality time you have to talk through the important details regarding remarriage. Instead of daydreaming that premarital sex will automatically make him love you, stick to the rules of the old lady. I see further while I am sitting down than you while you are standing up. I say this because I care and love you. Teach him to respect you and respect him too. Finally, both of you should do an AIDS blood test before being intimate. I repeat: do not change the rules of the game. Good luck!"

- Cohabitation before remarriage
  Based on the findings in a study by Ganong and Coleman (1989), cohabitating prior to remarriage had positive effects, but those effects were limited to the marital relationship only. The effects were most positive for men. Based on the same study, the results were surprising in indicating that pre-remarriage counseling for cohabiting partners was negatively related to remarriage success. Most of the cohabiting partners who sought counseling ended up separating before remarriage or after remarriage. According to Ganong and Coleman, a possible explanation may be that cohabiting partners seek

counseling to resolve existing problems, not to learn how to prevent problems. By the same token, the counselor may have been most likely focusing on problems lingering from divorce, not problems concerning remarriage and stepfamilies.

A significant number of couples seek counseling once problems have gotten out of control. Visher (1994) observed that many couples adapt an " if it is not broken, do not fix it" attitude and that keeps them from seeking professional help before their problems escalate.

- Reinforce marital stability and prevent divorce
In an effort to help couples attain and maintain the marital stability and satisfaction that prevent divorce, contemporary couple therapists encourage couples to invest themselves together in the foundation of their marriage, assess whether or not their expectations are realistic, develop emotional intelligence, learn to express emotions appropriately, prevent distress (especially because it affects communication motivation and sexual intimacy), promote marital adjustment, reinforce couple strengths, and validate interactive process in contrast to avoidant and volatile communication (Burleson & Denton, 1997; Gottman, 1994b; Johnson & Greenberg, 1994).

Professional therapists have suggested that marital partners should learn and practice problem-solving or conflict resolution skills, have open and mutual negotiation dialogues about finances, sexuality, parenting skills, set clear boundaries with in-laws, attain a level of acceptance that some aspects cannot be changed, stop attempting to change one another, maintain a significant level of shared spirituality and prayer time, learn to forgive oneself and the other, constantly maintain the purpose(s) of their marriage, learn to negotiate differences of opinion, and whenever necessary join a support group and seek professional help before the problems escalate (Ahrons, 2004; Ganong & Coleman, 1989; Kerr & Bowen, 1988; O'Leary, Heyman & Jongsman, 1998).

All in all, if the decision to remarry is final, then the custodial parent of minor children should:
- Discuss with the new partner their new financial arrangements
- Discuss disciplinary approaches
- Plan alone time with the children as well as family time with the new members of the family
- Children have to be helped to understand that boundaries exist and explain those boundaries to them

- The ex-spouse should not interfere with the discipline and boundaries set in the new home
- Children have to understand that private time is needed for the adults as well as for themselves
- If the new partner is a noncustodial parent, but has visitation with his/her children, discuss the living arrangements and house rules for those children when visiting
- Keep in mind that adult children may need some ground rules as well, especially if they are still living under the same roof

# Study Session 13.

## House Rules and Roles

*Description of House Rules and Roles*
*Experience of Others*
*My Experience*
*Keys to Proper Establishment and Management of*
*House Rules and Roles in Remarriage*

### Description of House Rules and Roles

Seven participants mentioned that because of the complexity of remarriage, rules are very important in second marriages. Some of the reasons they gave were that rules help to maintain structure and to establish a sense of discipline and order in the house. All seven of these participants had joint custody of their children with their former spouses, and they had realized that their children were finding it difficult to figure out what to do and not do in the households of their divorced parents.

Three of these participants had attended a seminar about remarriage in which they were helped to understand the importance of establishing rules and making them clear to the children in their households. One of the phrases which five participants reported as effective in helping their children to deal with the differences of guidelines while living in two households was the usage of the phrase:

"In this house, the rules are: ..."

### Experience of Others

Further individual discussions with those three parents revealed that the rules which had better helped their children in their second marriage were those that were clear, consistent, flexible, not rigid, and to which defined consequences were attached. One of the rules that Elías mentioned was:

> In this house, everybody who is at home during mealtime is expected to collaborate in the washing of the dishes after eating. Otherwise, whoever does not collaborate will have to wash the dishes alone after the next meal.

Six participants mentioned that the parents should make the rules in dialogue with their children, so that the children, especially teenagers and young adults, know what is expected of them. However, four participants emphasized that parents should not set the rules for their children exclusively. The parents should make rules or guidelines for themselves and abide by them, too. One of rules that six participants suggested for divorced parents was that, as parents, they should not criticize their former spouse in front of the children.

In addition to the house rules, four participants attributed the success of their remarriages to the fact that they made a conscious decision with their respective spouses not to get stuck into a rigid structure of abiding by the traditional gender roles. Abraham clarified:

> I help my second wife a lot with cooking, washing of the dishes, because I do not think that it is a job exclusively for women. This may sound or be perceived as a small thing by some people in traditional marriages, but it is a great relief to my wife. She likes it, and makes me feel supportive of her as we share some of the so-called traditional gender roles. Equally, too, I am not the only breadwinner in the house. We have a joint account, and we share all the expenses. However, there are other roles that we had to define clearly. For example, even if my stepson did not need any disciplinarian action because he grew up well-behaved, just in case any disciplinarian measures had to be taken, his biological parents would be the ones to do that, not me.

Five participants mentioned the need for couples to set a ritual for themselves alone and to schedule it in the form of a rule, so that they can comply by it. Elizabeth referred to that ritual as couple time and described it as a special time for her and her husband alone. Elizabeth mentioned: "I find myself during the week really crazy, very busy, with no time." By the same token, she encouraged other remarried people with tight schedules the following suggestion:

> Find time [together], let the dishes go, let the laundry go, don't wash the floor. It will be there. It is absolutely true. It will be

there. Find some time, even one hour a week, special time to go out to dinner. My husband does not like to go out to dinner, so we made a different special time. It is our date Saturday night. I find it very helpful for us, and it keeps us fresh.

House rules and roles are of paramount importance in remarriage settings. Three participants identified different house rules (bedtime for children) with a soft and firm tone of voice as a means of establishing order within the family and thereby helping each other to live in harmony. Based on their descriptions of the need for house rules, establishing clear house rules and the attached consequences for not abiding by them was a means to greater freedom within the family system, for dealing with the children, and for keeping clear boundaries with former spouses in order to provide collaborative parenting of the children.

Seven participants also made a distinction between traditional gender roles and flexible gender roles. Based on their inputs, it seemed that rigid, traditional gender roles (e.g., men as the sole breadwinners and women as the sole nurturers in a home) were not well suited for people in remarriage settings. Instead, they recommended mutual collaboration in many roles. Typical examples of such mutual sharing of roles included for some of the participants having the same bank account (joint method), so that the two partners responded to the payment of the house bills and other expenses.

Another example was the move away from emphasizing the biological parent as the only person responsible for the parenting responsibilities over his or her children from the previous marriage. Six participants mentioned that consulting their second spouses empowered them to become better parents, and they felt supported by the new spouse and more adult in their parenting role, especially those participants who did not have amicable relationships with their former spouses.

Henry's parenting style showed his wisdom. He had arranged with his second wife that he would be the disciplinarian of his children from the first marriage, and his second wife would be the one to reward them. He reported that this style had helped him to learn how to seek consultation from his second wife before disciplining his children. He felt supported by his second wife, put his wife into an active co-parenting role, and removed his wife from the position of being resented by his child and his former wife. Instead, she was well-respected as a stepmother without seeming to take away the mother-figure role from the children's biological mother, with whom the children have regular contact. The children like his wife very much because she reinforces their positive behavior by rewarding them.

**My experience**

Based on what you have read in this session, reflect on your own personal experience.

In order to facilitate the establishment and maintenance of a stable and satisfactory remarriage that involves custodial children from one and/or both spouses, I have a role as a custodial parent.

1.  What do I need to know, do and not do?

    _____
    _____
    _____
    _____
    _____

2.  What should I tell my and/or my new spouse's children and how?

    _____
    _____
    _____
    _____
    _____

**Keys to proper establishment and management of house rules and roles in remarriage**

As keys are important to open doors, consider the following keys to house rules and roles.

- Above all, respect is important. Treat each other with respect
- Have family meetings when needed
- Be flexible, but firm. Rules should be followed, but sometimes need to be negotiated
- Discuss rules for the house with your partner

# Study Session 14.

## Conflict Resolution

*Description of Conflict Resolution*
*Experience of Others*
*My Experience*
*Keys to Conflict Resolution*

### Description of Conflict Resolution

Partners in intimate relationships, especially in remarriage settings, need to understand and accept that given the complexity of remarriage as described in this book conflicts are likely to arise in stepfamilies. Some of the causes, risks and importance of conflict and an exploration of how it may be resolved will be considered in this section. Conflict is an interpersonal antagonism that occurs whenever one's values, actions, behaviors, desires, expectations, customs, points of view, traditions, priorities, interests, rules, power struggle and/or other interaction dynamics interfere with those of another person or group of people. Consequently, if the interference is not resolved using adequate means and in a timely fashion, the conflict may lead one or more people in a remarriage situation to experience psychological pain and misunderstanding. This may eventually escalate into withdrawal, open verbal attacks, depression, anger outbursts, domestic violence, separation, physical/ emotional abuse, divorce and/or death.

Therefore, it is important that partners in remarriage settings and other close family members plan on how they can reduce the risks of entering into conflict and do their best to resolve each conflict before it is too late. Some of the significant strategies they may use to achieve these goals may include but are not limited to setting ground rules of how to handle conflict (e.g., avoid attacking each other), learning some conflict resolution skills (e.g., deal with one issue at a time at an appropriate time), and being committed to finding a solution to the conflict. It is important to reach a consensus that enables the two partners or the individuals involved within a remarriage setting to process their available options, to choose the one(s) which they can mutually agree on, and then to be bound to follow through. All in all, conflict resolution requires the establishment of middle ground and a win-win situation for the parties involved.

## Experience of Others

Five participants stated that some conflict was inevitable and necessary to stay happily remarried. Felicia clarified:

> My [second] husband is a very peaceful gentleman, and both of us communicate very well. Nevertheless, however much we love one another, it is hard for us to live together without some moments of conflict between us. Once in a while, we have our arguments, but even then, we respect one another.

Elaborating on conflict in his remarriage, Henry said:

> Although it is sometimes very hard for my wife and I to maintain personal integrity during moments of conflict, whenever we resolve any given conflict, I feel good about myself, and we end up hugging one another. In a special way, I give credit to my wife because I have learned from her better skills of handling and resolving conflicts than I used to do in the past. I used to scream and nag at my wife, children, and coworkers.
>
> [Henry added:] I have learned to slow down, try to control my anger, keep my mouth shut as I think through the issues; not speak in self-defense, nor project blame on my wife because sometimes no one is to blame. In fact, sometimes conflicts arise out of misunderstandings, so to put the blame constantly on the other person or to make myself guilty for something I am not responsible for is not healthy. Additionally, as I force myself to slow down and delay passing judgment, I start to feel more comfortable to listen to my wife's perspective and put into context the motivations that might have contributed to what she thinks, feels, says, does, does not say, or decides not to do. Currently, I have also learned the importance of practicing the conflict resolution skills I have learned. Otherwise, without practicing them, I would not be any better at all than before.

With a smile on her face, Dora mentioned:

The conflicts I had in my first marriage have helped me to believe that nothing bad happens without some good coming out of it. I also noticed that some conflicts have strengthened my relationship with my spouse. My experience of conflict in marital relationships is that, if conflict does not escalate into the death of one or both spouses, it can influence those involved to make decisions and take actions that lead to positive change. Looking back on my life, even if the conflicts I suffered in my first marriage brought me a lot pain and humiliation, they prepared me to become more tolerant and persevering in life, especially during the divorce process and as a single mother of five children.

Beatrice clarified:

I have realized that taking the time to understand the source or sources of our conflicts has helped me to learn better ways of how to handle and resolve conflicts with my husband. I have learned not to minimize conflicts because in every conflict someone feels hurt. I also learned in my remarriage not to turn every minor conflict into a big issue. In a special way, I recall the night when I screamed at my husband for coming home delayed for two hours later than usual. He did not call me to inform me that he would be late nor inform me by phone that something had happened to him. I got mad at him, started thinking and imagining things that I cannot tell you now.

Beatrice added:

When he [her husband] came home, I screamed at him, and I left him in the sitting room. I told him to go to another bedroom. To cut the long story short, he told me that he was stuck in traffic for over an hour after a deadly accident had occurred in front of him. He did not have his cell phone that day because he had forgotten it in his other coat. When I read about that fatal accident in the newspapers the next day, I felt very bad. Not so much about the victims, whom I did not know, but because of the guilt I was feeling for having been unkind to my husband without knowing the cause of his delay and lack of communication.

Two participants (a man and a woman) mentioned that they lacked competency in handling conflict, especially in their first marriages and in the first five years of their second marriages. They were interested in learning some conflict resolution skills and how to control their anger during moments of conflict, especially with their former spouses and stepchildren.

Daniel, however, revealed:

> Although I had learned the hard way how to handle conflict more effectively than when I was in my first marriage and during the first 5 years of remarriage, I eventually learned how to choose my battles and to express my feelings without intentionally hurting my ex-spouse and/or second spouse.

Three participants suggested that if the conflict escalates in frequency and/or anger becomes intensely uncontrollable by one or both spouses, adequate measures must be taken before people seriously hurt one another. In retrospect, thinking over what had helped them in some moments of conflict, those three participants suggested that they found it very helpful to seek professional help because they managed to control their anger by attending anger management programs and through timely communication of their feelings.

Based on personal experience, Felicia suggested: "Each spouse should know that he or she may have the right answers or words, but may have to hold back to avoid the risk of speaking with anger." Dora also suggested: "In the case of on-going conflicts with the ex-spouse, the biological parents should avoid the risk of getting children caught up into those conflicts."

Four participants mentioned the likelihood of conflict and/or on-going expressions of abuse (i.e., physical, emotional, or verbal) in remarriage triad settings. However, one of the main problems highlighted by the participants is the lack of knowing the skills for resolving conflict and the ability to put them into practice during the moment of conflict.

Kiura (2004) observed: Couples can injure each other in the vain attempt to resolve conflicts. When this happens, matters become worse while the problem precipitating the conflict remains unresolved.

The participants identified the couple's abilities to resolve conflicts as one of the factors influencing stability and satisfaction in remarriage. Some of the skills that the participants recommended after having found them helpful in their remarriages included knowing how to channel anger constructively, discerning when to speak and when to keep one's mouth shut, being respectful of one another – even in the midst of strong differences of opinion, and the courage to deal with the problem in a timely fashion without attacking the other person or projecting all the blame onto oneself (LeBey, 2004).

## My experience

Based on what you have read in this session, reflect on your own personal experience.

1. In what areas do I have difficulty handling conflict?

_____
_____
_____
_____
_____

2. Whom do I have most conflicts with and what do we argue about?

_____
_____
_____
_____
_____

3. What types of conflicts do I tend to minimize and do they eventually turn into greater problems within myself and/or with others?

_____
_____
_____
_____
_____

4. What types of conflict resolution skills do I usually use and are they really effective without hurting myself and others?

_____
_____
_____
_____
_____

5.  What are the conflict resolution skills I have learned from the participants and other sources that I am going to implement in my life and interactions with others?

_____

_____

_____

_____

_____

## Keys to conflict resolution

As keys are important to open doors, consider the following keys to conflict resolution.

-   Stop minimizing conflicts
-   Resolve conflict from a win-win stance
-   Avoid a superiority or inferiority stance while resolving conflict
-   Learn to use "I" statements
-   Focus on the problem and how to resolve it without attacking the other or blaming oneself or the other
-   Take responsibility for actions, feelings and behaviors
-   Learn to negotiate with tact and respect

# Study Session 15.

## Clear Boundaries in Remarriage

### Description of Clear Boundaries in Remarriage

Clear boundaries are described here as the invisible barriers or limits that are designed within a given society, culture, family or system. These boundaries regulate the level of communication and the acceptable type of contact or separation between individuals involved within a given subsystem (e.g., stepfamily) so that they can interact with each other in healthy ways, respecting each other's space, time and rights. This allows the individual to become independent, to be dependent on others, as well as interdependent with them without becoming fused or caught up in rigid interactions with others.

### Experience of Others

Six participants mentioned that it was difficult for them to separate themselves completely from their former spouses, especially because four participants had joint custody of their biological children. Alicia said:

> Immediately after my divorce, I did not want to have any contact with my ex-spouse. I was so angry, frustrated, and fed up with him. Unfortunately, I had to live with the bitter truth that, because of the child we had together, I had to maintain constant contact. Secondly, I realized that as I kept being angry and distanced from him, the more I suffered because I could

not sit down with him to plan what would be in the best interest of our child.

Alicia added:

> I changed my attitude toward him, and my understanding of how his mother had badly treated him while growing up helped me to forgive him. So, when I changed the perspective and way of relating with him, he also changed. Then we started to communicate well. Ever since, we both respect each other, and planned together the wedding of our son, together with the help of my second husband and his second wife. Therefore, I have learned that, though divorce ends a marriage, it does not end the family. My ex-spouse and I are now close, and we can relate as friends.

On the other hand, Geoffrey mentioned:

> My divorce with my ex-spouse was generally amicable. I have never had any fight or major argument since I married my first wife and even after our divorce. Even now that makes me understand better why many relatives were shocked by our divorce. On the other hand, I have to clarify that, ever since I remarried, I have taken serious measures to make sure that my on-going amicable relationship with my ex-spouse does not become too intimate, and hence put my second marriage in jeopardy. We are very close as parents and friends, but distant enough to avoid the risk of falling back into romance. My second wife is also very respectful of my on-going friendship with my ex-spouse, and the two do some shopping together once in a while. All these healthy interpersonal relationships have also contributed to my remarriage stability and happiness.

Four participants also mentioned that having friendly relationships with their former and current in-laws were significant contributions to their stability and satisfaction in remarriage. Henry narrated how his former in-laws keep on sending him cards on his birthday and how his children enjoy spending part of their holidays with both their maternal and paternal grandparents.

Five participants highlighted that one of the things that had helped them in strengthening their remarriages was their on-going review, as individuals and as a couple, of how to become more conscious of protecting themselves from the negative influences of their neighborhoods and society at large. Catherine emphasized:

> Yes, I am a remarried divorcée, but I have realized that it is not very easy for me sometimes to live in a suburban neighborhood where most of my relatives and close friends are divorcing for the first, second, or third time. Fortunately, I have a very good supportive community at my church where I meet with other remarried parents. We empower one another and pray together for the success of our marriages. Therefore, I suggest that remarried couples need to learn how to take an objective stance in order to selectively appreciate what society offers, but also distance themselves from the negative influences from the media and the pressures from society which are detrimental to marital stability and happiness (e.g., drugs).

The type of relationship between the stepparent and a stepchild plays a significant role also in regard to the stability and satisfaction of a divorced parent's remarriage. This observation was reflected in Felicia's remarriage. Felicia mentioned:

> During the first years of my remarriage, I was very unhappy, and I was not sure whether my remarriage was going to last for long. This was because my second husband [Fausto] resented my son [José]. However, ever since I saw my husband interested in my son and doing his best to help my son, I experienced a lot of joy and tranquility in my remarriage.

As noted in the literature, a very strong attachment with the ex-spouse can be quite dangerous (Ahrons, 2004). Very close boundaries may create a possible risk of becoming sexually intimate again while currently in a second marriage with another person. However, very distant and/or conflictive boundaries with the former spouse may not be in the best interests of the children, especially in cases of joint custody.

It is important to establish clear boundaries and guidelines with one's children so that they do not break a remarriage in the dream of getting a parent together with a former spouse. No wonder one of the participants took a strong stand with his adolescent and young adult children at the time of remarriage and told them that his second marriage comes first before them. In that way, he managed to create clear boundaries with them, and they avoided the interruption of his remarriage and triangulation with their mother (McGoldrick & Carter, 1998).

The same participant also suggested that other remarried parents should learn from his experience and do likewise if necessary. It seems his suggestion and German background were reflected in his strong personality, but not all parents can manage to establish such rigid boundaries with their children. Parents of Italian, Jewish, or African American backgrounds, who tend to be quite attached to their children, may not find it very easy to exert such clear boundaries with their children as that participant managed to do (McGoldrick et al., 1996). This may sound like a tough decision but he said that it worked for him. He mentioned that his children later on thanked him for his stand and learned from that experience how to establish clear boundaries with him.

## My experience

Based on what you have read in this session, reflect on your own personal experience.

1. What are the benefits I have received by establishing and maintaining clear boundaries with my ex-spouse?

   _____
   _____
   _____
   _____
   _____

2. What is hindering me from establishing and maintaining clear boundaries with my children?

   _____
   _____
   _____
   _____
   _____

3. What are the dangers of involving my custodial child(ren) in all aspects of my personal life to the point that I tell the child(ren) everything about my life?

   _____
   _____
   _____
   _____
   _____

4.  What have I learned from the participants' experiences that I would like to integrate in my life in regard to clear boundaries?

    _____
    _____
    _____
    _____
    _____

**Keys to establishing and maintaining clear boundaries in remarriage**

As keys are important to open doors, consider the following keys to clear boundaries.

-   Know your own and others' boundaries and respect them
-   Do not get romantically involved with any adult child or relative of your spouse. [This is focused only on adults because sex with a minor is a crime and never to be tolerated!]
-   Respect and treat your stepchildren well

# Study Session 16.

## Cohabitation before Remarriage

*Description of Cohabitation*
*Experience of Others*
*My Experience*
*Keys to Explore before Cohabitation*

### *Description of Cohabitation*

Cohabitation refers to a relationship between two adult individuals living together as a couple without formalizing their relationship as a marriage/remarriage in a civil court and/or in a recognized religious denomination. Some partners start by cohabiting due to various reasons but with the intent of formalizing their relationship into a civil marriage and religious marriage. Other partners cohabite without any intention of getting married and stay together for as long as they want. Seven participants within the research study cohabited before getting remarried.

### *Experience of Others*

All seven participants highlighted that it was not an easy decision for them because of the criticisms they received from their family members who were against cohabitation before the official wedding in front of a municipal judge or a religious minister. Nevertheless, those seven participants managed to resist the criticisms from their relatives and the teachings of their churches that did not condone cohabitation.

Abraham said:

> After four prolonged conversations with my second wife [also a divorced custodial parent ], both of us decided to start living together without any formal ceremony at all. On my behalf, the primary motivation for prioritizing cohabitation was the fact that I was feeling insecure about committing myself to my

partner because I was still wounded in my heart based on what I had gone through with my previous spouse. Fortunately, the three-year period I cohabited with her helped me to know her in her true colors, and with no make-up. She is truly an adorable woman.

Beatrice stated:

> I was fearful to be hurt the second time. This was because I wanted to make sure that I was not getting into trouble the second time by marrying another abusive person and with a hidden agenda. So, I arranged with my fiancé [a divorced custodial parent too] to start living together before marriage. We did this so that we could know one another better. Furthermore, he had just spent two months in the United States since he left his native country. That also impacted our decision to live together before marriage. Two years later, we got married because both of us had come to know one another more closely.

Fred narrated in detail his cohabitation experience as follows:

> I dated many women after my first divorce primarily for sex, until one of them [a divorced parent too] asked me to marry her. During the next two months, I focused my exclusive attention to her and, as a result, she asked me to get married with her in church before we started living together. After a week or two, I eventually convinced her to postpone the church wedding, and asked her to start living together. She accepted and we started living together.
>
> [Fred added:] I spent the first three months very well and then we started to have problems related to finances and religion. Even if we were not married officially, we had established a real bond between us. However, due to the escalating problems, we decided to seek marital counseling to avoid the risk of separation. The counselor did his best and we also put our united effort to save the marriage. In the end we survived, but I realized that we made a mistake before we started living together.
>
> The truth of the matter was that both of us still had unresolved problems that were related to our divorces. Those problems made it harder for the counselor and for us because the counselor had to put aside our present problems that we

had presented to him about how our finances and religious differences were affecting our marriage. Instead, the counselor decided to focus on each individual's "baggage" that we had brought to the relationship. Therefore, I think that divorced persons should work toward resolving their problems before planning to live together and before they officially remarry.

On the other hand, Dora spoke of her cohabiting before remarriage (with another divorced custodial parent) as follows:

I do not advocate for everybody to live with his or her fiancé before they remarry, but in my case, it was very helpful, because that living together helped us to know one another. Therefore, when we made the decision for our official remarriage, both of us were convinced that we were making a life commitment to one another. We have come a long way because, when we started living together, we liked each other, but we didn't love each other. … I know, I don't love him. We didn't even go out. We just started to live together… Now we love each other, and we have been married for eighteen years.

It is important to note that transitional cohabitation as a step to remarriage is poorly documented in the existing literature. Further research is needed to better understand its impact on stability and satisfaction in remarriage. A study by Ganong and Coleman (1989) indicated that most of the cohabiting partners who sought counseling before remarriage or after remarriage ended up separating. However, the findings of this research-based book provided different results. All the participants who expressed having cohabited before remarriage said that seeking counseling helped them a great deal. All of them had been remarried for at least eight years and reported their remarriages as stable and satisfactory.

Therefore, given these mixed results about seeking counseling while cohabiting, the participants encouraged divorced parents contemplating remarriage to seek counseling before starting to cohabitate. In a similar vein, they might benefit from counseling by being helped to make realistic goals for cohabitation, and thus start working toward the process of successful family blending (Ahrons, 2004; LeBey, 2004).

**My experience**

Based on what you have read in this session, reflect on your own personal experience.

1. Did I ever cohabit before my first marriage or am I currently cohabiting before remarriage?

   _____

   _____

   _____

   _____

   _____

2. What is my experience regarding cohabitation?

   _____

   _____

   _____

   _____

   _____

3. What do I think hinders partners from getting married after cohabiting?

   _____

   _____

   _____

   _____

   _____

**Keys to explore before cohabitation**

As keys are important to open doors, consider the following keys to transitional cohabitation.

- Seek counseling before cohabiting
- Explore the advantages and disadvantages of cohabitation as an experiment for a stable and satisfactory remarriage

# Study Session 17.

## Permanent Sites for Professional Remarriage Services

*Description of Permanent Sites for Professional*
*Remarriage Services*
*Experience of Others My Experience*
*Keys to Permanent Sites for Professional Remarriage Services*

### Description of Professional Remarriage Services

Seven participants mentioned that it was very hard for them to know whom to turn to and where to receive a comprehensive pre-remarriage preparation, in order to get a better sense of what they were going into before making a final commitment to one another. All of them admitted that they needed guidance about stability and satisfaction in remarriage in an environment that is conducive to healing, reflection, prayer, and learning.

The site(s) for marriage and remarriage services should be permanently located so that interested people know where they could be referred and/or come back for professional help whenever needed in the near and/or distant future. The directors and the other personnel working in such buildings are cautioned not to stigmatize people who experience divorce. An atmosphere of hospitality and respect for the dignity every person need be held to the highest standards. Five participants recalled having attended, in a costly hotel, a weekend preparation course that was organized by three remarried couples and a priest. All five participants described that weekend experience as very inspiring, very loaded, expensive, and without an opportunity for any follow-up session, even if needed, because the directors admitted that they were not professionals, and there was no place to meet afterward.

Alicia stated:

> I have heard of many places where different types of training are offered (e.g., computer training centers, nursing schools, police training centers, sports centers, and schools for foreign

languages). However, I have never heard of a training center exclusively dedicated to the training of people for marriage and/ or remarriage. That bothers me a lot. I remember pronouncing my vows before the municipal judge the day I married for the first time and the second time, but I did not receive any training about marriage or remarriage. Above all, I really needed it before my remarriage because I did not want to run into the same problems without knowing how to address them.

Alicia clarified:

> The Pentecostal church I go to does not offer pre-remarriage training. In my local church and county there is no established site for remarrying parents where they can go and receive pre-remarriage counseling. To the best of my knowledge, I think only the Catholic Church is the one that has started to offer that kind of training, and I hear that it is only for Catholics who are widowed or divorced who have received their annulments from the previous marriage.

Daniel (a resident of a county other than Alicia's) mentioned:

> I haven't seen nor heard of any permanent building or center offering remarriage counseling in my local county. However, it is heart-breaking to see my close friends divorcing, remarrying within 6 months or so, and then re-divorcing. I wish I knew where to send them to seek guidance before they continue hurting their children also by those changes.

When asked if he thought his friends would go there to seek remarriage services, Daniel replied:

> I am not certainly sure. Probably, let me answer your question by referring to the people who go to the medical clinics. I do not go to my doctor unless I am sick or if he recommends me for a medical check-up. Honestly, who goes to the medical doctor without being sick? However, the good news is that, whenever you get sick, you can go to the hospital because it is there for you. You know where it is, or someone else takes you there. Therefore, it is my educated guess and heartfelt desire that people in need of remarriage services will have greater chances of going there, especially if they are accessible, with safe parking

lots, financially affordable for people with low income, and if the confidentiality is ensured.

Geoffrey said:

> Based on personal experience, most of remarriage problems became more explicit after I started living with my second wife, not during our courtship, and yet I did not know where to seek help when I most needed it. I am not sure whether I had idealized so much my wife while we were dating, and I felt I did not need any professional help before remarriage. However, I think that, if I had known of any established buildings with qualified personnel (particularly remarried spouses), I would probably have sought post-remarriage counseling to address the problems which we faced in the first 5 years of remarriage.

Eight participants (four males and four females) expressed that they had observed increasing numbers of divorces, remarriages, and second divorces in their neighborhoods. All of them made the suggestion regarding an urgent need for establishing permanent buildings where people can receive remarriage services. Those participants also suggested that the buildings should be geographically accessible, within safe neighborhoods, with parking spaces, and where people can be referred for help at affordable cost for the professional services they receive.

Fred stated:

> There is a school almost for everything, for example, driving schools, agriculture and seminaries where religious ministers are trained. However, the government has almost nothing set in place to help the people prepare themselves for marriage or remarriage. The marriages in civil courts are primarily focused on paper work and writing signatures. Beyond that, there is no preparation at all for married life.
>
> I do not know of any other church, apart from the Catholic Church, where a selected number of Catholics, those whose marriages have been annulled, are offered a one-day or one-weekend pre-remarriage preparation workshop. I hear the content is good, but the workshop is too rushed, with limited numbers of participants, and very costly.

Fred added:

> Based on my marital experience of twenty-five years in both marriages, I have realized that I have made many mistakes because of my ignorance about first marriages and the complexity of remarriage. Hopefully, I would have avoided some of those mistakes if I had participated in a comprehensive premarital preparation program within a formalized institution.

The participants highlighted that some of the workshops that professionals could offer would include those focused on how to help couples communicate better, to learn and practice different skills. Examples of such skills include: problem-solving and/or conflict resolution skills, open and mutual negotiation dialogues about finances, sexuality, parenting and step-parenting skills and setting clear boundaries with in-laws. Couples should also be counseled on how to attain a level of acceptance that some aspects of life cannot be changed and how to stop attempting to change one another.

Based on the consulted literature, remarrying parents may be helped in such workshops to learn about how to maintain a significant level of shared spirituality and prayer time, to learn to forgive oneself and the other, to constantly recall the purpose(s) of their marriage, to learn to negotiate differences of opinion, and, whenever necessary, to join a support group and to seek professional help before the problems escalate (Ahrons, 2004; Ganong & Coleman, 1989; Kerr & Bowen, 1988; O'Leary et al., 1998).

## My experience

Based on what you have read in this session, reflect on your own personal experience.

1. What do I think family therapists, psychologists and other professional (e.g., religious ministers and social workers) need to do in order to help me and/or my partner contemplating remarriage to seek pre-remarriage counseling and psychological education regarding forming and maintaining satisfactory relationships?
2. What suggestions or ideas can I make for family therapists, psychologists, and other professionals so that they become more efficient counselors for divorced custodial parents who are preparing for a second marriage.

## Keys to Permanent Sites for Professional Remarriage Services

As keys are important to open doors, consider the following keys to permanent sites for professional remarriage services. There are several components needed(e.g., personnel, location, facilities and affordability) at permanent sites in order to provide a variety of professional remarriage services.

- Personnel must be qualified and properly trained. They need to have the necessary materials and equipment available. Staff must be hospitable and caring. If needed, security staff should be on hand.
- Location needs to be accessible and have adequate parking available. It should be near public transportation. The site should be permanent (not changing location all the time)
- The facility must be well maintained (inviting, not run down) and have sanitary rest rooms. If possible, it should include a designated spiritual space (chapel) and have a cafeteria. It should be family friendly (e.g., provide babysitting services, play room, snacks, etc.)
- It must be affordable

# Part III

## Roles for Divorced Persons Contemplating Remarriage

Role 1. Healing from the Trauma of Divorce

Role 2. Annulment Process in the Catholic Church

Role 3. Remarriage Preparation in the Catholic Church

When contemplating remarriage after divorce, it is recommended that the person do whatever it takes to heal from the wounds of divorce before entering into a remarriage. Otherwise, the risk of a subsequent divorce (re-divorce) is high and filling in another person in the unhealed wounds may be emotionally and psychologically more harmful than anticipated.

Part III is designed to include three steps or roles to undertake before remarriage. **Role 1** is meant for anyone who has experienced divorce. **Role 2** is specifically designed for those divorced Catholics or other baptized Christians who have experienced divorce after being married within a Catholic or other Christian Church. After receiving a civil divorce decree, they have to apply for an annulment through the tribunal of their respective dioceses or archdioceses before remarriage within the Catholic Church. **Role 3** is specifically designed for Catholics contemplating remarriage within the Catholic Church after receiving an annulment. However, even for non-Catholics, preparing for remarriage with the help of a third party is highly encouraged.

# Role 1.

## Healing from the Trauma of Divorce

*Barbara Leahy Shlemon's Divorce and Spiritual Healing Story*
*Alex's Healing Process from Divorce and Other Traumas*
*Identifying the Pain and Working through It*
*Taking Steps toward Healing*
*Questions for Reflection and Action*

In order to establish a stable and satisfactory remarriage, it is better to work through trauma from the previous marriage(s) and other unresolved painful experiences in one's life. Even if the annulment process and the receiving of an annulment can bring about some healing and peace, they are not enough. Divorce brings a lot of damage to the individual and the other significant people in his/her life at many levels. These damages include, but are not limited to, one's emotional, physical, spiritual, psychological, moral, relational, intellectual well-being and professional functioning. All these levels need healing. Here the focus will be on exploring how spirituality has contributed to the healing process of two Catholics who experienced divorce. The coined phrase for this type of healing is healing spirituality and its scope goes beyond spiritual healing. It is important to highlight that there are many Catholics who have been granted annulments, remarried and then divorced in a couple of months or years. One wonders what went wrong or what is missing from what the Catholic Church has to offer in addition to annulments! Therefore, the Catholic Church is already responding in her pastoral mission to help couples and individuals undergoing the trauma of divorce. Much more still needs to be done by the Church and other professionals. We are all one body. Whenever one part of the body suffers, every part suffers with it; if one part is honored, every part rejoices with it (cf. 1 Corinthians 12: 14 26).

The goal is not to point fingers, not to assign blame and not to put people on a guilt trip. Instead, it is to raise awareness about the need for paying attention to one's pain, identifying the type of suffering and making a commitment to work through that pain. All of that is what may contribute to attaining holistic healing. If the pain is unresolved, then with the help of a professional, better coping skills may be developed to live with it.

During the period an individual in a divorce situation is working through the grief, it may be very valuable for him or her to have access to a person in whom to confide and verbalize one's thoughts, fears, concerns, anger, guilt, and other feelings (Berry, 1998). Straudacher (1994, p. 128) emphasized that there "are hundreds of thoughts, feelings, conditions, questions, and assumptions that can be cleared up or lessened by talking them over with someone else, particularly with another person who has also experienced a loss."

Additionally, for those contemplating remarriage, they may be well disposed to effectively implement the influencing factors of stability and satisfaction in remarriage discussed previously in this book. Therefore, this section is designed to search for ways of helping Catholics and non-Catholics who are still suffering from the experience of divorce and/or other unresolved trauma.

Keenan's (2004) discussion clarifies the impact of suffering and the need the pay attention to another person's story of suffering. According to Keenan (2004, p.67): "When we examine suffering, we need to recognize two very different types of discussions on this topic. The more familiar occurs in academic gatherings, which produce many philosophical and theological works about suffering and its 'meaning.' The less familiar occurs in those intimate settings in which we are called to respond to someone who is suffering and who wants to talk with us about her or his suffering; in that setting, we usually listen rather than talk."

Therefore, listening to others in pain is important instead of doing most of the talking. Listening and/or paying attention to people narrating their suffering may help them to heal. Two responses to the suffering that is significantly impacted by divorce are presented here. These responses explore the trauma of divorce, other traumas and the need for holistic healing. First, Barbara Leahy Shlemon is one of the many Catholics whose written divorce experiences, challenges, spiritual struggles, honesty and faith continue to inspire. The second story is that of a friend, fictitiously referred to as Alex.

### Barbara Leahy Shlemon's Divorce and Spiritual Healing Story

Shlemon (1992) understands and makes excellent connections to how Christian spirituality can be an important healing resource from the wounds of divorce. A typical example of the need for healing from divorce is based on the feelings of rejection experienced by most divorced persons.

Shlemon guides the reader to some verses and passages in the Bible that "can provide help for the seemingly hopeless devastation of rejection. The Bible constantly gives reminders of the Father's everlasting love, compassion, and caring. 'Does a woman forget her baby at the breast, or fail to cherish the son of womb? Yet, even if these forget, I will never forget you,' says the Lord (Isaiah 49:15).... Finding quiet moments throughout the day to just sit in the presence of the one who loves unconditionally can console the ravages of rejection" (Shlemon, 1992, p. 26).

Shlemon's divorce and healing story seems to affirm what many people go through during and after divorce, their search for God and the experience of God's consolation at a deeper level than ever before in their lives.

## Alex's Healing Process from Divorce and Other Traumas

The following is a prolonged interview with a close friend about suffering, with specific reference to divorce-related suffering and his experience of spiritual healing. At the time of the interview, Alex had been divorced for fifteen years. When asked how people respond to suffering after divorce, he replied:

> People going through a bitter divorce respond to suffering and pain in different ways. Unfortunately, most of those ways are more destructive than constructive. For instance, some turn to alcohol, drugs, pornography, sex outside of marriage, blaming others, blaming themselves, overworking, overspending, losing hope in God and ultimately some kill themselves or other innocent people.

Alex clarified:

> It is hard to predict how each person will respond to divorce, including those who are believers and regular churchgoers. Some people turn to God in the midst of all types of suffering, and specifically in what may be called the "divorce trauma." However, sometimes suffering takes people away from God. Others need to learn more about divorce to become consolers to people who seek God in their sufferings.

Alex emphasized:

> Learn to help divorced Christians who are using destructive ways to learn how to unite their sufferings to those of Christ.

When questioned about how he is handling his divorce trauma, he answered:

> Well, in retrospect, I may say that through all those years, I used to handle intensely those sufferings, especially of stress, loneliness and frustration, by overdrinking and playing the blame game. Above all, I was blaming my ex-wife and God for all my sufferings. I used to wonder whether really God cares about me. I was feeling abandoned by God, empty within me, depressed and lonely.

[After a minute-long silence Alex eventually continued:]

> One Sunday morning, in frustration and seeking what to do with my life, I was standing in my driveway. My neighbor saw me on his way to Sunday Mass and invited me to accompany him because the Mass was in memory of his wife who had died a month ago.

Alex mentioned:

> I accepted for the sake of my neighbor and we went together. Part of my shame was that although I am Catholic, I had not put [stepped] my foot into any Catholic Church in twenty years. Surprisingly, on the way to the Church, a thought passed my mind that made me realize that overdrinking was not solving my problems. I was hurting internally about my lost marriage and started to feel remorse for all the suffering that I had inflicted upon my ex-wife and children. I felt profound grief and pain that I cannot put in words. I did not say anything to my neighbor. I kept it all to myself but deep down, I was hurting.

Alex added:

> I understood on that day what my mother used to say: 'God works in mysterious ways.' I say this because, the Gospel reading

for that Sunday made me feel that Jesus was speaking directly to me. I remember it was taken from the Gospel according Matthew. The verse that touched me the most was that where Jesus says: 'Come to me, all you who labor and are burdened, and I will give you rest' (Matthew 11: 28).

Alex elaborated:

I started attending Sunday Mass. I got to know the priest better in that Church and I felt confident eventually to share my divorce story with that priest. He told me about the annulment and I did it. The annulment brought me some healing but I feel I have a long way to go. I am still in pain and I am fearful to enter into another relationship because I am still broken-hearted.

Alex clarified:

In retrospect, I am very grateful to God for sending my neighbor into my life. Accompanying him to Church turned out to be a life-long benefit for me. I really needed another human being to bring me to God. Above all, accepting the invitation from Jesus saved my life. I was overburdened and I came to him. I started going to the Catholic Church and the rest is history. It is now seven years and I feel so much better to be in the company of Jesus.

Alex added:

Now I feel more peace knowing that I can turn to Jesus who is God, who experienced suffering at many levels. His suffering was not only being crucified. He suffered rejection, he suffered when he saw people mistreating others and he suffered betrayal by a close disciple, Judas Iscariot. I love Jesus because he is God and I can turn to him for solace.

Alex revealed:

Jesus experienced many sufferings as we do and I have learned to constantly unite my ongoing sufferings to his sufferings. Sometimes I feel so much pain in my inner being from invisible wounds. In such moments, I find great relief in uniting my sufferings to the sufferings of Christ. I have changed my attitude and questions about suffering. Appreciating the good people, things and resources in my life has also been beneficial in coping with suffering.

Alex also shared what else has helped him on his healing journey:

I realized that God loves us unconditionally, coming back to the Catholic Church, prayer, acknowledging my sins and asking for God's forgiveness in the sacrament of confession, attending Sunday Mass and receiving the Eucharist, reading the Bible and the Catechism of the Catholic Church, trusting in God. I will also add: the love and support from my family members, friends with good manners, my pastor and my neighbors.

Alex's journey of spiritual healing and his allowing Jesus to become his model for handling suffering is exemplary. He expressed thanks for listening to him because it is hard to talk about suffering.

*Prayer*: The following prayer about suffering may offer healing and consolation to those who are hurting:

Heavenly Father, I thank you for the gift of life, loved ones and all the resources you give us. As Jesus turned to you in his sufferings, I turn to you too for consolation, courage, mercy and unconditional love. I pray for myself and on behalf of all the suffering people in the world. Help me to unite my sufferings and those of others to the sufferings of Christ for the salvation of your people.

Grant us faith, courage and serenity so that our sufferings, temptations and joys may never separate us from the love of Christ. Give us your grace to become active consolers and mediums of transformation for those whose invisible wounds and silent cries go unnoticed. In a special way, I offer you the sufferings of the babies in abortion clinics, the hungry, homeless, sick, caregivers, family members and friends, people in difficult marriages, abandoned senior citizens and orphans, people who have lost jobs, lost faith and hope, and the souls in purgatory. Send us your Holy Spirit in our sufferings and joys as we make our journey to heaven. I ask this through Christ, our Lord, who suffered death for our salvation. Amen.

## Identifying the Pain and Working through It

So many devoted Catholics and non-Catholics who believe in God have experienced the pain of divorce. They have shared some of the questions they ask themselves to which they have no immediate answers. For instance:

"Why has God abandoned me?"

"Why am I suffering?"

"What am I going to do with life?"

Questions of this nature are also discussed in the letter of Blessed John Paul II on the Christian meaning of human suffering (Salvifici Doloris). The Pope observed that at some point in our lives, our experience of suffering causes bodily and spiritual pain and leads us to ask the question "Why do I suffer?" Particularly anguishing is "the daily drama of so many cases of undeserved suffering" (Salvifici Doloris, paragraph 9).

The lack of sufficient answers to such questions often causes more anguish and suffering. Unfortunately, the number of people experiencing suffering influenced by divorce in both first and second marriages is on the increase. Furthermore, there are an increasing number of people who are remarrying or cohabiting after divorce while they are still experiencing so much pain. Hence, this suffering seems to contribute to divorcing again and more suffering or staying in unsatisfactory relationships.

Often remarried and cohabiting partners ask themselves additional questions to which they do not have satisfactory answers. For instance:

"Why am I still suffering the pains of divorce after so many years?"

"Why do I keep thinking about my former spouse who hurt me so much?"

"How can I get my former spouse out of my thoughts?" "How can I establish a stable and satisfactory remarriage?" "What next? "

"Why me?"

There are no easy answers and each case is unique. It is important to acknowledge one's resources in moments of suffering and integrate them with gratitude to God into our healing process. Ryan (1999, p. 129) noted a beautiful insight by Joan Borysenko: "Thank God for what doesn't need healing."

*Taking Steps toward Healing*

Another observation that needs clarification is in regard to whether or not a Catholic can receive communion if he/she is divorced and has not received an annulment. Divorced Catholics who have not remarried may receive Communion. However, because of the human condition, he/she is encouraged to receive the sacrament of Reconciliation before receiving Eucharist. They are not excommunicated from the Church and are welcome to attend Mass and participate in their parish activities.

Finally, Catholics who have experienced a divorce and have not started the annulment process are encouraged to get the right information about the annulment process and take action to start it (see Role 2 for details) . Many questions may come to mind, doubts and/or moments of anxiety may be experienced before starting the process. Starting the process of annulment may seem to be intimidating. Such experiences need be perceived as expected human reactions that can be overcome. Therefore, seek the help of someone trained in Canon Law (that is, Law of the Catholic Church), for instance, a trained priest, religious, lay person and/or professionals in the Tribunal of your diocese/archdiocese. Contact any of them if you need help. If the one you contact does not offer you the help you need, ask another until you get the one who is willing and able to help you.

## Questions for Reflection and Action

Consider the following questions for reflection regarding suffering and as pathways for resolving suffering, reducing it and/or coping better with it.

1.  What kind of suffering am I experiencing? Try as much as possible to express the pain in terms of feelings, e.g., shame, guilt, loneliness, anxiety or lack of self-esteem.

_____

_____

_____

_____

_____

2. What is its source?

_____

_____

_____

_____

_____

3. When did it start?

_____

_____

_____

_____

_____

4. Is it a remembrance?

_____

_____

_____

_____

_____

5. How does pain affect me physically?

_____

_____

_____

_____

_____

6. How does pain affect me emotionally?

_____

_____

_____

_____

7. How does pain affect me mentally?

_____

_____

_____

_____

8. What am I doing or saying to myself that does not contribute to my healing?

_____

_____

_____

_____

_____

9. What is going well in my life and/or in that of my loved ones in these current days, months, years, decades? Identify it and give thanks to God for it.

_____

_____

_____

_____

_____

## My situation

1. What part(s) of me still needs to be healed?

_____

_____

_____

_____

_____

2. What is the description of the healing process that I need to engage in?

_____

_____

_____

_____

_____

3. What are the dangers of rushing into remarriage before I heal from the wounds of my divorce?

_____

_____

_____

_____
_____

4. Whom can I turn to in order to take the first steps toward the needed healing process and when am I going to start?

_____
_____
_____
_____
_____

## Situation of my prospective spouse

1. What are the risks of entering into remarriage with my prospective spouse if he/she has not healed from divorce and/or has other problems, such as illness, addictions and/or mental disorder?

_____
_____
_____
_____
_____

2. What part(s) of him/her need healing?

_____
_____
_____
_____
_____

3. How committed is he/she to the needed healing process before we remarry?

_____
_____
_____
_____
_____

# Role 2.

## Annulment Process in the Catholic Church

*Annulment Process for Divorced and Civilly Remarried Catholics*

Some divorced Catholics have experienced both profound spiritual transformations and challenges in regard to the annulment process. Many lack the necessary and correct information about an annulment. The majority of individuals are searching for holistic strategies and resources for healing so that they are able to move on with their lives after divorce. Some have remarried in the Catholic Church after receiving an annulment, while others have remarried civilly without seeking an annulment and still wonder about the annulment process.

This section is specifically designed to focus on the annulment process for Catholics of the Roman Rite who divorced after a Church wedding and are currently single or have civilly remarried before getting a Church annulment. The initial marriage could have been between a Catholic and another Catholic, or another Christian, a non-Christian believer, or a nonbeliever in God. The information in this section is by no means exhaustive in regard to the complex and unique situations in every individual case. However, it does offer an easy to understand introduction to the process of annulment.

It is recommended that those seeking annulments and/or those interested in learning more about annulments and related topics should consult the experts who work in the Catholic marriage tribunals of their diocese. Two Canon lawyers have reviewed the information provided in this section and have approved it. Many sources as well have been utilized to help provide adequate insight on this topic (e.g., Beal, Coriden & Green, 2000; Coriden, Green & Heintschel, 1985; Catoir, 1996; Robinson, 1984; and Zwack, 1983).

Because of the complex nature of the ideas expressed in this section, some repetition is necessary to help the reader better understand some of these ideas. As the adage states: "Repetition is the mother of learning."

## Roman Catholic Church's Understanding of Marriage

According to the Bible, the teaching of the Magisterium, and the Tradition of the Roman Catholic Church, the Catholic Church acknowledges marriage between a man and a woman only. "From the very beginning, the Creator 'made them male and female' and said, for this reason ... (Genesis 2:24) a man shall leave his father and mother and be joined to his wife and the two shall become one flesh" (Matthew 19: 4 -5; cf. Ephesians 3:31). Therefore, this section is limited to the annulment of heterosexual marriages.

Likewise, Code 1055 of the Church's Canon Law states: "The Matrimonial covenant, by which a man and a woman establish between themselves a partnership of the whole of life and which is ordered by its nature to the good of spouses and the procreation and education of offspring, has been raised by Christ the Lord to the dignity of a sacrament between the baptized" (Beal, Coriden & Green, 2000, p. 1240).

Consequently, because marriage has its origins in Divine Law, every marriage (Protestant, Jewish, nonbeliever, etc.) is presumed by the Church to be a true marriage unless the opposite is proven beyond a reasonable doubt. To marry is, thus, one of the most important decisions a person will make in his/her life because it entails a lifelong commitment.

It is no wonder then that every Church Tribunal has the responsibility of investigating and studying every case presented for annulment to make sure that there are sufficient grounds for granting an annulment. Once a marital bond has been formed, that bond cannot be broken by any human being. "Therefore, what God has joined, no man must separate" (Matthew 19:6). A marriage cannot be annulled whenever a marriage bond is acknowledged to be valid. It follows, therefore, that NOT all annulment applications are granted by the Tribunal.

Nevertheless, all individuals who have completed a civil divorce process are encouraged to apply for an annulment from the Tribunal. However, each person should know beforehand that there is no guarantee that an annulment will be granted. "Both grounds for nullity and positive proof must be produced" (www.diometuchen.org, 2012).

Because of various misconceptions and complexities about the annulment process (Cantoir, 1996), this process of annulment in the Catholic Church is explained further, with special emphasis on its meaning, scope, limits, healing benefits, importance and using justice as a background.

## Description of an Annulment

An annulment is a declaration by the Tribunal that a marital union must have lacked, from the beginning, some element essential to marriage as ordained by God, our Creator, and taught by Jesus Christ. The annulment as a decree is designed to indicate that the marriage in question never legally existed as a sacramental union according to Canon Law. In other words, there was never a canonical marriage and a true marriage bond never came into existence (Zwack, 1983).

However, it is important to emphasize that a Catholic annulment does not deny the existence of the marriage. It essentially establishes that the marriage was not a sacramental union. Consequently, a person who has been granted an annulment by the Tribunal is free to enter into a future marriage that is a sacrament. For example, a Catholic who has gotten a divorce is allowed to remarry in the Catholic Church only after receiving an annulment from the Tribunal. A marriage or remarriage outside the Catholic Church is considered invalid by the Catholic Church.

Conceptually, the annulment process can be compared to the process of obtaining a valid passport. The comparison may not fully reflect the meaning and value of an annulment, but it highlights some points that are so important on many levels. The process of getting a passport involves dedicating time to the process, patience after providing the requested information to the passport office, spending energy and money and taking on responsibilities. Sometimes, for specific reasons, someone's passport or visa application may be denied. So is the case with annulment applications.

Once you get the passport, you can use it for international travel whenever the need arises, provided that you have the necessary requirements for international travel: an airline ticket, proper visa, money or credit card, and vaccinations. If traveling with another adult, he or she too must fulfill the requirements for international travel. The other adult person in this analogy represents the person to whom one would marry in the Church after receiving an annulment.

## Description of a Tribunal

The Tribunal may be described as the "Church court" (Catoir, 1996, p. 55). It is under the direction of the Bishop and is supervised by his delegate, the Judicial Vicar. This vicar works with a staff of trained priests, religious, and laity who specialize in offering assistance to persons who request that the Church investigate and determine whether a marriage has grounds for an ecclesiastical annulment. The Tribunal makes that determination after conducting a thorough investigation according to the laws and procedures of the Church. Part of this investigation involves examining the history of the relationship in order to determine if there was a valid bond according to the laws of the Roman Catholic Church.

Listing the Church laws and procedures is beyond the scope of this section. As mentioned before, the following are excellent resources: Beal, Coriden and Green (2000), Catoir (1996), Robinson (1984) and Zwack(1983).

Divorced Catholic singles, as well as those in current civil remarriages after divorce, are encouraged to apply for an annulment so that the Tribunal may determine whether or not there are grounds for nullity of their prior marriage.

## Benefits of an Annulment

An annulment seeks only the spiritual welfare of the parties involved. There is no attempt to assign blame for the breakup of the marriage. A Church annulment has no civil or legal ramifications. It does not affect the legitimacy of any children from the marriage; their status remains unchanged.

It may be beneficial for some to initiate the annulment application so that they are prepared in the event that they decide to remarry. The possession of an annulment is like having a valid passport so that the person can travel at the desired time with the right companion for the journey. It is important to remember the Church does not acknowledge the remarriage of a divorced Catholic who has not received an annulment.

## Overcoming Common Misunderstandings about Annulments

Catholics who were married in the Catholic Church and have gone through a process of civil divorce may have significant misunderstandings about an annulment that can endanger their faith and integrity. In order to overcome these misunderstandings, Cantoir (1996) made a list of statements, which follow, that are false. Many people who still believe these statements to be true. Become familiar with these statements in order to dispel the many misunderstandings that still exist among Catholics today.

> It is FALSE that divorced Catholics who have not remarried are automatically excommunicated from the Catholic Church, can no longer consider themselves Catholics, are in a state of permanent mortal sin, may not serve as sponsors at Baptism or Confirmation, may not receive the sacraments of Eucharist and Penance, and are not allowed a funeral in the Catholic Church or burial in a Catholic cemetery.
>
> It is FALSE that divorced Catholics who have remarried without an annulment are automatically excommunicated from the Catholic Church, may not attend Mass and are not welcome at parish activities, may not receive the sacrament of Reconciliation, should no longer consider themselves Catholic, may not have their children baptized or confirmed in a Catholic Church, and are not allowed funeral in the Catholic Church or burial in a Catholic cemetery.
>
> It is FALSE that marriage Tribunals in the Catholic Church require you to pay exorbitant fees for an annulment, only grant annulments to people with power and influence, refuse annulments to people who were married a long time, refuse annulments to people with children, consider the children from annulled marriages to be "illegitimate," and take many years to process even the simplest case (Cantoir, 1996, p. 3).

## Suggested Questions for Potential Annulment Applicants

One of the Canon lawyers made the suggestion that while the Tribunal is responsible for discerning the validity or nullity of a marriage, annulment applicants should ask themselves the following questions:

1.  Was I pressured to marry by my parents or my spouse's parents for any reason, for example, an unexpected pregnancy?
2.  Did my spouse marry to conceal a same-sex orientation?

3. Did I find out after years of humiliation that my spouse was an alcoholic or a drug addict with no intention of getting help and lacked the necessary freedom to make a commitment?
4. Did I discover that my spouse was incapable of sexual fidelity?
5. Did my spouse conceal a history of psychological problems?
6. At the time of the wedding, did my spouse intend to stay with me only for a limited period?
7. Did either one of us refuse to have children?
8. Was my spouse married to someone else at any time prior to our marriage without telling me?
9. Did I marry before a civil official?
10. Did my spouse conceal from me that he/she was marrying in order to get immigration papers?
11. Was I the one who had a hidden agenda and never revealed it to my spouse?
12. What was that hidden agenda?

## Starting the Annulment Process and Information Required by the Tribunal

First, consult your parish priest, a parochial vicar, a religious or a deacon to help you obtain the necessary documents and fill out the forms. You may also contact the Tribunal in your diocese for the necessary papers. The required paperwork may also be found on your diocesan website.

Generally, you will be required to submit the following information to the Tribunal:

1. Written summary of the courtship and marriage (autobiography)
2. Necessary documents: baptismal certificate (for Catholics only), marriage certificate, divorce decree
3. Filing fee
4. Completed marital history
5. Summary petition
6. Applicant's signature and initials on the agreement requesting the nullity of the former marriage

Variations in requirements may occur from one diocese/ archdiocese to another. Do not hesitate to ask for help from a priest or directly from any member of the Tribunal personnel. After the petitioner sends the application, a member of the Tribunal staff will be assigned to assist the petitioner until the case is finalized.

## Contacts with the Former Spouse

Tribunals do not require the spouses to have any contact with each other. However, Church law and basic human justice require the Tribunal to notify the former spouse and to give him/her an opportunity to present a history of the marriage and introduce witnesses. It must first be ascertained, however, if a given Tribunal has the authority to handle the case. Jurisdiction is determined by where the marriage took place or where the former spouse now lives. This is one of the reasons why it is mandatory to provide the Tribunal with a current address of the former spouse when the petition is filed.

If the petitioner cannot get the current address of the former spouse, then the address of a family member through whom the Tribunal may contact the spouse should be provided. Furthermore, if a current address is unattainable, proof of attempts to secure an address may be submitted instead. The Tribunal cannot process the petition unless a serious effort has been made to contact the former spouse.

The participation of the former spouse is usually helpful to the Tribunal in providing a different view of the marriage. It is possible that the former spouse may choose not to exercise the right to participate in the annulment process. However, if he/she chooses not to participate, it will not prevent the Tribunal from studying and processing the case.

## Duration of the Annulment Process

It is impossible to predict the length of this process because of a number of variable factors. No two cases are the same. In many dioceses, under ideal circumstances, a case takes about a year, but it can take two years or even longer. Even the "Briefer Process" does not apply in every case. The uniqueness and complexity of each case, the firm beliefs and active participation of both parties involved in the annulment process, proof process for the proposed grounds for nullity, the workload at the tribunal, staff, resources and other factors affect the time it takes to process the application. The problem, more often than not, is that people never get started with the process. This reminds me of what a friend once told me: "It is amazing to realize how long it takes to finish something you never started and followed through with to its completion!"

CAUTION: No plans for a future marriage in the Church should be made until the Tribunal communicates an affirmative decision. Not every annulment application is granted. Every application is studied and decided on by at least two tribunals: one from the diocese of application and then by the tribunal from another diocese.

## Choosing Witnesses during the Annulment Process

Marriage is never totally a private relationship. It has a profound effect on the family, society and the Church. Witnesses are required by Church law to aid the Tribunal in a deeper understanding of the parties involved, the marriage and the reasons for its failure. The person applying for an annulment must be aware of the need for knowledgeable witnesses who knew the couple prior to the wedding day and who can provide information that is crucial to the annulment process. Witnesses may be relatives, friends or acquaintances.

The witnesses will be asked to submit written statements, without any input whatsoever from the parties involved, directly to the Tribunal in support of the petitioner's application. Any evidence of or reason to suspect collusion will render a witness's statement inadmissible. The statements should be signed, dated, and mailed directly to the Tribunal. Most Tribunals require that each spouse choose two witnesses. As mentioned before, witnesses may be relatives, friends or acquaintances.

## Catholic Church's Strict Rationale for Granting Annulments

Once a man and a woman who have all the canonical requirements for marriage in the Catholic Church exchange their marriage vows in the presence of the Church's minister and two witnesses, then no one can annul that marriage. This is the truth of the matter. It should be noted that the truth is not the truth because the Catholic Church proclaims it. The truth is the truth––and the Catholic Church proclaims it. Likewise, the Catholic Church proclaims that marriage is sacred and a sacrament between a man and woman.

Therefore, those preparing for marriage must be educated and helped to fully understand before the wedding the significant responsibility involved. Catholics and the Tribunal have to obey Christ's teaching: No human being must separate what God has joined together (Matthew 19: 6). No wonder then that no annulment is granted before serious investigations are made to ensure that a marriage was canonically defective from the beginning (even if it had the appearance of being valid). Hence, the union is held indissoluble till the death of one or both of the spouses.

## *Difference between a Civil Divorce and an Annulment*

A divorce is a formal dissolution by a civil court of an existing union; an annulment declares that there never was a valid marriage despite appearances to the contrary. The Church does not consider the civil authorities capable of breaking a sacramental bond. In the eyes of the Church you are still considered married to your first spouse. If you are content to remain single for the rest of your life, there is no Church penalty for divorce, but if you ever wish to remarry, you must have the first union annulled in the eyes of the Church.

## *Addressing One's Internal Struggles Regarding an Annulment*

Some divorced Catholics have dilemmas about applying for an annulment and have shared their struggles and spiritual concerns. One of them asked: "How can my marriage be annulled given that I consciously made my marriage vows before God and I do not believe in annulment?" A Catholic may not believe in annulment but an annulment in the Church is not a matter of personal opinion or belief. An invalid marriage in the eyes of the Catholic Church is invalid and a valid marriage cannot be invalidated by anyone.

Therefore, any divorced Catholic who has concerns about an annulment should motivate himself/herself to start writing a summary of his/her marriage and the related details. Send that summary with the other needed paperwork and trust the decision of the Tribunal. The Tribunal is composed of experts who make a decision only after a thorough investigation of each case.

## *Annulments that Involve Domestic Violence and/or Other Addictions*

During the wedding vows, the celebrants of the marriage (husband and wife) promise to love one another, to love each other in sickness and in health, in poverty and in richness, all the days of their lives. Therefore it is important to document all the complications that became manifest during the course of marriage and present them to the experts in the Tribunal. They will determine whether there are sufficient grounds for the annulment of each given case. These complications include, but are not limited to, domestic violence, serious addictions, on-going marital infidelity and/or cases of serious mental illness. Likewise, Cantoir (1996, p. 23) noted: "Sometimes there is an element of fraud or psychological incapacity present. It's a matter of justice to help the party who was defrauded or deceived."

It is also important to clarify that Tribunal experts work in consultation with other professionals. In many cases doctors, psychiatrists, psychologists, professional counselors or clergy have been consulted before or during a marriage. The Tribunal asks the petitioner to provide the complete names, addresses and dates of consultations with a professional, along with a signed release form. These professionals may then, confidentially, supply the Tribunal with insight regarding the party(ies) and the marriage. All in all, it is "a matter of justice to help the party who was defrauded or deceived" (Cantoir, 1996, p. 23).

## Receiving the Eucharist after Divorce

Another observation that needs clarification is in regard to whether or not a Catholic can receive Eucharist if he/she is divorced and has not received an annulment. Divorced Catholics who have not remarried may receive Communion. However, because of the human condition, he/she is encouraged to receive the sacrament of Reconciliation before receiving Eucharist. Divorced Catholics who have remarried civilly without obtaining an annulment are not excommunicated from the Church and are welcome to attend Mass and participate in their parish activities. However, they cannot receive the Eucharist until the previous marriage is annulled and the current civil marriage is convalidated in the Church.

## Description of Convalidation

Whenever two heterosexual Catholics or a Catholic and a non-Catholic partner are married outside the Catholic Church, they have entered as a couple into a marriage that the Catholic Church considers invalid. Therefore, in order for a marriage to be considered valid and a sacrament in the Catholic Church, the contracted marriage or remarriage has to be convalidated. In other words, convalidation is the Catholic Church's procedure to validate a marriage contracted outside the Church into a marriage that is acknowledged by the Catholic Church of the Roman Rite (cf. Beal, Coriden & Green, 2000, Codes 1156 – 1165 for details).

The annulment process may bring some healing, but it is usually not enough for people to move on with their lives. Identify your pain and seek professional help if needed. Whether you decide to stay single for the rest of your life or to remarry, the choice is yours. What is important is to get "unstuck" by working through the ravages of divorce and other unresolved trauma and to develop better coping skills. Recalling the advice of a friend: "Start slowly, take the baby steps, do what you have to do, ask for help if needed, put one foot in front of the other and keep walking."

**Questions for Reflection and Action**

1. How and where do I start the process for getting remarried in the Catholic Church?

   _____

   _____

   _____

   _____

   _____

2. What is hindering me from applying for an annulment?

   _____

   _____

   _____

   _____

   _____

**My situation**

1. Do I need an annulment?

   _____

   _____

   _____

   _____

   _____

2. Have I gotten an annulment?

   _____

   _____

   _____

   _____

   _____

3. How do I start the annulment process?

   _____

   _____

   _____

   _____

   _____

4. Where can I obtain the requirements for filing an annulment in my (Arch)Diocese?

_____
_____
_____
_____
_____

5. When am I going to contact my pastor to walk me through the preliminary steps for processing my annulment?

_____
_____
_____
_____
_____

6. What is the current mailing address of my former spouse?

_____
_____
_____
_____
_____

7. Who are the two people that can serve as my witnesses regarding the events in my first marriage and divorce process?

_____
_____
_____
_____
_____

## Situation of my prospective spouse

1. If previously married, did he/she get married in the former marriage(s) a religious ceremony?

_____
_____
_____
_____
_____

2. Does he/ she need an annulment?

_____

_____

_____

_____

_____

3. Did he/she get an annulment?

_____

_____

_____

_____

_____

4. What am I going to do if he/she has decided not to apply for annulment?

_____

_____

_____

_____

_____

# Role 3.

## Remarriage Preparation in the Catholic Church

*Sacrament of Matrimony after an Annulment*
*Remarriage Preparation*
*Requirements for a Valid Remarriage in the Catholic Church*
*Impediments to Marriage and Remarriage in the Catholic Church*
*Questions for Reflection and Action*
*Keys for Those Contemplating Remarriage in the Catholic Church after Receiving an Annulment*

### Sacrament of Matrimony after an Annulment

A significant number of people who experience divorce, sooner or later, cohabit and/or remarry, then stay together or experience divorce again. Catholics are no exception. Since the 1960's there has been a significant increase in the number of cohabiting or civilly remarrying Catholics after divorce (Zwack, 1983). Some have processed their annulments, but many are staying away from attending Mass and receiving the sacraments. Based on these observations, this section is designed to offer encouragement to the engaged divorced and civilly remarried Catholics who have been granted annulments to come back to the Catholic Church and receive the necessary preparation for remarriage and the sacrament of Matrimony in the Catholic Church.

The Catholic Church has its own unique requirements and guidelines for remarriage. Some of those requirements are identified here in order to make them more accessible to whoever may benefit from them. Many Catholics want to receive God's blessing in their remarriage but they do not know the requirements for remarriage in the Catholic Church. Some have expressed their frustrations and lack of knowledge of the Church's rationale in regard to the various remarriage requirements in the Catholic Church. Others wonder why the Church requires a lot of paper work and attendance at premarriage preparation courses.

The Church asks the engaged couple to do so for their well-being and because the Church cares for her own. In other words, reinforced by the teachings of Vatican II, the Catholic Church is a "Mother" (cf. Lumen Gentium, paragraph 8) who makes specific requirements to engaged partners for their greater benefit, for the well-being of the significant people in their lives, and for the good of the Church and society. Some recommendations based on pastoral experiences are included that remarrying partners may need to know, do or not do in order to remarry validly in the Catholic Church and to embrace a stable and satisfactory remarriage.

Furthermore, this section does not replace the required remarriage preparation training offered by the Catholic Church in different parts of the world. One should consult one's respective parish or diocese for additional details or requirements. Consistent with the main objective of this book, this section is also designed to help people embrace stability and satisfaction in remarriage.

### Remarriage Preparation

First of all, receiving an annulment from the Marriage Tribunal is not an expression of readiness for remarriage. Second, even if you have never been married, getting married in the Catholic Church to someone who was previously married requires participation in the remarriage program offered by the Church. Therefore, engaged partners after being granted an annulment have to contact their respective parish priest or other assigned personnel in the parish (e.g., associate pastor, deacon, religious or laity). The initial contact with the parish to speak to the priest should be done one year in advance of the prospective wedding date.

The preparation in the Church begins with an initial interview in which the partners discuss whether they are free to marry and can complete the required documentation depending on the uniqueness of each case. After completing the initial interview, the priest or other designated personnel will determine if both partners are free to marry. If there are impediments to the partners' prospective marriage, the partners will be informed as well (see section below about impediments). Then, a formalized counseling process will begin, covering different areas, including the role faith plays in the sacrament of marriage and the unbreakable bond of this sacrament.

Additional preparation topics before the Church wedding include, but are not limited to, family of origin, money, step-parenting, the context of marriage today, communication, the meaning of permanence, responsible parenthood, the requirements of a sacramental marriage, the role of faith, prayer, expectations, responsibilities within marriage, meaning of wedding vows, gender and sexuality, the value of children, natural family planning, and spirituality.

## Requirements for a Valid Remarriage in the Catholic Church

The required paperwork for remarriage in the Catholic Church after divorce includes, but is not limited to:

1. Recent copy of the baptismal certificate (and possibly Confirmation)
2. Certified copy of the civil divorce decree
3. Prenuptial investigation form permissions or dispensations (if needed)
4. Affidavit of free status (if necessary)
5. Letter of annulment from the Tribunal indicating that the previous marriage has been annulled or a death certificate for the previous spouse
6. Copy of civil marriage license for previous marriage
7. Copy of Church marriage license for previous marriage

In addition to the required paperwork, the following Church laws must be observed:

1. The partners must be capable of being married (they must be a woman and a man who are free of any impediment that would prevent marriage)
2. The partners must give their individual consent to be married (by an act of the will each partner irrevocably gives and accepts the other in order to establish marriage; cf. Canon 1057)
3. The partners must follow the canonical form for marriage (they must be married according to the laws of the Church so that the Church and the wider community will be certain about the validity of their marriage)

The wedding must take place in a Catholic Church. If you have married someone of another faith in their place of worship, your marriage must be convalidated in the Catholic Church. You should also receive the sacrament of Penance prior to the sacrament of Matrimony.

## *Impediments to Marriage and Remarriage in the Catholic Church*

The following impediments apply to marriage and remarriage. It is important to take them into account before dating and to maximize the importance of starting on the right foot. Each partner must be capable of entering a valid marriage and free of any impediment or obstacle that would prevent marriage in the Catholic Church. These impediments to marriage include: age, impotence, previous marriage bond, lack of dispensation in cases that involve disparity of cult, sacred orders, public religious vows, abduction, a crime involving the murder of a spouse to pave the way for a new marriage, affinity, consanguinity, de facto relatives and adoption (Robinson,1984).

Elaborating on some of those impediments, the minimum age required by Church law for a valid marriage is sixteen years for a man and fourteen years for a woman. However, the Conference of Bishops can raise that age for a licit marriage celebration (Canon 1083). Likewise, both partners need to have the psychological maturity to contract marriage (Canon 1095). In regard to a previous marriage, Church law impedes marriage with anyone else if one or both is currently married.

Additionally, one should not marry someone who is already his or her relative (Canons 1091-1094). There is no dispensation for a marriage involving siblings. The same applies to marrying a parent or child of one's deceased partner or living partner after divorce. Church law also impedes marrying an adopted son/daughter or brother/sister. Anyone who is incapable of understanding what marriage is and the responsibilities that come with it (e.g., because of mental impairment) cannot enter marriage (Canon 1095). Furthermore, no one can be forced into marriage either directly or because of some "grave fear" (Canon 1103).

The above-mentioned requirements and impediments are the most common ones. Other requirements deal with special circumstances and administrative details. Additionally, each diocese has its own rules regarding marriage and remarriage. Each parish may also have specific policies regarding remarriage preparation and the wedding ceremony. Consequently, engaged and civilly remarried partners should check with the pastor or designed personne in the parish for additional details and clarifications. For baptized Catholics who have not received Confirmation and Eucharist they should plan to complete the sacraments of initiation. A confession is generally recommended before celebrating the sacrament of Matrimony.

**Questions for Reflection and Action**

1. How am I committed to receive preparation for remarriage?

   _____
   _____
   _____
   _____
   _____

2. Am I registered in any parish as a member of that parish?

   _____
   _____
   _____
   _____
   _____

3. In what Catholic parish does my prospective spouse and I want to be married and what are our reason for choosing it?

   _____
   _____
   _____
   _____
   _____

4. When are we going to contact the parish office to have an appointment with the Pastor or other designated person to walk us through the requirements for remarriage in that particular Church?

   _____
   _____
   _____
   _____
   _____

**My situation**

1. What are the various types of paper work that I need to present to the Catholic Church in order to remarry in Church?

   _____
   _____
   _____

_____
_____

## Situation of my prospective spouse

1. Is this going to be his/her first marriage?

_____
_____
_____
_____
_____

2. What is his/her religion?

_____
_____
_____
_____
_____

3. Does he/she want to get married in the Catholic Church?

_____
_____
_____
_____
_____

4. Has he/she received an annulment from any previous marriage?

_____
_____
_____
_____
_____

5. What are the various types of paper work that my prospective spouse needs to present to the Catholic Church in order to remarry in the Church?

_____
_____
_____
_____
_____

## Keys for those contemplating remarriage in the Catholic Church after receiving an annulment

- If you are seriously contemplating remarriage, you must take your time in choosing the person you want to remarry. If possible, choose another Catholic or someone who will allow you to practice your faith. Put God in the middle of your relationship. Whoever is contemplating remarriage in Catholic Church should start with one's self.
- Prepare stability and satisfaction in remarriage.
- After experiencing a divorce, lessons should be learned from that experience to avoid the risk of another divorce (cf. Adage: "Once bitten, twice shy.")
- If you have done your own work of healing, do not presume that the person you want to marry has also done his/her self-study. Prepare to get married to someone who has an integrated psychological maturity and is free to consent to the marriage vows. Enter into marriage with someone who has the ability to assume and maintain the responsibility of marriage. Marriage is for integrally independent people. You do not marry the other person to fill your needs. You have to be a happy single person to get married with another happy independent person so that you can become mutually interdependent.
- Marriage needs first to be consented to by each partner independently before it becomes a mutual agreement. Loving the idea of being married and/or being caught up in the ideals of marriage without taking the time to identify one's needs and to know one another can be very risky. Each partner must freely consent to the marriage without inner and external coercion, conditions, restrictions or reservations. Each partner should not be dragged into the remarriage, neither one should drag the other into it and/or both of them drag themselves into it. Said in metaphorical terms, without mutual consent, one or both partners may experience what looks like a dog wagged by its tail instead of the dog wagging its tail.
- When entering marriage and to stay remarried learn how to integrate spirituality, committed love, intimacy and passionate love. This reminds me of the advice I overheard my grandmother giving to one of my uncles just before he remarried: "Develop an on-going practice of sharing your innermost feelings and thoughts with your partner

to reinforce intimacy. Listen to her as well and share hugs with her frequently. Commitment without passion breeds sadness and resentment. Passion without commitment is lust. Intimacy without commitment is like telling your secrets to a stranger whom you do not expect to see again."

- After the wedding, you and your spouse are encouraged to participate in a remarriage encounter weekend at least once every five years. This will help to reinforce your remarriage in different areas (e.g., stepparenting, money, sex, in-laws and spirituality).

- If you are experiencing difficulties in your marriage, consider participating in the Retrouvaille program (a seminar for helping troubled marriages; www.retrouvaille.org/pages for more information).

- Remarried partners are encouraged to attend Church and participate in Mass to celebrate every marriage anniversary. Do not wait for the silver jubilee or golden jubilee. Remember to celebrate your wedding anniversary and renew your wedding vows every year. Married partners seem to be empowered as they celebrate their wedding anniversaries (e.g., by participating in Mass together, receiving the Eucharist and inviting a few loved ones to celebrate with them. As the adage says: "Whatever is not celebrated dies." Jesus came so that we may have life and have it more abundantly. So, celebrating Jesus' presence and receiving him in the Eucharist may bring more vitality into the sacrament of Matrimony between husband and wife with Christ in their midst.

- Review all the suggestions made by the research participants and consulted literature as mentioned in the various sections of this book and/or other resources. Seek advice, professional help and spiritual direction if needed and before it is too late.

# Part IV:

# Categories of Significant People for Custodial Parents

Community Healers
Category 1. The "Self" of the Custodial Parent
Category 2. Custodial (and Older) Children
Category 3. Relatives of the Custodial Parent
Category 4. Close Friends of the Custodial Parent
Category 5. Remarriage Partner or Remarriage Spouse
Category 6. Ex-Spouse (and Ex-In-Laws)
Category 7. Stepchildren of the Custodial Parent
Category 8. The Other Parent of One's Stepchildren
Category 9. Current or Prospective In-Laws
Category 10. Close Friends of Current or Prospective Spouse
Category 11. Coworkers and Employers
Category 12. Lawyers
Category 13. Lawmakers and Judges
Category 14. Politicians and Local Governmental Leaders
Category 15. Religious Leaders
Category 16. Mental Health Professionals
Roles and Challenges for All Community Healers

# Community Healers

*Identifying Community Healers*
*Rationale for Including Community Healers(CH)*
*Description of Each of the Categories and Key Questions for People in Each of*
*These Categories*

## Identifying Community Healers

The adage or common saying that "It takes a village to raise a child" can also be applied to stability and satisfaction in remarriage. Even if the parents do their best to raise their children in the best way possible, still other people are needed. These include, but are not limited to, grandparents, teachers, relatives, doctors, farmers, religious ministers, police personnel, employers of parents, and other indirect personnel, for example, the military who protect the citizens of a given country. In the same way, although the custodial parent and his/her remarriage partner do their best to make remarriage work, other people's contributions are also necessary. Therefore, as mentioned in the Preface, this book is also designed for the people who profoundly impact (in positive and/or negative ways) the integral life of each custodial parent in divorce and/or remarriage situations.

Because the emphasis should be from negative influences to positive influences, these people are referred to as community healers (CH). Consequently, Part IV of this book is designed to explore what the significant people in the lives of the custodial parent should do and not do in order to reinforce the stability and satisfaction in remarriage of the remarrying /remarried custodial parent. Throughout the book the abbreviation CH (community healers) is used for such significant people in the lives of custodial parents.

It is beyond the scope of this book to present a detailed discussion of the all the significant people and the roles they may play in regard to one's stability and satisfaction in remarriage. However, it is important to take into consideration the following selected categories in light of the feedback received from the research participants and the literature review. The reader is encouraged to think of other categories in addition to those presented and also to reflect on how a person or people and faith in God may be positive influences in regard to stability and satisfaction in remarriage.

In the Introduction to this book, the phrase remarriage triad was explained as the interconnections among divorce, recoupling and stepfamily realities (see Figure 1). Within the same triad, each member of the community of healers is represented in the middle of Figure 6.

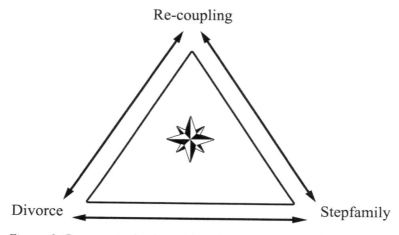

Figure 6. Community healers within the remarriage triad.

The icon within the remarriage triad represents the presence and roles of any member who, like a shining star, forms part of the community healers for the custodial parent. Examples of such healers may include a custodial parent's relative, friend, former spouse, religious minister or mental health professional. In order to qualify as a member of the community of healers, that member's role and interactions with the divorced custodial parents, who are contemplating remarriage, should be geared toward reinforcing the stability and satisfaction in remarriage of those partners, so that the children involved may also be happy within the stepfamily.

## Rationale for Including Community Healers (CH)

Another reason for including the CH is to empower them with research-based information because they are the ones who ought to offer the needed support (instead of destructive criticism and unnecessary burdens) to the custodial parent before and after remarriage. In other words, it seems that CH have a profound influence on the integral life of the custodial parent in remarriage situations. The influence may be in terms either of reducing the stress to the custodial parent by means of their multilayered support or by reinforcing tension, conflict, blame, guilt, other relational constraints and in the worst scenario contributing to the death of the custodial parent or child. No wonder Kelley and Burg (2000) highlighted: Do you know what chimpanzees do? They kill the offspring first!

Therefore, Part IV of book is designed to help significant others to continue or start working toward becoming members of the community of healers for the custodial parent. Everyone can have a profound positive influence on the multilayered healing and growth process that every custodial parent needs instead of making his or her life more burdensome. Custodial parents need support, not attacks or indifference from the significant people in their lives. Another rationale for making the CH a special audience for this researchbased book is because the advice a custodial parent may get from one (some or all) of them may be helpful, but it may also be biased, opinionated or dangerous if followed blindly. In some cases, it seems that one or more of the CH themselves may be in need of professional help to address the personal emotions and challenges related to the custodial parent's remarriage plans or remarriage status.

Elaborating on the importance of empowering the CH is to help them understand better the complex dynamics within each remarriage. Accordingly, Covey's (1989, p. 238) general recommendation may be applied to the CH to become more effective: "Unless you understand me and my unique situation and feelings, you won't know how to advise me or counsel me. What you say is good and fine, but it does not pertain to me". Likewise, this quotation may be implemented by the CH as a means of making a radical paradigm shift with regard to seeking to understand the custodial parent's problems and complex dynamics before making any intervention.

Furthermore, because of the stigma still attached to divorce and remarriage in some of the organized religions (Ahrons, 2004; Himes & Coriden, 1996), it is hoped that the results of this research-based book may inspire more religious leaders to extend pastoral care to custodial parents who find it hard, after divorce, to be accepted and full communion in their religions (Shelmon, 1992). Based on such results and understanding, religious pastors may become more effective while ministering to custodial parents preparing for remarriage after divorce and/or to currently remarried parents.

Some examples of community healers that may influence a custodial parent preparing for stability and satisfaction in remarriage include:

1. The "Self" of the custodial parent
2. Custodial (and older) children
3. Relatives of the custodial parent
4. Close friends of the custodial parent

5. Remarriage partner or remarriage spouse
6. Ex-spouse (and ex-in-laws)
7. Stepchildren of the custodial parent
8. Other parent of one's stepchildren
9. Current or prospective in-laws
10. Close friends of current or prospective spouse
11. Coworkers and employers
12. Lawyers
13. Lawmakers and judges
14. Politicians and local government leaders
15. Religious ministers
16. Mental health professionals

## Description of Each of the Categories

and Key Questions for People in Each of These Categories
Some of the categories are easy to understand, so more time will be dedicated to mentioning the experiences and suggestions of the participants for those specific categories of people. Questions for reflection and action have also been added to help the community healers to take the necessary time to answer them and take action that will empower the stability and satisfaction in remarriage of the custodial parents who remarry after divorce.

All the people in the categories mentioned and others who want to support custodial parents to establish and maintain stability and satisfaction in remarriage are encouraged to read the entire book. The experiences of the participants are highly informative, formative and transformative. Additionally, every significant person in the lives of custodial parents in remarriage situations needs to make an honest evaluation of his/her feelings about divorce, remarriage and stepfamilies.

The community healer cannot effectively help a stepfamily in crisis if he or she holds negative attitudes or stereotypes toward them. Community healers may need to first educate themselves about specific issues in stepfamilies in order to be of any help (Ferch, 2001; Framo, 1985). They need to consider the people within the remarriage triad as people and not as pathological specimens (Nichols, 1996). In other words, CH may have to assess their own attitudes and beliefs about the remarriage of divorced parents and should obtain the necessary training they need so that they can better understand, empathize, and offer help to the diversity of people in remarriage situations (Ferch, 1999; Fincham, Beach & Davila, 2004).

More often than not, custodial parents tend to seek support from one or more of the significant people in their lives before seeking professional help. Sometimes, the person whose advice is sought feels incompetent, but goes ahead and gives personal opinions instead of admitting one's incompetency. Irrespective of one's good intentions, in situations where one feels incompetent, it is recommended that the relative or close friend advise their loved one to seek help from a competent professional. Bad advice is worse than no advice. On the other hand, some people make life as difficult as they can for the custodial parent. Consequently, their actions end up being a negative influence to the stability and satisfaction in remarriage of the custodial parent and life in general.

Therefore, based on the above observations, it is recommended that those CH in categories 2 – 16 discern better when, how and in what area each can help or advise a custodial parent in a divorce/remarriage situation by carefully reflecting on the questions specific to them.

# Category 1.

## The "Self" of the Custodial Parent

In this book, the "self" of the custodial parent is described as his/her self-awareness. It is reflexive quality of taking himself/herself as the object of his/her own perception, attention and and/or being (Brown,1998). For example, the custodial parent may refer to his/her "self" by using a phrase like: I see myself as ….or I think of myself as ….. Consequently, a positive self-perception of the custodial parent is manifested in his/her conscious center of psychic life which enables him/her to grow and develop by overcoming egocentrism as he/she cares for oneself and others (Kennedy, 1995). Therefore, each custodial parent contemplating remarriage or already remarried to become more aware of the role played by his/her "self" before focusing on the other selected categories. The people in the other categories too need to respect the well-informed, formed and transformed "self" of the custodial parent.

A common adage is: "We are our own worst enemies." This may lead to false self-fulfilling prophecy, low self-esteem, depression, self-blame, negative self-perception and a failure in life. All these variables are likely to have a negative impact on the self of the custodial parent and thus on his/her stability and satisfaction in remarriage. Therefore, rather than being one's worst enemy, be your best friend by developing your "self." It is also important to explore how one's self has been impacted by the custodial parent's divorce, single-parenthood phase, remarriage, integrity and other variables.

"Know thyself" is an ancient maxim but not all people pay attention to it. Therefore, for any custodial parent, before other people in the community contribute to your healing, "study and investigate yourself until you arrive at knowing yourself! This knowledge … would suffice to reform the world" (O'Connell, 1958, p. 17).

As an individual, it is important to have faith in God. There are some things that one can change about oneself. This awareness of self helps when reflecting on the phrases the following serenity prayer (formulated by Reinhold Niebuhr) and committing to seek ways of putting it into practice:

God grant me the serenity
to accept the things I cannot change;
courage to change the things I can;
and wisdom to know the difference.
Living one day at a time;
Enjoying one moment at a time;
Accepting hardships as the pathway to peace;
Taking, as He did, this sinful world
as it is, not as I would have it;
Trusting that He will make all things right
if I surrender to His Will;
That I may be reasonably happy in this life
and supremely happy with Him
Forever in the next.
Amen.

## Questions for Reflection and Action

1. What type of messages do I tell my "self".

   _____

   _____

   _____

   _____

   _____

2. What do I think about myself?

   _____

   _____

   _____

   _____

   _____

3. Who am I? (Socrates: "To thy own self be true.")

   _____

   _____

   _____

   _____

   _____

4. What do I think other people think about me?

    _____

    _____

    _____

    _____

    _____

5. What does God's think about me?

    _____

    _____

    _____

    _____

    _____

6. What do I need to do with the rest of my life?

    _____

    _____

    _____

    _____

    _____

7. What makes me to believe that the message(s) I keep telling myself is (are) true? Where is the evidence?

    _____

    _____

    _____

    _____

    _____

8. What are my needs?

    _____

    _____

    _____

    _____

    _____

9.  Who/what do I want to be for the rest of my life on earth?

_____

_____

_____

_____

_____

# Category 2.

## Custodial (and Older) Children

Every child who has reached the age of reason can contribute to the stability and remarriage of his/custodial parent.

**Questions for Reflection and Action**

1.  What is my reaction on seeing my custodial parent dating another man /woman?

    _____
    _____
    _____
    _____
    _____

2.  What is my reaction on hearing about remarriage plans of my custodial parent?

    _____
    _____
    _____
    _____
    _____

3.  In what ways can I as a custodial child facilitate in the establishment and maintenance of a stable and satisfactory remarriage of my mother and/or father?

    _____
    _____
    _____
    _____
    _____

4.  What do I have to do and not do in order to help my mother/
    father establish and maintain a stable and happy remarriage with
    my stepparent?

    _____

    _____

    _____

    _____

    _____

# Category 3.

## Relatives of the Custodial Parent

Parents, siblings, and extended family members may be supportive of the custodial parent's divorce and/or remarriage, whereas others may be against it. Family loyalties are challenged.

If you have doubts about the prospective remarriage partner of your relative or have major concerns about him/her, find constructive ways of expressing your observations without being sarcastic.

### Questions for Reflection and Action

1. Am I aware of being a significant person in the life of the custodial parent contemplating remarriage or already remarried?

   _____

   _____

   _____

   _____

   _____

2. If so, in what way(s) am I significant in his/her life?

   _____

   _____

   _____

   _____

   _____

3. What are my beliefs about remarriage after divorce and how do they influence my attitude toward remarrying people?

   _____

   _____

   _____

   _____

   _____

4. On hearing about an upcoming remarriage of a relative who experienced a divorce and has custody of his/her children, what would be my response and attitude after being informed about his/her the upcoming remarriage?

_____
_____
_____
_____
_____

5. What kind of mechanisms is the custodial parent using to cope with divorce that I consider dangerous to self and/or others (e.g., excessive drinking, working too much, using drugs, becoming promiscuous, taking on additional loans or excessive spending).

_____
_____
_____
_____
_____

6. What do I think is motivating the custodial parent to remarry now or in the near future?

_____
_____
_____
_____
_____

7. Would I advise him/her to stay single even if he/she has decided remarry?

_____
_____
_____
_____
_____

8. What are the reasons for my advice?

_____
_____
_____

_____

_____

9. What are the factors that I think influence stability and satisfaction in remarriage?

_____

_____

_____

_____

_____

10. How can I help a custodial parent to establish a stable and satisfactory remarriage?

_____

_____

_____

_____

_____

11. Whom do I turn to for support /guidance by virtue of being one of the CH?

_____

_____

_____

_____

_____

# Category 4.

## Close Friends of the Custodial Parent

Evaluate the advice you give to your friend (the custodial parent) in a divorce situation. Whether you have also experienced a divorce or not, sometimes you do a better job by listening than giving your opinions. It may be hard to keep the friendship with both partners who were friends with you when they were still a couple, but do not abandon them after their divorce. Avoid getting pulled into conflict or taking sides but be objective.

### Questions for Reflection and Action

Based on the descriptions, experiences and recommendations by the participants in the study:

1. Who of the participants has impacted me the most and why?

_____

_____

_____

_____

_____

2. What is my current attitude about divorce and remarriage after reading about the self-disclosures of the participants in this book?

_____

_____

_____

_____

_____

3. What have I learned from the descriptions of each participant that I should take into account when interacting with my close friends whose first marriage has ended in divorce?

_____
_____
_____
_____
_____

4. What are the factors that I think influence stability and satisfaction in remarriage?

_____
_____
_____
_____
_____

5. What are the main ideas I have learned from this book, that I can share with a close friend who is also a custodial parent and is contemplating remarriage after divorce?

_____
_____
_____
_____
_____

6. Who of the participants mentioned in this book seems to have almost similar experiences and insights like the custodial parents I know and care about?

_____
_____
_____
_____
_____

# Category 5.

## Remarriage Partner or Remarriage Spouse

It is important for the partner of a custodial parent to know the impact and dynamics between stepparents and stepchildren. As prospective stepparents, such partners need to understand that the relationships between stepparents and children are more likely to be conflictive than those of nuclear families. This is partly because some new stepparents jump right into attempting to establish close relationships with their stepchildren without considering first the children's emotional status and gender. For instance, boys and girls in stepfamilies prefer verbal affection, such as praise or compliments, rather than physical closeness, such as hugs and kisses from their stepparents. In particular, girls in stepfamilies reported that they were uncomfortable with the physical expressions of affection from their stepfathers. According to a study by James and Johnson (2001) most boys were reported as being more readily accepting of their stepfathers than girls.

### Questions for Reflection and Action

1. Based on the experiences of the participants described in this book, what are the main ideas that that I have learned that I intend to incorporate in my marriage with a custodial parent?

   _____

   _____

   _____

   _____

   _____

2. Am I also a custodial parent?

   _____

   _____

   _____

   _____

   _____

3. If yes, how am I preparing my child(ren) to share the same roof with the child(ren) of my partner?

_____
_____
_____
_____
_____

4. What concrete strategies am I taking regarding committed love, maturity, stepparenting, finances, spirituality and other factors that have been identified in this book as contributing factors to stability and satisfaction in remarriage?

_____
_____
_____
_____
_____

5. What do I need to do to prepare myself to embrace marriage with a custodial parent who has children from the previous marriage?

_____
_____
_____
_____
_____

6. Based on the knowledge I have about my relatives and close friends, whom do I have to establish clear boundaries with to prevent/stop him/her from having a negative impact on my prospective/current marriage with my partner who is a custodial parent?

_____
_____
_____
_____

# Category 6.

## Ex-Spouse (and Ex-In-Laws)

Accept the fact that the marriage has ended, but the children involved continue to make you family members. Hard as divorce may be, a lot of pain is reduced when both parties practice civility toward one another. On-going battles with the ex-spouse hurt everybody and are damaging to many people. In the event the ex-partner or ex-in-law has found someone to remarry, do not make it difficult for them either to remarry or to maintain a stable and satisfactory remarriage.

**Questions for Reflection and Action**

Based on the fact that my ex-spouse and I are divorced:

1. How can I positively support him/her in raising our child(ren)?

   _____
   _____
   _____
   _____
   _____

2. What strategies am I going to take to prevent myself from being a negative influence in the life of my exspouse?

   _____
   _____
   _____
   _____
   _____

3. How am I resolved to handle the jealous feelings that I may experience if my ex-spouse decides to remarry?

_____
_____
_____
_____
_____

4. What concrete strategies am I going to take to support my ex-spouse to establish and maintain a stable and satisfactory remarriage with another partner?

_____
_____
_____
_____
_____

5. What am I struggling with that does not let me leave my ex-spouse in peace and/or to remarry another person?

_____
_____
_____
_____
_____

6. What am I doing to support my ex-spouse to raise our child(ren) in the presence of his/her remarriage partner?

_____
_____
_____
_____
_____

7. In addition to avoiding bad-mouthing my ex-spouse, especially in front of our child(ren), what else should I avoid/stop doing in order to honor and respect the dignity of my ex-spouse?

_____
_____
_____
_____
_____

8. How am I going to communicate my disagreements to my ex-spouse if I am not satisfied with the way he/she is raising our child(ren) in his/her remarriage?

_____

_____

_____

_____

_____

# Category 7.

## Stepchildren of the Custodial Parent

The child(ren) of the remarriage partner also have a significant impact on the stability and satisfaction in remarriage of the custodial parent. The other parent of that child or those children also has a profound impact on the remarriage

**Questions for Reflection and Action**

1. What are my feelings about my custodial parent planning to remarry with another custodial parent?

   _____
   _____
   _____
   _____
   _____

2. What kind of support does my custodial parent need that I can provide to facilitate his/her establishment of a stable and satisfactory remarriage?

   _____
   _____
   _____
   _____
   _____

3. How can I help these custodial parents to prevent the risk of experiencing another divorce?

   _____
   _____
   _____
   _____
   _____

4.  What are my feelings about attending the wedding of my custodial parent with another woman/man?

    _____
    _____
    _____
    _____
    _____

5.  How can I show loyalty to both divorced parents and also embrace the new partner of my father/mother as a stepparent?

    _____
    _____
    _____
    _____
    _____

6.  Even if I have accepted that my parents will never get back together as a couple, what do I need to do to feel comfortable when I see each them dating another man/woman?

    _____
    _____
    _____
    _____
    _____

7.  How can I voice my feelings and thoughts to my father/mother that if he/she chooses to remarry another person, he/she has my support?

    _____
    _____
    _____
    _____
    _____

8.  What will help me overcome the feelings of jealousy for sharing my father/mother with the children of his/her remarriage partner?

    _____
    _____
    _____
    _____

9. How am I going to address directly my stepparent: by his/her first name or _____ ?

_____

_____

_____

_____

_____

10. If my custodial parent is not at home, am I resolved to take to heart any advice and/or disciplinary action from my stepparent?

_____

_____

_____

_____

_____

11. How can I prevent/stop my father/mother with whom I have visitation times from badmouthing my step-parent without being disloyal to him/her?

_____

_____

_____

_____

_____

12. Based on personal experience, what recommendations do I have for a custodial parent planning to remarry with another partner who also has custodial children?

_____

_____

_____

_____

_____

# Category 8.

## The Other Parent of One's Stepchildren

It may sound ironic for an ex-spouse to be asked to support remarriage of his/her ex-partner with another custodial parent, but that support is extremely necessary toward the stability and satisfaction in remarriage of custodial parents. The support may be done in many forms. For instance, accepting that that he/she will not get back with her/his ex-spouse allows the ex-spouse to make his/her remarriage plans without interference. In other words, by virtue of the partner having a child(ren), his/her ex-spouse has a role to play in the growth of those children and that father or mother may have a positive or negative impact on the stability and satisfaction of the remarrying or remarried parents. That other parent needs to have sufficient maturity, compassion and integrity to avoid disrupting the remarriage of his/her ex-spouse.

**Questions for Reflection and Action**

Based on the fact that I have children with my ex-spouse who is getting remarried with another custodial parent:

1. Am I aware of being a significant person in the life of the custodial parent contemplating remarriage or already remarried with my ex-spouse?

   _____
   _____
   _____
   _____
   _____

2. If so, in what way(s) am I significant in his or her life?

   _____
   _____
   _____
   _____
   _____

3. What lessons have I learned from the experiences of the participants and the interactions they had with their exspouses?

_____
_____
_____
_____
_____

4. What strategies do I need to avoid/stop badmouthing my ex-spouse and his/her remarriage partner, especially in front of our children?

_____
_____
_____
_____
_____

5. How can I support the woman/man who is currently the step-parent of my children after her/his marriage with my ex-spouse?

_____
_____
_____
_____
_____

6. What can I do to empower my children to become more respectful of their stepparent who has replaced me as the spouse of their mother/father?

_____
_____
_____
_____
_____

# Category 9.

## Current or Prospective In-Laws

A custodial parent may enter a remarriage with a person having the same or a different cultural background, economic status, education, career, age, geographical area, religion and other variables. Even if the two partners love one another, such a remarriage brings with it other sets of in-laws of the new partner. Some or all of his /her family members may be supportive of the marriage, whereas others may be indifferent or completely opposed to it.

As a relative of the prospective or current remarriage partner, one needs to be supportive of the remarriage for its stability and satisfaction. If there are legitimate concerns about the person marrying your relative, you should express these concerns in a civil and constructive manner.

**Questions for Reflection and Action**

Based on the fact that my relative is planning to enter into marriage with a partner who has children from a prior marriage that ended in divorce:

1.  What are my concerns about their prospective marriage?

    _____
    _____
    _____
    _____
    _____

2.  How can I express my concerns without attacking the person involved and thereby safeguard his/her dignity?

    _____
    _____
    _____
    _____
    _____

3.  In what concrete ways can I help the partners to establish a stable and satisfactory remarriage?

    _____

    _____

    _____

    _____

    _____

4.  What have learned from the participants' experiences that I can use in helping the partners remarry and count on my support?

    _____

    _____

    _____

    _____

    _____

# Category 10.

## Close Friends of Current or Prospective Spouse

Some people confide in their close friends more so than in their relatives. Consequently, the close friends of the partner planning to get married with a custodial parent may be consulted for advice and he/she should not limit his/her response to personal opinions because his/her friend may take them at surface value.

As a close friend of the current or prospective spouse, you can share informed advice and give support to him/her in establishing a stable and satisfactory (re)marriage with a custodial parent.

### Questions for Reflection and Action

1. What have l learned from the experiences of the participants in the study on which this book is based?

   _____

   _____

   _____

   _____

   _____

2. What do I know about my friend that may hinder him/her from establishing a stable and satisfactory (re)marriage?

   _____

   _____

   _____

   _____

   _____

3.  How can I best advise my friend on what he/she has to do before committing him/herself to a (re)marriage with a custodial parent?

    _____
    _____
    _____
    _____
    _____

# Category 11.

## Coworkers and Employers

Many people spend a great amount of time interacting with their coworkers and /or employers. During coffee breaks and lunchtime, some of them share personal conversations, for instance: talks about one's divorce, children, exspouse, new fiancé, new fiancée, alimony, vacations and other topics. At the same time, lot of advice is given by one's coworkers and/or employer. However, some of that advice is based on personal opinions and some people are often willing to give unsolicited suggestions that may have a negative influence on the recipient and his/her significant others.

Therefore, coworkers and employers of custodial parents are also invited to read this book and reflect on the following questions in order to provide profound insights that may help your custodial parents to establish stable and satisfactory remarriages.

**Questions for Reflection and Action**

1. What have I learned from the experiences of the participants in the study on which this book is based?

_____

_____

_____

_____

_____

_____

_____

_____

2. What questions should I ask a custodial parent contemplating remarriage that may stimulate his/her thinking in order to establish a stable and satisfactory remarriage?

_____

_____

_____

_____

_____

_____

_____

_____

_____

_____

# Category 12.

## Lawyers

Lawyers should review the laws periodically and evaluate the impact of divorce and the different kinds of custody (e.g., sole and joint) as the children grow.

Five participants in the study felt undermined by the legal system during their divorce process as they experienced the greed for money from their lawyers. Unfortunately, the judges involved also kept prolonging the cases and made them feel helpless. One of the participants mentioned:

> "It is understandable that making money is important, but over-focusing on the money to collect from one's clients leaves many people hurt in the process, including the children." Another participant suggested that lawyers should ask themselves: "What is in the best interest of the people involved in the case at hand? Dragging cases, intensifying the fighting between the divorcing parties and innocent children suffer in the process, while the lawyers are benefitting from the money that would have helped the children."

Two other participants suggested that lawyers should advise the divorcing partners to settle their financial battles and be civil to one another. One participant mentioned that the people involved in the divorce should use their consciences and common sense rather than leaving the lawyers to decide for them. Minor cases become bigger and prolonged for clients who put more trust in their lawyers in comparison to the partners who settle their disputes in mutual respect.

Fausto reminded and cautioned the lawyers who work with either party in the divorce proceedings as follows:

> Lawyers, you are in the profession that not only helps people not only to win cases but also to care for them by advocating for justice that leads to peace. Therefore, [lawyers] do not engage in endless negotiations. Advise your client to settle quickly

his/her differences with the other partner by being fair, civil, and sensible to his/her soon to be ex-spouse. Encourage your client to pay child support and alimony as agreed upon. Inform him/her that not doing so hurts the children and brings-up endless disputes with the ex-spouse. If the same client and his/her ex-partner are continually showing up with custody issues or payment default , find ways of contacting the other party's lawyers to advise your clients with the same message of responsibility, being civil, accountable and peaceable. In this way, lawyers will regain their reputation and they will be promoters of lasting justice, peace and contribute to healing within the community.

## Questions for Reflection and Action

Based on the experiences of the participants in this study:

1. What have I learned the most about stability and satisfaction in remarriage?

   _____

   _____

   _____

   _____

   _____

2. What have I learned about my client that makes me think that he/she may benefit from professional mental health services, counseling or therapy?

   _____

   _____

   _____

   _____

   _____

Regarding the divorce of spouses with young children:

3. What would be my response and attitude after being informed about the upcoming divorce of my loved ones who have children that are under eighteen years of age

   _____

   _____

_____
_____
_____

4. Would I advise one of them, or both, to stay together for the sake of the children or to divorce?

_____
_____
_____
_____
_____

5. What are the reasons for my advice?

_____
_____
_____
_____
_____

6. When in my interactions with the custodial parent (and other parties involved in the case) do I decide to recommend to him/ her that he/ she seek professional counseling before remarriage?

_____
_____
_____
_____

# Category 13.

## Lawmakers and Judges

Five participants emphasized during the post-interview sessions the need for lawmakers to design laws that help judges to establish shorter time limits on divorce cases. Such laws will also motivate the parties involved to make up their minds and settle their disputes. Likewise, lawyers will also be encouraged to work on the cases more quickly, save the parties from unnecessary charges due to proceedings that are dragged on.

The participants indicated that lawmakers, judges and lawyers need to understand that endless divorce negotiations and child-custody arrangements only create hostility and frustration on both sides, financial drain, and tension for the children involved. If divorce is inevitable, then the judge should set a time limit for the parties to just get it done. The judge must make sure that the child support amounts, as well as the visitation rights, are fair.

### Questions for Reflection and Action

1. What new laws need to be enacted that will help a custodial parent continue to receive alimony if one establishes a stable and satisfactory remarriage with a partner of minimal financial resources?

 

2. How do I think I can best use my position as a lawmaker, judge or lawyer to support the establishment and maintenance of stability and satisfaction in remarriage for the people involved?

3. Based on personal experience from interacting or working with cases of the people experiencing divorce, financial proceedings, custody battles, remarriage problems and/or divorce after remarriage, what do I think professionals in my field need to do to help people contemplating remarriage?

_____
_____
_____
_____
_____

4. What are some of the mistakes that I have witnessed committed by people in divorce, remarriage and stepfamily situations which I can reference in formulating laws or enforcing laws geared at correcting those mistakes?

_____
_____
_____
_____
_____

5. How can I use my professional position to become a ministry to caring for people in remarriage situations in addition to a job that generation income for me?

_____
_____
_____
_____
_____

# Category 14.

## Politicians and Local Government Leaders

Based on the feedback of the participants in the study on which this book is based, it was suggested that there is an urgent need for permanent buildings where people can go to receive premarital training and post-marital support or on-going marital training. However, the costs of constructing such permanent buildings and maintenance is very expensive. Therefore, politicians and local government leaders are urged to work with Church leaders and mental health professional to help them financially with building costs and designate the facilities as tax-exempt. Politicians need to be motivated and to understand that such facilities will aid their constituents in establishing stable and satisfactory (re)marriages, nuclear families and stepfamilies, a benefit for the entire community.

**Questions for Reflection and Action**

1.  What have I learned from the experiences of the participants in the study on which this book is based?

    _____
    _____
    _____
    _____
    _____

2.  Given the increasing number of first marriages ending in divorce and many more remarriages, what policies can I put into place to support custodial parents establish and maintain stable and satisfactory remarriages.

    _____
    _____
    _____
    _____
    _____

3.  How has my reading about the factors that influence stability and satisfaction in remarriage awakened in me a commitment to establish policies that support the institution of marriage and family life?

    _____
    _____
    _____
    _____
    _____

4.  What have I learned from the participants' gender and cultural differences that will affect my policy decisions?

    _____
    _____
    _____
    _____
    _____

# Category 15.

## Religious Ministers

Seven participants experienced judgmental attitudes from their religious leaders as they turned to them for emotional support and spiritual guidance during the divorce process. One of them exclaimed:

> I wish my pastoral leaders would stop being judgmental and understand the sufferings and abuses I have suffered in my first marriage. Even if I consciously said 'I do' on my wedding day, I did not understand fully what I was getting into.

Over the years into the marriage, some spouses change for the best, others for the worst. Some start excessive drinking, gambling, get involved in extramarital affairs and/or become physically abusive. Additionally, five Catholic participants in the study made the following suggestions for their Catholic religious ministers:

1. They should allow parents contemplating remarriage to participate in remarriage workshops that are organized and funded by the Catholic Church. In other words, pre-remarriage preparation should be open to all people, including divorced Catholics who have not received annulments of their prior marriages

   _____

   _____

   _____

   _____

   _____

2. They should be more compassionate and less judgmental about divorced and remarried persons

   _____

   _____

   _____

_____

_____

3. They should have a positive pastoral attitude toward divorced persons with and without annulments, remarried couples in a civil court, and the divorced who are cohabitating

_____

_____

_____

_____

_____

4. The hierarchy within the Roman Catholic Church needs to seriously reflect and take action with nonjudgmental pastoral care to the increasing numbers of divorced, cohabiting and remarried Catholics

_____

_____

_____

_____

_____

## Questions for Reflection and Action

1. Where are my opinions and biases about remarriage after divorce?

_____

_____

_____

_____

_____

2. What are the risks of having a lack of knowledge about the differences between first marriages and the remarriage?

_____

_____

_____

_____

_____

3. What are the major differences between a first marriages and the marriage of custodial parents who remarry after divorce?

_____

_____

_____

_____

_____

4. How can I best use my position as a religious minister to help custodial parents establish and maintain stability and satisfaction in remarriage?

_____

_____

_____

_____

_____

# Category 16.

## Mental Health Professionals

These include, but not limited to marriage and family counselors, psychologists, psychiatrists and social workers.

### Questions for Reflection and Action

Based on my professional training about remarriage after divorce and knowledge of a custodial parent planning to remarry:

1. What kind of mechanisms is this specific custodial parent using to cope with divorce that I consider dangerous to self and/or others (e.g., excessive drinking, workaholic, using drugs, becoming promiscuous, taking on additional loans or excessive spending)?

   _____
   _____
   _____
   _____
   _____

2. What do I think he/she must work on before remarriage?

   _____
   _____
   _____
   _____
   _____

3. How am I going to communicate my thoughts to him/her in the best way that I can for his/her benefit and/or that of other people who will be impacted by his/her remarriage?

   _____
   _____
   _____

_____

_____

_____

4. In what way(s) do I perceive this custodial parent to be stuck in nonproductive behaviors?

_____

_____

_____

_____

_____

5. How can I help the custodial parent caught up in unproductive emotions, actions, behaviors and unfinished business from his/her family of origin or first marriage?

_____

_____

_____

_____

_____

6. What are my nonbiased opinions about the custodial parent's prospective spouse?

_____

_____

_____

_____

_____

7. What kind of support does the custodial parent need that I can provide to facilitate his/her establishment of a stable and satisfactory remarriage?

_____

_____

_____

_____

_____

8. What do I think is motivating the custodial parent to remarry now or in the near future?

_____

_____

_____

_____

_____

9. How can I help the custodial parent prevent the risk of another divorce based on my knowledge of his/her unrealistic motivations and expectations for remarriage?

_____

_____

_____

_____

_____

Based on the results of this study:

10. How have my views about custodial parents changed?

_____

_____

_____

_____

_____

11. How has the description of the results in this study helped me to understand that custodial parents may need professional help in order to establish and maintain stable and satisfactory remarriages?

_____

_____

_____

_____

_____

Based on the cultural and ethnic backgrounds of the participants:

12. Which cultural differences manifested in this study have helped me to think deeply about the impact of the cultural backgrounds of the custodial parents in remarriage situations?

_____

_____

_____

_____

_____

13. What lessons have I learned from each participant's cultural background in this study?

_____

_____

_____

_____

_____

Based on the gender of the participants:

14. Which gender differences manifested in this study have helped me to think deeply about the impact of gender differences in regard to custodial parenthood?

_____

_____

_____

_____

_____

15. What lessons have I learned from the results of each female participant in this study?

_____

_____

_____

_____

_____

16. What lessons have I learned from the results of each male participant in this study?

_____

_____

_____

_____

_____

17. Based on the experiences of the participants in this study, what do I think a custodial parent should focus on as he/she prepares for remarriage?

_____

_____

_____

_____

_____

18. What new ideas have I learned from each of the participants that I had not thought about?

_____

_____

_____

_____

_____

19. Whom do I turn to for support and/or guidance as I offer professional services to custodial parents in remarriage situation?

_____

_____

_____

_____

_____

20. What is my theoretical orientation while working with custodial parents contemplating remarriage after divorce?

_____

_____

_____

_____

_____

21. In what ways would my theoretical orientation differ if the custodial parent is contemplating remarriage after widowhood instead of divorce?

_____
_____
_____
_____
_____

22. Based on my experience of helping custodial parents, what factors do I consider need to be added to the developed theory in order to reinforce stability and satisfaction in remarriage?

_____
_____
_____
_____
_____

23. What is my attitude about custodial parents who have experienced a divorce or multiple divorces and are currently planning to enter remarriage?

_____
_____
_____
_____
_____

24. What kind of help do I need myself to better serve custodial parents in remarriage situations?

_____
_____
_____
_____
_____

25. Which books, DVDs and/or CDs would I recommend to somebody experiencing any of the following stages in his or her life:
    o   Preparation for first marriage
    o   First marriage enrichment
    o   Parenting in first marriage

- o Complicated or ambiguous (seemingly amicable) divorce Process
- o Healing from divorce
- o Life after divorce
- o Single-parenthood
- o Preparation for remarriage
- o Remarriage after divorce
- o Stepparenting
- o Remarriage reinforcement

26. What are the main ideas that have impacted me in each of the books, DVDs and/or CDs that I have identified in question 25?

_____

_____

_____

_____

_____

27. Which of the ideas in each the books, DVDs and/or CDs have I found least helpful and why?

_____

_____

_____

_____

_____

28. How do I handle my emotions, opinions and beliefs to maintain a professional attitude as I work with divorcing spouses nearing retirement?

_____

_____

_____

_____

_____

29. How do I handle my emotions, opinions and beliefs to maintain a professional attitude as I work with divorcing retired and/or elderly spouses?

_____

_____

_____

_____

_____

———————— ⬦ ————————

30. How do I handle my emotions, opinions and beliefs to maintain a professional attitude as I work with an individual in his/her fifties considering remarriage with a partner in her/his thirties?

_____

_____

_____

_____

## Keys for mental health professionals

- It is important for all mental health professionals to remember that counseling people for remarriage is different from counseling for a first marriage. Hence, a need for a paradigm shift . Each remarriage situation is unique. For instance, each divorced parent has his or her unique way of mourning divorce, sometimes even involving delayed grief. Likewise, divorced parents who rush into the second marriage before mourning the previous marriage handle their unresolved grief differently. The same is true for the children of divorced parents and their respective stepsiblings (Baum, 2003; Sager et al., 1983).
- Professionals should be nonjudgmental, able to maintain confidentiality, and ask for affordable prices for their services from the people who need help. Very high costs hinder some people from seeking the professional help they need. Assess their needs: physical, sexual, financial, step-parenting, and other important topics related to remarriage with the partners before formalizing the remarriage. Assess for the emotions surrounding the stages of the divorced's grieving of divorce.
- Professionals providing services related to stability and satisfaction in remarriage should encourage remarrying and remarried parents, especially the biological parents, to be very supportive and empathetic to adolescents during the process of identity formation.

The significant others should be encouraged to contribute to every adolescent's process of identity formation by being trustworthy and caring about the integral growth of the adolescent.

- Likewise, professionals are reminded to help couples address some of the micro and macro social-contextual challenges by establishing workshops (especially in school settings) about prevention of substance abuse, substance dependence, self-control, sexuality awareness, teenager pregnancy, self-esteem and supportive groups for students grieving the loss of their loved ones. They are based on the participants' suggestions for professionals working with the divorced, remarried parents and children in stepfamilies.

# Roles and Challenges for All Community Healers

All the people within the categories presented and those perhaps not mentioned yet play significant roles in the lives of custodial parents in remarriage situations. They need to understand that remarriage is complex and different from a first marriage. Therefore, all community healers (CH) need to be aware of the different problems and issues that stepfamilies face. Stepfamilies cannot be advised or counseled exactly as a nuclear family would be. There are specific issues such as children's loyalty conflicts between the biological parent and the stepparent, feelings of not belonging (within the family and society in general), and feelings of his and hers when it comes to children and stepchildren (Nichols, 1996; Richmond, 1995; Sager, 1985).

Custodial parents need a lot of help as they plan for remarriage. A stable and satisfactory remarriage requires comprehensive premarital preparation, especially if it involves adolescent children (Ahrons, 2004; Berger, 2000; Lutz, 1983) because remarried partners are likely to face more challenges than in their first marriages (Cherlin, 1992; MacDonald & DeMaris, 1995). Consequently, in the preparation planning before remarriage, CH should help divorced parents contemplating remarriage focus on the following three key areas: financial planning and living arrangements, resolving feelings and unresolved concerns about the previous marriage, and profound discussions regarding parenting and decision-making (Kelley & Burg, 2000; Shlemon, 1992; Smoke, 1995; Wallerstein & Blakeslee, 1989; 1995).

Elaborating on these three preparatory areas, CH can help divorced parents preparing for remarriage to agree on where they will live, how they will sustain themselves financially, how they will share their wealth and how they will spend their money (Kelley & Burg, 2000; Wolcott, 1999). CH can help the partners decide on whether they want to keep their money separately (each with a different bank account, credit card) or have a joint account (one-pot method) and spend it together. However, based on Kelley and Burg's (2000) qualitative research, custodial parents are advised to understand that the results of this study indicated that remarried couples who were using the one-pot method generally reported higher marital and family satisfaction than those who separated their funds.

Remarrying parents should therefore resolve feelings and concerns about their previous marriages (Smoke, 1995). CHs may need to understand that, for both adults and the children involved in the post-divorce transitions, remarriage usually reawakens old unresolved anger and hurts from previous marriages. A typical example is when a child hears that his/her parent is getting remarried. Consequently, the child is forced to give up on the ultimate hope that his or her biological parents will ever reconcile (Nichols, 1996; Rutter, 1998).

Some divorced men and women have felt hurt or angry and have exacerbated stormy relationships with their former spouses after hearing of their remarriage arrangements (Shlemon, 1992; Wang & Amato, 2000). Therefore, such men and women should be encouraged to seek professional help in order to resolve unfinished issues and thus work toward reinforcing their stability and satisfaction in remarriage.

Additionally, CH also need to understand the unique resources and constraints of each stepfamily. They should help stepparents understand that most frequently a threat to the stepparent-stepchild relationship might arise over questions of loyalty and sexuality (Ganong & Coleman, 1989; Rutter, 1998). For example, a stepfather may wonder whether his new wife is more loyal to her children or him. This attitude can create an inappropriate triangle within the remarriage triad among children, custodial parent, and stepparent. The same attitude also reveals that the stepfather assumes that he and the children are at the same hierarchical level within the family (Carter & McGoldrick, 1998). Encourage custodial parents to let children have contacts with nonresidential parents.

Divorced parents need to understand that the less a noncustodial parent visits the children living in stepfamily households, the more likely those children are to feel abandoned by the noncustodial parent (Lofas, 1998; Lutz, 1983). Consequently, CH have to understand how to help parents reconnect with their children (e.g., by encouraging them to develop special activities and rituals that involve only the children and the noncustodial parent) (Lewis, 1980). Furthermore, CH may have to caution parents to avoid the risk of bad mouthing their former spouses in front of the children. Otherwise, such a practice undermines the child's self-esteem and may put the child in the position of defending a parent (Kelley & Burg, 2000).

## Keys for all community healers

- Know that every remarriage case is unique. Each couple has a specific history and personality differences. There are many factors that vary from one marriage to another

- Orientate remarrying partners to assess their motivations for remarriage and to avoid the risk of remarrying on the basis of the partner's money
- Coach the partners to ask themselves the "What if ...?" questions (e.g., What if all your expectations are not fulfilled in remarriage, what will you do?")
- Help the partners to understand differences between remarriage after divorce and after the death of a spouse
- Advocate for involving children in the pre-remarriage arrangements in order to listen to their concerns, pay attention to their needs, address their fears, losses, conflict of loyalties, and help them in their adjustment process to life within a stepfamily
- Acknowledge people's spirituality: Religion and spirituality empower people to live by and be motivated by an ethical component within the marriage, thereby being empowered to practice family values, e.g., justice, fairness, and charity
- Double-check with the remarrying partner if he/she has accepted his/her personal responsibility for the previous marriage ending in divorce
- Help partners to set clear boundaries with one's exspouse, family members and friends
- Clarify to the partners that nobody changes the other, but a change in oneself can change the other
- In regard to resolving conflict, help each one to realize that he or she is only seeing part of the whole picture
- Clarify to each party that it is hard to get outside of one's own view. So, encourage each to do so
- Be knowledgeable about how to normalize the anger and let each party know that anger is not necessarily a good response to constructive handling of differences
- Different professional disciplines and professionals are needed to reinforce stability and satisfaction in remarriage
- Be aware of the developmental stage and needs (e.g., the specific needs of adults entering remarriage and the needs of each custodial child)
- Acknowledge that remarriage is not an event, but an ongoing process and reawakens diverse memories in the people involved

- Help partners to understand the importance of resolving their unfinished problems from the previous marriage and other related problems which may interfere with the stability and satisfaction in remarriage
- Coach the remarrying partners about the different needs and challenges in remarriage (e.g., physical, emotional, sexual, financial, stepparenting, and other important topics related to remarriage with the partners before formalizing their marriage
- Offer psychological education or referral to partners by paying attention to the demographic differences (e.g., age, gender, cultural backgrounds, social economic status, level of formal education and religion) of the remarrying and/or remarried individuals
- Pay attention to women going through menopause and men with declining sexual expressiveness
- Know the unique needs and challenges of the remarrying individuals, partners, and children involved (e.g., handicapped, recovering alcoholics, immigration status)
- Help parents to involve their children from the very onset of the parent dating another person
- Help the partners to think through what kinds of risks are anticipated
- Because money seems to be a major contributing factor to divorce for partners living in suburbs and for very rich couples, pre-remarriage contracts are highly recommended for financially rich partners; and if possible wealthy partners should attend separate sessions from those partners with lesser finances
- Biological parent's awareness that his or her children do not have the option of choosing their stepparent
- Be sensitive to the children's developmental stage, needs, fears, emotions, and jealous feelings toward the stepparent who might be perceived by the children as the person coming to take the parent away
- When disciplining stepchildren, the biological parent should do the disciplining most of the time, especially at the beginning of the marriage
- Attempts must be made by the prospective stepparent to win the children's trust before and during the marriage

# Part V:

## Looking Forward

Additional Contributions by the Participants

Writing the Conclusion

# Additional Contributions by the Participants

- *Remarriage Stability Does NOT Automatically Imply Remarriage Satisfaction and Vice Versa*
- *Factors Influencing Remarriage Stability*
- *Factors Influencing Remarriage Satisfaction*
- *Factors to Consider for Re-divorce Prevention*
- *Two Memorable Milestones: Day of Divorce and Day of Remarriage*
- *Mental Health of Either Partner*
- *Empowerment of the Participants*

Although the research study focused on identifying the factors that influence both stability and satisfaction in remarriage, the participants mentioned several other points as well. In addition to the primary and secondary factors mentioned in the previous sections, different participants reported that there were specific factors that had contributed to their remarriage stability but not to their remarriage satisfaction or vice versa. However, it is important to clarify that the responses that some of the participants specifically attributed to remarriage stability were reported by other participants as exclusively applicable to their remarriage satisfaction.

Although some of the reported specific factors for remarriage stability are similar to those for remarriage satisfaction, the differences were based in every participant's perceptions of what he or she had significantly perceived as his or her remarriage stability or satisfaction. A possible explanation for these unique perceptions may be related to every participant's personal needs, needs of his or her significant others, and achieved expectations for remarriage. The following factors were identified as exclusively contributing factors to remarriage stability.

*Remarriage Stability Does NOT Automatically Imply Remarriage Satisfaction and Vice Versa*

During the interviews, the experiences of nine participants suggested that remarriage satisfaction could not be determined by focusing on the longevity or duration of time the partners had been remarried. By the same token, those participants mentioned specific moments in remarriages when they experienced no satisfaction with their spouses, especially in regard to money, sexuality, and disciplining of the children; yet they remained in the remarriage.

Catherine clarified: "I am happy in my remarriage, but every day is not a honeymoon." The results of this study were primarily focused on factors influencing both stability and satisfaction in remarriage. Otherwise, as those nine participants indicated, it is possible to stay in a remarriage (e.g., for the sake of the children), but without being happy.

*Factors Influencing Remarriage Stability*

Two males and three female participants attributed marital stability to having a respectful partner (especially one who is not verbally, emotionally and/or physically abusive), having the right motivations for remarriage (e.g., a focus on realistic expectations about remarriage and the prospective spouse). Two other female participants mentioned marital compatibility, selection of the right partner, and a life commitment to one's partner as exclusive factors to remarriage stability.

Three other males highlighted every partner's level of integral maturity, temperament, high level of emotional stability, perseverance, and good attitude (e.g., loving, calming influence, easy going, kind and/or optimistic) as influencing factors to remarriage stability. Four females identified the need for structure, flexibility with self and others, and the wisdom that is focused on knowing one's position and roles in the marriage.

Two females and two males emphasized the need for each partner to be able to handle and resolve conflicts with a balanced control of emotional outbursts and the importance of negotiating differences of opinions in order to arrive at mutually acceptable decisions. They added the need for keeping up with the lessons learned from one's past mistakes that contributed to the end of the first marriage (e.g., marital infidelity and an over-focus on work at the expense of the marriage and family life) in order to avoid the risk of making the same mistakes again.

One female participant reported that her remarriage stability had been highly influenced by her need for a co-parent and a real model for her children from her first marriage. Based on these "two benefits" which were provided by her second husband, she resolved to stay remarried, especially for the benefit of her children. Two males and two female participants acknowledged the pains and losses suffered by the children as a result of parental conflict and divorce. Consequently, they were resolved to stay in the second marriage so that their children would not face the same fate again.

Given the scarcity of research studies focusing on remarriage stability, further studies are needed to evaluate how the reported factors are congruent and/or incongruent with a broader range of people from diverse backgrounds and groupings. More research studies and clinical cases have been reported regarding marital stability in first marriages (Gottman, 1993) in comparison to second marriages.

## Factors Influencing Remarriage Satisfaction

Four males and two female participants attributed remarriage satisfaction to in-depth communication with their second spouses, deeper perception of feeling respected by second spouses in comparison to the first ones, and harmonious relationships between their second spouses and biological children from the first marriages. Two other female participants highlighted the satisfaction they received from being actively involved in decision-making processes.

Two males and two female participants said that having peaceful and wellbehaved biological children and stepchildren had significantly contributed to remarriage satisfaction. These children were described as keeping themselves out of trouble, helping with house chores, being responsible about school work, accepting of the stepparent, being open to receive constructive criticism from the biological parent and stepparent, being drug-free, knowing how to choose their friends, not sexually active (especially before finishing college), and being self-motivated and healthy, both physically and emotionally.

For their remarriages four females and four male participants said that they chose the right partners, who helped them to find satisfaction in that marriage. In elaborating about choosing the right partners to remarry, these participants described a right marital partner as follows: someone you can trust, communicate with spontaneously, handle conflicts with by negotiating and resolving them maturely, someone who is respectful, generous, outgoing, loving, mature, friendly to his or her stepchildren, and spiritual. These observations are in agreement with Cox's (2002) research findings.

Five females and four male participants reported that social support from trusted friends, sharing humor with their spouse, doing some household activities with their spouse (e.g., shopping), eating together, and relaxed moments of sexual intimacy with their spouse were significant buffers for their remarriage satisfaction. Three females emphasized that acknowledgment of how second husbands related to them as equal partners helped them to feel happy and raised their levels of self-esteem. Some of the ways in which these participants perceived equal treatment from their husbands included their spouse's expressions of kindness and generosity, involving their wives in the daily decision-making processes, as well as consistent and mutual respect for one another.

Four males and four female participants reported that learning to share and to appreciate what each partner brought and/or started to bring to the remarriage relationship (e.g., material resources, personal talents, such as spirituality, conflict resolution skills, optimism, parenting skills, and humor) had significantly contributed to remarriage satisfaction.

It is important to clarify that the identification of the specific factors that had contributed to the participants' remarriage stability and remarriage satisfaction indicated that some remarriages are stable and yet the spouses are dissatisfied. In contrast, other spouses are satisfied, but their remarriages break up in less than 7 years. This observation is consistent with the literature findings and reviews (Ahrons, 2004; Berger, 1998; Carter & McGoldrick, 1998; Gottman, 1994b; Nichols, 1996; Sager, 1985).

Therefore, the above findings seem to indicate that a stable remarriage does not automatically equate to being a satisfactory one and vice versa for each remarried partner. However, as Charles indicated, the factors that influenced his remarriage stability also reinforced his remarriage satisfaction.

Charles mentioned:

> Having a caring spouse has empowered me to stay longer in my remarriage [stability]. The more I stay with her, the happier I feel and the more she continues to care for me, particularly when I am sick. I perceive her to be living by her vows because she loves me in good times and bad. This brings a chain reaction of stability and satisfaction in remarriage because now I feel more committed to her than ever before [stability influences satisfaction and vice versa].

## Factors to Consider for Re-Divorce Prevention

In addition to the specifically reported factors for either remarriage stability or satisfaction, different participants said that remarrying and remarried parents should take into account the following factors in order to prevent risking their remarriages to another divorce. These factors included: emotional and financial stress in raising a handicapped child (2 participants), domestic violence (2 participants), unpaid credit debts (5 participants), marital incompatibility (7 participants), marital infidelity (7 participants), jealousy

(6 participants), verbal and/or physical abuse (7 participants), and over-prioritizing work at the expense of marital and family life (6 participants).

## Two Memorable Milestones: Day of Divorce and Day of Remarriage

All the participants had almost live memories of the day they signed the divorce papers because each participant said that that day had marked a real beginning in his or her life. As long as each had not signed the divorce papers, he or she knew that he or she was still legally married. The signing of the divorce papers was reported by some of those who took the initiative for divorce (the leavers) as a day of great relief and/or guilt, while most of those who did not take the initiative for divorce recalled it with greater feelings of anger. After divorce, some of the participants' children had held onto the idea that their parents might reunite. So the day one of the parents remarried with another person, then those children's dreams were shattered.

Since the moment of formal remarriage, the children from the previous marriage have a stepparent. Once remarried, one may wonder if that marriage will last or will also end in another divorce. The date of the divorce marks a closing of one door and remarriage seems to mark the opening of another door within the mysterious building of marital life. Hence the adage: "When one door closes, another opens." Based on the participants' input, the metaphor of a milestone seemed to represent each of those two days in the lives of the participants.

## Mental Health of Either Partner

The mental health (cognitive and emotional functioning) of each partner has a significant impact on marital stability and satisfaction. A typical example of the negative effects on his marital success as a result of poor mental health was reported by Geoffrey, especially after his excessive dependence on alcohol.

The other case illustrates the impact of cognitive and emotional functioning on marital stability and satisfaction was the one that Hilda narrated. She described how the lack of mental health services might have contributed to the divorce of her parents and her feelings of being triangulated between her parents after they divorced. Hilda clarified:

> My parents divorced during the time when . . . mental health services were not as available as they are today. My mother filed for divorce after realizing that she could not bear any longer my father's drastic mood changes. After signing the divorce papers, my father was diagnosed with a mental illness, and the cause of this divorce was emotional stress. Unfortunately, after

knowing the diagnosis of my father's mental illness, namely, post-traumatic stress disorder, my mother started to blame herself for having abandoned a mentally abnormal person. However much I tried to convince her that it was not her fault, she did not manage to forgive herself. She spent the rest of her life with a profound sense of guilt, and that also affected me.

Hilda's description emphasizes the need to consider taking a comprehensive mental exam for people who plan to enter married life and probably to encourage them to consider undertaking a 2-year periodic mental-health checkup. Such checkups might be necessary particularly for aging partners who may be at a greater risk of dementia and/or Alzheimer's disease (Groth-Marnat, 1999).

## Empowerment of the Participants

During and after the interviews, the participants affirmed, clarified and bridged many knowledge gaps about stability and satisfaction in remarriage. They openly shared their stories of pain, suffering, trust and resilience. They spoke of the empowerment of their life experiences. On the one hand, as they narrated their first-marriage and post-divorce experiences, they shared their pain, shame, loneliness, incidents of domestic violence, rejection from family members and/or humiliation. On the other hand, they also related their stories of resilience and experiences of satisfaction and stability in their second marriages. Almost all of them spoke of having recovered self-esteem and dignity and of having found meaning in life. All of them seemed to be more resolved to stay with their second spouses "till death do us part."

# Writing the Conclusion

The Author acknowledges that without the participants' contributions this book would not have come into existence in its current format. Each participant had a significant impact on the Author and for that he is most grateful. The process of developing a grounded theory was tedious, but the theory developed is very encouraging due to its congruence with the existing literature and research studies.

The Author learned from the research participants that one must consistently work on stability and satisfaction in remarriage and that work needs to be done before it is too late. In the meantime, whoever contemplates remarriage or is remarried, the author suggests that you should:

i. Think remarriage stability, seek it and practice it and work on it every day

ii. Think remarriage satisfaction, seek it, practice it and work on it every day

iii. Think remarriage triad, it is a reality, harmonize it, and work on it every day.

Therefore, the conclusion to this book can only be written by "YOU." What have the participants taught you? How do you plan on implementing what you have learned regarding stability and satisfaction in remarriage? Now it is time for you to write your own story!

# Glossary

Axial coding: The process of relating categories to their subcategories, termed "axial" because coding occurs around the axis of a category by linking categories at the level of properties and dimensions (Strauss & Corbin, 1998, p. 123)

Category: A theme which represents a unit of information composed of events, happenings, and instances (Creswell, 1998).

Concepts: The building blocks used to develop the theory (Strauss & Corbin, 1998).

Credibility: The trustfulness criterion in conventional research comparable to internal validity in conventional research (Guba & Lincoln, 1985). Many techniques can be used to facilitate credibility in a study(e.g., in this study, prolonged engagement with the participants, persistent observation, peer debriefing, and member checking).

Confirmability: Precautions implemented to make sure that the findings of the inquiry were established by the participants and conditions of the inquiry instead of the biases, motivations, interests, or perspectives of the researcher who interviewed the participants.

Dependability: This term is used in qualitative studies in a manner comparable to the notion of reliability in quantitative research. It refers to the need of determining that the findings of this study may be repeated if the inquiry would be replicated with the same (or similar) participants in the same (or similar context). A rough coding system and analysis of the raw data were some of the strategies the researcher used to establish dependability and to maintain its consistency.

Dimensions: The ranges used to analyze how the general properties of each category varied, and what was specific to each category.

Informed consent form: A document which every participant signs before participating in the study to express his or her voluntary willingness to participate after being informed about the necessary details (Appendix E) regarding the study and his or her well-being.

Insightful understanding: Reflective understanding and a unifying field of knowledge as described by Lonergan (1957).

Gatekeepers: Individuals whom the researcher contacted in writing to ask for permission in order to recruit participants in their respective social work agencies (Appendix A) and ministers of different religious denominations (Appendix B).

Open coding: An analytic process for identifying concepts, their properties, and discovered dimensions in the collected data (Strauss & Corbin, 1998)

Phenomena: The concepts used to summarize the central ideas in the data. Properties: The characteristics of each category.

Prospective participants: Individuals contacted by the researcher on the assumption that those individuals had the potential for providing information that would be relevant to the study.

Purposeful sampling: The criteria which the researcher used to explore the factors that influence stability and satisfaction in remarriage from selected participants (Creswell, 1998).

Reflective journal: A personal diary in which the researcher recorded a variety of information about self, process notes, observations about participants, insights, and reflections about what was happening in terms of his own beliefs, values, and interests.

Remarriage satisfaction: The custodial parent's responsibility to establish a second marriage, in which the custodial parent perceives the relationship as generating happiness and meaning through his or her interactions with his or her spouse, learning to persevere by doing his or her best to make marriage a success, and in a mutually life-giving structure with his or her spouse and children (Gottman, 1994b; Jacobson & Greenburg, 1994; James & Johnson, 2001; LeBey, 2004; Strauss & Corbin, 1998).

Remarriage stability: The custodial parent's responsibility to develop and maintain a permanent marital commitment with his or her spouse until biological death separates them (Berger, 1998; Champlin, 1997; Himes & Coriden, 1996).

Remarriage triad: A term designed by the researcher to illustrate the need for conceptualizing the dynamics of relationships and interactions of remarried parents and their significant others by focusing on their resources and constraints within a framework of three interconnected domains: divorce, re-coupling and living in a stepfamily context.

Resilience: This term used is in this study from the standpoint of the "psychology of human effectiveness" (Gelso & Fassinger, 1992, p. 293), and in reference with Kelley and Burg's (2000) research findings which indicated that in spite of the challenges related to divorce, remarriage, and stepfamilies (e.g., personal, social, cultural, legal, gender, and financial constraints), some of the people involved are able to overcome them and start to live normal lives. In this book, resilience refers to the interpersonal strengths and interpersonal empowerments (Walsh, 2002) that help the divorced and / or children of divorced parents to develop positive coping strategies before, during, and / or after divorce. Rutter (1998) clarified, "Although divorce and remarriage may confront families with stresses and adaptive challenges, they also offer opportunities for personal growth and more harmonious, fulfilling family and personal relationships" (p. 186).

Selective cording: The process of integrating and refining the theory.

Selection criteria: The common elements or set of requirements that every participant had to have before being selected by the researcher to participate in the study, (e.g., one of the selection criteria for this study required all participants to be heterosexual individuals).

Snowball approach or chain approach: A method of obtaining participants by identifying cases of interest from people who knew other people to be information rich.

Subcategories: The concepts that pertained to a category and which are helpful in giving further clarifications and specification to each category.

Theoretical sampling: The process whereby the researcher interviewed individuals who could contribute to the evolving theory.

Theoretical saturation: The point in category development at which no new properties, dimensions or relationships emerged during analysis (Strauss & Corbin, 1998). However, it is important to clarify that theoretical saturation was not yet attained after interviewing the anticipated 12 participants (six men and six women). Consequently, as preplanned, I consulted my adviser to decide whether to stop interviewing additional participants or to agree on how many more participants to interview. The adviser told me to interview more participants until saturation. After interviewing four more participants (two females and two males), based on their additional input, saturation was attained.

Transferability of results: The potential for the findings of the study to be applied to other people in different or similar contexts. In other words, transferability in qualitative research may be compared to external validity in quantitative research (Mertens, 1998). However, it is important to note that unlike quantitative studies which provide results that can be generalized, qualitative studies are geared at providing only working hypotheses along with an account of the time and context in which they were collected. The person interested in applying those hypotheses has to use his or her judgment before transferring them (Creswell, 1998; Mertens, 1998).

# References

Adams, J. (1980). *Marriage, divorce, and remarriage in the Bible: A fresh look at what scripture teaches.* Grand Rapids, MI: Zondervan.

Ahrons, C. (1994). *The good divorce: keeping your family together when your marriage come apart.* New York: HarperCollins.

Ahrons, C. (2004). *We are still family: What grown children have to say about their parents' divorce.* New York: Harper Collins.

Amato, P. R. (1987). Family processes in one-parent, stepparent, and intact families: The child's point-of-view. *Journal of Marriage and Family, 49,* 327 – 337.

Amato, P., & Ochiltree, G. (1987). Child and adolescent competence in intact, one-parent, and stepfamilies: An Australian study. *Journal of Divorce, 10,* 75 – 96.

Amen, D. (1998). *Change your brain - change your life: The breakthrough program for conquering anxiety, depression, obsessiveness, anger and impulsiveness.* New York: Three Rivers Press.

American Association of Marriage and Family Therapy (AAMFT) (1998). *Code of ethics.* Washington, DC.

Anderston, T., & White, G. (1986). An empirical investigation of interaction and relationship. Patterns in functional and dysfunctional nuclear families and stepfamilies. *Family Process,* 407 – 422.

Aponte, H. (1994). *Bread and spirit: Therapy with the new poor, diversity of race, culture, and values.* New York. Norton.

Baum, N. (2003). The male way of mourning divorce: When, what, and how. *Clinical Social Work Journal, 31* (1), 37 – 50.

Beal, J., Coriden, J., & Green, T. (Eds.). (2000). *New commentary on the code of canon law.* New York: Paulist Press.

Berger, K. (1998). *The developing person through the lifespan* (4th ed.). New York: Worth.

Berger, R. (2000). Remarried families of 2000: Definitions, description, and interventions. In W. Nichols, M. Pace-Nichols, D., Becvar, &

A.Napier (Eds.), *Handbook of family development and intervention*, pp. 371 – 390. New York: John Wiley & Sons.

Berry, D. (1998). *The divorce recovery source book.* Los Billings, A. (1979). Conflict resolution in distressed and nondistressed married couples. *Journal of Consulting and Clinical Psychology, 23,* 362 – 371.

Black, D. (1998). *Smart dating: A guide to starting and keeping a healthy relationship.* New Orleans, LA: Paper Chase Press.

Bohr, D. (1999). *Catholic moral tradition: In Christ, a new Creation.* Huntington, IN: Our Sunday Publishing Division.

Boszomenyi-Nagy & Krasner, B. (1986). *Between give and take: A clinical guide to contextual therapy.* New York: Brunner/Mazel.

Bowlby, J. (1980). *Attachment and loss (Vol. 3).* New York: Basic Books.

Bowen, M. (1972). On the Differentiation of Self. First published anonymously in J. Framo (Ed.), *Family Interaction: A Dialogue Between Family Researchers and Family Therapists*, pp. 111-173. New York: Springer.

Brehm, S. (1992). *Intimate relationships* (2nd ed.). New York: McGraw-Hill.

Breunlin, D., Schwartz, R., & Kune-Karrer, B. (1992). *Metaframeworks: Transcending the models of family therapy.* San Francisco: Jossey-Bass.

Brown, J. (1998). *The self.* Boston: McGraw-Hill.

Brown, S., & Booth, A. (1996). Cohabitation versus marriage: A comparison of relationship quality. *Journal of Marriage and Family, 58(* 3), 668 – 679.

Burleson, B., & Denton, W. (1997). The relationship between communication skill and marital satisfaction: Some moderating effects. *Journal of Marriage and Family, 59,* 884 – 902.

Carter, B., & McGoldrick, M. (1998). *The expanded family life cycle: Individual, family, and social perspectives* (3rd ed.). Boston: Allyn & Bacon.

Catoir, J. (1996). *Where do you stand with the church? The dilemma of divorced Catholics.* New York: Alba House.

Champlin, J. (1997). *Together-for-life.* Notre Dame, IN: Ave Maria Press.

Cherlin, A. (1992). *Marriage, divorce, remarriage (revised and enlarged).* Cambridge, MA: Harvard University Press.

Coleman, M., & Ganong, L. (1985). Remarriage myths: Implications for helping professions. *Journal of Counseling and Development, 64,* 116 – 120.

Covey, S. (1989). *The 7 habits of highly effective people: Powerful lessons in personal change.* New York: Simon & Schuster.

Cox, F. (2002). Remarriage: A growing way of American life. In F. Cox (Ed.). *Human intimacy: Marriage, the family, and its meaning,* pp. 513 – 537. Australia: Wadsworth.

Creswell, J. (1998). *Qualitative inquiry and research design: Choosing among five traditions.* Thousand Oaks, CA: Sage.

Cunningha, C., & Foley. W. (1994). The relative stability of remarriages: A cohort approach using vital statistics. *Family Relations, 43* (3), 305 – 311.

Davidson, M. (2003). *The everything divorce book: Know your rights, understand the law, and regain control of your life.* Avon, MA: Adams Media Corporation.

Demo, D., & Acock, A. (1997). Singlehood, marriage, and remarriage: The effects of family structure and family relationships on the mother's well-being. *Journal of Family Issues, 17,* 388-407.

de Shazer, S. (1985). Keys to solution in brief therapy. New York: Norton.

Dulton, D., & Aron, A. (1999). Some evidence of heightened sexual attraction under conditions of high anxiety. In E. Aronson (Ed.), *Readings about the social animal* (8th ed.), pp. 486 – 499. New York: Worth Publishers/W. H. Freeman.

Erera-Weatherley, P. (1996). On becoming a stepparent: Factors associated with the adoption of alternative stepparenting styles. *Journal of Divorce and Remarriage, 25,* 155 – 174.

Erlandson, D., Harris, E., Skipper, B., & Allen, S. (1993). *Doing naturalistic inquiry: A guide to methods.* Newbury Park, CA: Sage.

Falicov, C. J. (1988). *Family transitions: Continuity & change over the life cycle.* New York: The Guilford Press.

Ferch, S. (1998). Intentional forgiving as a counseling intervention. *Journal of Counseling and Development, 76,* 261 – 270.

Ferch, S. (1999). Marital forgiveness: A case study of forgiveness and multiple extra-marital affairs. *Marriage and Family: A Christian Journal, 2,* 169 – 170.

Ferch, S. (2001). Relational conversation: Meaningful communication as a therapeutic intervention. *Journal of Counseling and Values, 45* (2), 118 – 138.

Fincham, F., Beach, S., & Davila, J. (2004). Forgiveness and conflict resolution in marriage. *Journal of Family Psychology, 18* (1), 72 – 81.

Fitzpatrick, M. (1990). Models of marital interaction. In H. Giles & W. Robinson (Eds.). *Handbook of language and social psychology, pp. 433 – 451. Chichester,* NY: Wiley.

Fisch, R., Weakland, J., & Segal, L. (1982). *The tactics of change: Doing therapy briefly.* San Francisco: Jossey-Bass.

Fivaz, R. (1991). Thermodynamics of complexity. *Systems Research, 9,* 19-32.

Floyd, F. (1988). Couples' cognitive/affective reactions to communication behaviors. *Journal of Marriage and Family, 50,* 523 – 532.

Framo, M. (1985). Remarried families: Couple's issues. In H. Grunebaum, R. Chasin, & D. Jacobs (Directors of Course Syllabus), *Family therapy – Working with couples,* pp. 29 – 30. Harvard Medical School: Department of Continuing Education, Cambridge, MA

Frankl, V. (1963). *Man's search for meaning.* New York: Washington Press.

Freedman, J., & Combs, G. (1996). *Narrative therapy: The social construction of preferred realities.* New York: Norton.

Ganong, L., & Coleman, M. (1989). Preparing for remarriage: Anticipating the issues, seeking solutions. *Family Relations, 38,* 28 – 33.

Gelso, C., & Fassinger, R. (1992). Personality, development, and counseling psychology: Depth, ambivalence, and actualization. *Journal of Counseling Psychology, 39,* 275 – 298.

Glaser, B. (1992). *Basics of grounded theory analysis.* Mill Valley, CA: Sociology Press.

Glaser, B., & Strauss, A. (1967). *The discovery of grounded theory: Strategies for qualitative research.* New York: Aldine Hawthorne.

Glick, P., & Norton, A. (1977). Marrying, divorcing and living together in the United States today. *Population Bulletin, 32* (5), 4 – 8.

Gordon, K., Baucom, D., & Snyder, D. (2004). An integrative intervention for promoting recovery from extramarital affairs. *Journal of Marital and Family Therapy, 30* (2), 213 – 231.

Gottman, J. (1991). Predicting the longitudinal course of marriage. *Journal of Marital and Family Therapy, 17,* 3 – 7.

Gottman, J. (1993). A theory of marital dissolution and stability. *Journal of Family Psychology, 7*, 57 – 75.

Gottman, J. (1994a). What predicts divorce? Hillsdale, NJ: Lawrence Erlbaum Associates.

Gottman, J. (1994b). *Why marriages succeed or fail… and how you can make yours last.* New York: Simon & Schuster.

Gottman, J., Coan, J., Carrere.A., & Swanson, C. (1998). Predicting marital happiness and stability from newlywed interactions. *Journal of Marriage and Family, 60* (1), 5 – 23.

Gottman, J., & Levenson, R. (1988). The social psychophysiology of marriage. In P. Noller & M.A. Fitzpatrick (Eds.), *Perspectives on marital integration,* pp.182-199.Clevedon, England: Multilingual Matters.

Gottman, J., Notarius, C., Gonso, J., and Markman, H. (1976) *A couple's guide to communication.* Champaign, IL: Research Press.

Gottman, J., Ryan, K., Carrere, A., Erlay, P. (2001). Toward a scientifically based marital therapy. In H. Liddle, D. Santisteban, R. Levant, & J. Bray (Eds.), *Family psychology: Science-based interventions,* pp. 147 – 174. Washington, DC: American Psychological Association.

Gottman, J., & Silver, N. (1999). *The seven principles for making marriage work: A practical guide from country's foremost relationship expert.* New York: Crown.

Gray, C. (1996). When therapy is not in the client's best interest: Adapting clinical interventions to the stages of divorce. *Journal of Divorce & Remarriage, 26*, 117 – 127.

Groth-Marnat, G. (1999). *Handbook of psychological assessment* (3rd ed.). New York: John Wiley & Sons.

Hackney, H. & Cormier, S. (1994). *Counseling strategies and interventions.* Boston: Allyn & Bacon.

Haley, J. (1984). *Problem solving therapy* (2nd ed.). San Francisco: Jossey-Bass.

Heínísch, P. (1955). *Theology of the Old Testament: Be holy as I Yahweh our God am holy.* Collegeville, MN: The Liturgical Press.

Hendrick, S. (1995). Close relationships research: Application to counseling psychology. *The Counseling Psychologist, 23*, 649 – 665.

Himes, K., & Coriden, J. (1996). Current theology: Pastoral care of the divorced and remarried. *Theological Studies, 57* (1), 97 – 124.

Hollingshead, A. (1975). *Four factor index of social studies.* Unpublished manuscript.

Jacobson, N., & Christensen, A (1996). *Integrative couple therapy: Promoting acceptance and change.* New York: Norton.

James, S., & Johnson, D. (2001). Social interdependence, psychological adjustment, and marital satisfaction in second marriages. *Journal of Social Psychology, 128* (3), 287 – 303.

Johnson, S., & Greenberg, L. (1994). Emotion in intimate interactions: A synthesis. In S. Johnson & L. Greenberg (Eds.), *The heart of the matter: Perspectives on emotion in marital therapy,* pp. 297 – 323. New York: Brunner/Mazel.

Kaslow, F. (1996). *Handbook of relational diagnosis and dysfunctional family patterns.* New York: John Wiley & Sons.

Kelley, P. (1995). *Developing healthy stepfamilies.* New York: The Harrington Park Press.

Kelley, S., & Burg, D. (2000). Why remarriages succeed. In S. Kelley & D. Burg (Eds.), *The second time around: Everything you need to know to make your marriage happy.* New York: HarperCollins.

Kennedy, T (1995). *Doers of the word: Moral theology for the third millennium.* Liguori (Missouri), Triumph Books.

Kerr, M., & Bowen, M. (1988). *Family evaluation: The role of the family as an emotional unit that governs individual behavior and development.* New York: W. W. Norton.

Kiura, J. (2004). *Success in marriage.* Nairobi, Kenya: Paulines Publications Africa.

Kupisch, S. (1987). Children and stepfamilies. In A. Thomas & J. Grimes (Eds.), *Children's needs: Psychological perspectives.* Washington, DC: National Association of Psychologists.

Kurdek, L. (1994). Conflict resolution styles in gay, lesbian, heterosexual nonparent, and heterosexual parent couples. *Journal of Marriage and Family, 56,* 705 – 722.

Larson, H., & Holman, T. (1994). Premarital predictors of marital quality and stability. *Family Relations, 43,* 228 – 237.

Larson, H., Nowell, K., & Nichols, S (2002). A review of three comprehensive premarital assessment questionnaires. *Journal of Marital & Family Therapy, 28* (2), 233 – 239.

LeBey, B. (2004). *Remarried with children: Ten secrets for successfully blending and extending your family.* New York: Bantam Books.

Levant, R., & Philpot, C. (2002). Conceptualizing gender in marital and family therapy research: The gender role strain paradigm. In H.

Liddle, D. Santisteban, R. Levant, & J. Bray (Eds.). *Family psychology: Science-based interventions*, pp. 301 – 329. Washington, DC: American Psychological Association.

Lewis, H. (1980). *All about families: The second time around.* Atlanta, GA: Peachtree.

Lincoln, Y., & Guba, E. (1985). *Naturalistic inquiry.* Beverly Hills, CA: Sage.

Lofas, J., & Sova, D. (1995). Stepparenting: *The real problems. The real solutions* (Revised and updated). New York: MJF Books.

Lofas, J. (1998). *Family Rules: Helping stepfamilies and single parents build happy homes.* New York: Kensington Books.

Lofas, J., & Sova, D. (1985). *The family challenge of the nineties: Stepparenting* (Revised and updated). New York: Kensington Books.

Lutz, P. (1983). The stepfamily: An adolescent perspective. *Family Relations, 32,* 367 – 375.

MacDonald, W., & DeMaris, A. (1995). Remarriage, stepchildren and marital conflict: Challenges to the institutionalization hypothesis. *Journal of Marriage and Family, 57* (2), 387 – 399.

Maslow, A. (1961). Peak experiences as acute identity experiences. American Journal of Psychoanalysis,21, 254-260. Reprinted in A. Combs (Ed.), *Personality theory and counseling practice.* Gainesville, FL: University of Florida Press.

McCulullough, M., Spence, N., & Worthington, E. (1994). Encouraging clients to forgive people who hurt them: Review, critique, and research prospectus. *Journal of Psychology and Theology, 33,* 3 – 20.

McFarland, F. (1992). Counselors teaching peaceful conflict resolution. *Journal of Counseling and Development, 71,* 18 – 22.

McGoldrick, M. (1995). *You can go home again: Reconnecting with your family.* New York: Norton.

McGoldrick, M. (1998). Becoming a couple: In M. McGoldrick & B. Carter (Eds.), *The expanded family life cycle: Individual, family, and social perspectives* (3rd ed.), pp. 231 – 248. Boston: Allyn & Bacon, McGoldrick, M., & Carter B. (1998). Remarried families: In M. McGoldrick & B. Carter. *The expanded family life cycle: Individual, family, and social perspectives* (3rd ed.), pp. 417 – 435. Boston: Allyn & Bacon.

McGoldrick, M., Gerson, R., & Shellenberger, S. (1999). Genograms: *Assessment and intervention* (2nd ed.). New York: Norton.

McGoldrick, M., Giordano, J., & Pearce, J. (Eds.). (1996). *Ethnicity & family therapy* (2nd ed.). New York: The Guilford Press.

Megan, Z. (1998). *Exploring adolescent happiness: Commitment, purpose, and fulfillment.* Thousand Oaks: Sage.

Mertens, D. (1998). Research methods in education and psychology: Integrating diversity with quantitative and qualitative approaches. Thousand Oaks, CA: Sage.

Miller, A. (1985). Guidelines in stepparenting. *Psychotherapy in Private Practice, 3,* 99 – 109.

Miller, W. (Ed.). (1999). *Integrating spirituality into treatment: Resources for practitioners.* Washington, DC: American Psychological Association.

Minuchin, S. (1974). *Families and family therapy.* Cambridge, MA: Harvard University Press.

Minuchin , S., & Nichols, M. (1993). *Family healing: Strategies for hope and understanding.* New York: The Free Press.

Morrow, S., Rakhsha, G., & Castaneda, C. (2001). Qualitative research methods for multicultural counseling. In J. Ponterotto,

M. Casas, L. Suzuki, & C. Alexander (Eds.), *Handbook of multicultural counseling* (2nd ed.), pp. 575 – 603. Thousand Oaks: Sage.

Myers, J., & Schwiebert, V. (1999). Grandparents and stepgrandparents: Challenges in counseling the extended-blended family. *Adultspan Journal, 1,* 50 – 60.

Nakonezny, P., & Shull, R. (1995). The effect of no-fault divorce law on the divorce rate across 50 states and its relation to income, education, and religiosity. *Journal of Marriage and Family, 57* (2), 477 – 488.

Nichols, W. (1996). *Treating people in families: An integrative framework.* New York: The Guilford Press.

O'Leary, D., Heyman, R., & Jongsman, A., Jr. (1998). Communication. In D. O'Leary, R. Heyman, & A. Jongsman, Jr. (Eds.). *The couple's psychotherapy treatment planner,* pp. 51 – 59. New York: John Wiley & Sons.

Oyebade, J. (2005). *Love guide: Top secrets for peace of mind, success and happiness in your love-life.* London: Good Publications International.

Papernow, P. (1998). *Becoming a stepfamily: Patterns of development in remarried families.* Cambridge, MA: Gestalt Institute of Cleveland Press.

Parkes, C., Laungani, P., & Young, B. (Eds.). (1997). *Death and bereavement across cultures.* London: Routledge.

Paul VI. (1969). *Evangelii nuntiandii.* Rome: The Vatican Press.

Peck, M. (1997). *Further along the road less traveled: The unending journey toward spiritual growth.* New York: Simon & Schuster.

Rafuls, S., & Moon, S. (1996). Grounded theory methodology in family therapy research. In D. Sprenkle & S. Moon (Eds.). *Research methods in family therapy*, pp. 64 – 80. New York: The Guilford Press.

Reis, H., Senchak, M., & Solomon, B. (1985). Gender differences in the intimacy of social interaction: Further examination of potential explanations. *Journal of Personality and Social Psychology, 48,* 1204 – 1217.

Richmond, V. (1995). Amount of communication in marital dyads as a function of dyad and individual marital satisfaction. *Communication Research Reports, 12,* 152 – 159.

Robinson, G. (1984). *Marriage, Divorce & Nullity: A guide to the annulment process in the Catholic Church.* Collegeville, MN: The Liturgical Press.

Russell-Chapin, L., Chapin, T., and Sattler, L. (2001). The relationship of conflict resolution styles and certain marital satisfaction factors to marital distress. *The Family Journal: Counseling and Therapy for Couples and Families, 9* (3), 259 – 264.

Rutter, S. (1998). Lessons from stepfamilies. *Journal of Marriage and Family Therapy 38,* 185 - 190.

Sager, C. (1985). Second marriages: Working with the couple. In H. Grunebaum, R. Chasin, & D. Jacobs (Directors of Course Syllabus): *Family therapy – Working with couples*, pp. 47 – 48. Harvard Medical School: Department of Continuing Education, Cambridge, MA.

Sager, C., Brown, H., Crohn, H., Engel, T., Rodstein, E., & Walker, L. (1983). Treating the remarried family. New York: Brunner/Mazel.

Satir, V., & Baldwin, M. (1983). *Step-by-step: A guide to creating change in families.* Palo Alto, CA: Science and Behavioral Books.

Shlemon, B. (1992). *Healing the wounds of divorce: A spiritual guide to recovery.* Notre Dame, IN: Ave Maria Press.

Skeen, P., Covi, R., & Robinson, B., (1985). Stepfamilies: A review of the literature with suggestions for practitioners. *Journal of Counseling and Development, 64,* 121 – 125.

Smoke, J. (1995). *Growing through divorce.* Eugene, OR: Harvest House.

Spinier, G., & Thompson, L. (1984). *Parting: The aftermath of separation and divorce.* Beverly Hills, CA: Sage.

Sprenkle, D., & Moon, S. (1996). *Research methods in family therapy.* New York: Guildford.

Staudacher, C. (1987). *Beyond grief: A guide for recovering from the death of a loved one.* Oakland, CA: New Harbinger.

Staudacher, C. (1991). *Men & grief: A guide for men surviving the death of a loved one; A resource for caregivers and mental health professionals.* Oakland, CA: New Harbinger.

Stepfamily Foundation (2004). *Stepfamilies.* http:/www.stepfamily.org

Staudacher, C. (1994). *A time to grieve: Meditations for healing after the death of a loved one.* New York: HarperSanFrancisco.

Strauss, A. (1987). *Qualitative analysis for social scientists.* New York: Cambridge University Press.

Strauss, A., & Corbin, J. (1998). *Basics of qualitative research: Techniques and procedures for developing grounded theory* (2nd ed.). Thousand Oaks, CA: Sage.

Subortnik, M., & Harris, G. (1994). *Surviving infidelity: Making decisions, recovering from the pain.* Holbrook, MA: Adams Publishing.

Tatelbaum, J. (1980). *The courage to grieve: Creative living, recovery & growth through grief.* New York: Harper & Row.

Tessman, L. (1978). *Children of parting parents.* New York: Norton.

Thies, J. (1977). Beyond divorce: The impact of remarriage on children. *Journal of Clinical Child Psychology, 6,* 59 – 61.

Treadway, D. (1989). *Before it's too late: Working with substance abuse in the family.* New York: Norton.

Visher, J. (1994). Stepfamilies: A work in progress. *The American Journal of Family Therapy, 22* (4), 337 – 344.

Wallerstein, J., & Blakeslee, S. (1989). *Second chances: Men, women, and children a decade after divorce.* Boston: Houghton-Mifflin.

Wallerstein, J., & Blakeslee, S. (1995). *The good marriage: How and why love lasts.* New York: Warner Books.

Walsh, F. (1998). *Strengthening family resilience.* New York: Guilford.

Walsh, F. (2002). A family resilience framework: Innovative practice applications. *Family relations, 51,* 130 – 137.

Walsh, W. (1992). Twenty major issues in remarriage families. *Journal of Counseling and Development, 70* (6), 709 – 716.

Wang, H. & Amato, P. (2000). Predictors of divorce adjustment: Stressors, resources, and definitions. *Journal of Marriage and Family, 62* (3), 655 – 669.

White, L. (1990). Determinants of divorce: A review of research in the eighties. *Journal of Marriage and Family, 52,* 904 – 912.

White, M. & Epson, D. (1990). *Narrative means to therapeutic ends.* New York: Norton.

Worden, W. (1991). *Grief counseling and grief therapy: A handbook for mental health practitioner* (2nd ed.). New York: Springer.

Wolcott, I. (1999). Strong families and satisfying marriages. *Family Matters, 53,* 21 – 30.

Yalom, I. (1995). *The theory and practice of group psychotherapy* (4th ed.). New York: Basic Books.

Zwack, J. (1983). *Annulment: Your chance to remarry within the Catholic Church: A step-by-step guide using the New Code of Canon Law.* Cambridge, MA: Harper & Row.

CPSIA information can be obtained
at www.ICGtesting.com
Printed in the USA
FSHW021928100819
60871FS

9 781948 828215